TAKE IT TO THE BRIDGE

TAKE IT
TO THE BRIDGE

Dundee's Rock & Pop History

Lorraine Wilson

BLACK & WHITE PUBLISHING

For Catherine

First published 2011
by Black & White Publishing Ltd
29 Ocean Drive, Edinburgh EH6 6JL

1 3 5 7 9 10 8 6 4 2   11 12 13 14
ISBN: 978 1 84502 363 8
Copyright © Lorraine Wilson 2011

The publisher has made every reasonable effort to contact copyright holders
of images in the picture section. Any errors are inadvertent and anyone who,
for any reason, has not been contacted is invited to write to the publisher
so that a full acknowledgement can be made in subsequent editions of this work.

Hopin' (They'll Be Open) Words and Music by Gary Clark
© Copyright 1993 Nettwerk One Music Limited. All Rights Reserved. International Copyright
Secured. Used by permission of Music Sales Limited.

A CIP catalogue record for this book is available from the British Library.

Typeset by Ellipsis Digital Ltd, Glasgow
Printed and bound by MPG Books Ltd, Bodmin, Cornwall

Contents

Acknowledgements

My sincere thanks to everyone who gave up their time to have a blether about their involvement in the musical history of Dundee. With more than sixty interviewees to mention, your names all come in the following pages – I could have spent countless hours with every one of you. However, special mention must go to Alastair 'Breeks' Brodie and Donny Coutts, who opened up their 'loaby presses' allowing years of treasured photography and memorabilia to spill out. The teabags, milk and many biscuits will be repaid. Also to Gordon Gurvan at Retro Dundee.

Hugs and kisses to those who had the belief, especially Ewan (for dog-walking and tea-making and just nodding at the ranting). Also Migs, Washie, Heid and Kat, Poppy, Shenagh, and JB. Thanks to Aarti Joshi at DF, to Dundee City Archives and to Bill McLoughlin and Susan Dailly at D.C. Thomson for their help through the archives there. Also everyone at Black & White Publishing for their support and guidance.

Kudos to my brothers Alfie and Graham for having most excellent music taste and fuelling the fires from an early age. And finally, thanks to my wonderful mum and dad – for everything.

Foreword

If something remains a strong childhood memory, there's a good chance it has something of an effect on adult life.

Ingrained in my memory are the occasions when my mum would be getting 'dolled up' for an all-too-rare night out with my dad. I would follow her around like a puppy, choking in the vapour trails of Estée Lauder Youth Dew she created. As she rushed around, sparks flew from her Crimplene frock – the whole house was energised and the sense of anticipation was immense.

My dad usually worked twelve-hour shifts, seven days a week, so these were the good suit and Brylcreem times for him. I wondered what could be so magical, so important, so grown-up? Why were they all dressed up and leaving me in the hands of a babysitter? Invariably a not-much-older cousin who would proceed to taunt me, steal my sweeties and want to 'toy fight'.

The destination would be no huge stadium or even a cool jazz club. It was usually the Longhaugh Hotel, no more than five minutes' walk from our front door in Fintry. From memory, the 'turn' was more often than not someone called Tony Vincent. On other occasions, they would venture into the town centre to a dinner dance at the Hong Kong, where a 'big act' like Christian might have been booked. To me, it didn't get much more exotic than that. Other nights it would have been out to meet friends or family at the mythical 'clubby'.

When they spoke about the night afterwards, the highlight was always the same thing – the music, and particularly the live music. It was an escape. Without getting too 'jute mill', people worked hard in Dundee and when they played, music was generally a big part of it.

The wealth of bands that Dundee has produced and nurtured could fill a book (luckily enough!) but the community of those musicians, and how some of their stories are interwoven with the venues, record shops, music shops and even music hacks, shows how music has always been such a strong part of its culture.

After watching older brothers and sister teeter off in platforms to go to dancehalls and discos like the JM, Teazers and Tiffany's, it was my turn in the 1980s. At the start of my live music journey, I was dressed like a modern-day Doris Day in hat, gloves and probably the same kind of Crimplene frocks my mum had more than a decade earlier. The highlight of the week was taking the 33 bus from Fintry on a Sunday night (never battered once, despite the gear!), walking up the Westport to hook up with chums, having a couple of those newfangled imported lagers in the Blue Mountains and then the real purpose of the night, heading over to Dance Factory at Fat Sams.

No matter what I've done, where I've been or how life has been treating me, music has remained at the centre. I've been fortunate enough to earn a living writing 'the pop' for D.C. Thomson teen magazines like *Jackie*, working with music magazines and also writing music articles, where I've interviewed some genuine heroes.

Being a member of many bands over the years has been an absolute joy. The names I heard as a child, as a teenager and a more musically savvy adult (not Tony Vincent or Christian I hasten to add) have been an inspiration and the deeper I dig into Dundee's musical history, the prouder I am of this city.

As a young child in the seventies, Dundee didn't seem to offer much, but digging deeper, it's clear that it's a city that has always been able to carry a tune.

THE SIXTIES

The Sixties

A GLITTERING FUTURE

It was a long way up to the balcony for a ten-year-old. Up well past his bedtime and dressed in his Sunday best, Andrew Lothian took his mother's hand to climb the stairs, but his pace quickened when he heard a familiar voice in the distance announcing, 'and that's all . . .' It was the first time he would hear the famous call sign of his bandleader father.

From the vantage point of the balcony in the Palais de Danse, almost high enough to touch the glitterballs hanging from the ceiling, he could look down upon the ballroom and its swirl of dancers, awaiting the next foxtrot or quickstep from Andy Lothian and his band.

'When I looked down, I saw him in a white-tailed suit, with a white bow tie. As he spoke, the band disappeared, the lights dimmed, and two spotlights turned on to the glitterballs – the whole ballroom was so beautifully lit.

'He stepped down from the bandstand and started to move among the couples with his violin, playing a waltz. I didn't know what a pop star was then, but I know now that's what my dad was. Even at that age, I realised that every woman in the room was in love with my father, and would manoeuvre themselves to be near him wherever he went. It was a magical experience for me.'

When his son saw him play for the first time, Andy Lothian Snr had been bandleader at the Palais in South Tay Street for more than a decade. Born in a Glasgow tenement as one of seven in 1910, he was something of a musical prodigy and he left school at thirteen to play violin professionally.

He played in cafés and for silent movies, but when the talkies came in he moved into playing on cruise liners, leaving the *Athenia* just before it was sunk by German torpedoes on the first day of the Second World War.

In a bid to make his mark in Scotland, he expanded his band to a fourteen-piece outfit and became a popular draw on the touring circuit. At that time bands would play for six months at one ballroom, then move on to the next. In the last few months of 1937 and into 1938, Andy Lothian and his band were resident at the new Beach Ballroom in Aberdeen, which wasn't doing particularly well before they arrived. The fact that this new band was attracting the crowds did not go unnoticed.

The late 1930s was a boom time for dancehalls. In Dundee, blissfully ignorant of the increasingly unstable political situation across Europe, there was an appetite for dancing.

The Empress had opened in 1938 on Shore Terrace and proved popular under the ownership of the Duncan family, who also ran the Chalet Roadhouse in Broughty Ferry and the Marine Ballroom in Aberdeen. The Locarno in Lochee Road underwent a refurbishment and reopened in 1939 as the New Locarno – when war broke out the ads of the day carried a reminder for dancers to carry their gas masks.

The West End Palais, or Robie's as it was popularly known, was in Well Road off the Hawkhill. It had been opened in 1910 by John Robertson and was the place to go to learn to dance. The JM Ballroom in North Tay Street came later, around 1954, and was operated by a family who had a significant impact on entertainment in the city, headed at that time by Murdoch (Murdie) Wallace.

The Palais de Danse was a popular dancehall in the 1920s but had recently reopened and decided to cater for more refined tastes.

'The manager, George Dundas, was having the same struggle as the

Beach Ballroom,' says Andy Lothian. 'The Empress and the Locarno were both doing well but for some reason the Palais hadn't taken off. So, without telling the owner of the ballroom, Dundas offered to double my father's money if he came to Dundee.'

Andy Lothian Snr agreed to come for six months – and stayed for thirty-five years. By the time he retired, he was the longest-standing residential bandleader in Britain – and he owned the ballroom. The Palais was a long, narrow space. It danced 1000 people, but was licensed for 860. On a Saturday night, however, there were close to 600 couples in there.

The bandleader inadvertently played Cupid and later was often the messenger of good news. In 1988, he told journalist Mary McCormick, 'I was forever announcing engagements and marriages of couples who'd fallen for each other on the Palais floor.'

This relationship with the Dundee public was broken only by the outbreak of war (during which time the Palais had a temporary bandleader). As a radio operator in the RAF, Andy Lothian saw some active service but also took up the baton as bandleader, providing entertainment for the forces in India and the Far East.

'My first memories of my dad are around VE Day, when I was four years old,' Andy recalls. 'I wasn't aware that he had been away, but it was clear that the fact that he was coming back was something to celebrate. We lived on the ground floor at 6 Bellfield Avenue and I remember standing at the window and seeing Dad coming round the corner with his kitbag. Out of his kitbag he presented what seemed like a sack of chocolates. He had saved his sweetie ration through the whole war to buy me these. Thinking about it now, it was probably a ruse to get my mum to himself for the next two days.'

THE PIPER CALLS THE TUNE

Andy Lothian Jnr's musical career began in the second year of secondary school, when he ditched the trombone in favour of the double bass, and was soon playing with the City of Dundee Schools Orchestra.

But this was the late 1950s and jazz was where it was at (man). From the age of fifteen, he would play with local jazz bands, travelling as far as Perth for a residency in the Salutation Hotel on Saturday nights.

In 1958 he formed the East Coast Jazzmen, and opened the Dundee Jazz Club in Parker Street, although for a while it found a home in Nicoll Street, where Andy, 'painted the whole place black and hung strange spider web things around. Don't ask me what I was thinking.'

When school was over, there was more time to devote to the band, but to make ends meet he also took a job in quality control at Smedley's fruit and vegetable canning factory in Blairgowrie, the epicentre of the Angus soft fruit industry.

The East Coast Jazzmen had a following but Andy admits that the band reached its peak in 1960, when they entered the Scottish Jazz Band Championships for the first time and reached the finals in Glasgow. 'Our van broke down on the way. When we eventually arrived at the City Halls it was a sell-out, and we could hear the buzz in the hall from the other bands playing. We had to bang on the stage door and eventually they let us in, but they weren't convinced about letting us play. I was most upset. I was only nineteen and had spent my own money on new jerseys for the boys – one pound each as I recall!'

The management relented and the East Coast Jazzmen were allowed to play last. As they stood at the side of the stage to watch the competition, they were impressed but knew they had something special up the sleeves of those new jerseys.

Andy Snr had asked what the band were planning to play in the final and suggested that, rather than the usual jazz classics, they take songs and give them a new interpretation, suggesting 'Sentimental Journey'. Batting off his son's protestations that it was a pop tune, he also suggested something which at first seemed a strange choice to his jazzer son. 'My dad had worked out an arrangement for a traditional tune called "The Piper o' Dundee". It started with my bass and then everything came in gradually.

From the off it was obvious how much the audience were enjoying it . . . you could feel it in the room and I thought . . . we just might win this.'

They did, becoming the first band to take the title away from Glasgow. The van was fine on the road home.

The late 1950s and early 1960s saw a decline in Dundee's dancehalls, the Empress being demolished around 1964 to make way for an approach to the new road bridge, and the West End Palais a victim of university expansion. The Locarno had already closed in 1953.

HEP REPLACEMENTS

Musical tastes were also changing in the early 1960s. Stuart McHardy grew up in a resolutely communist household where the soundtrack included the music of Django Reinhardt, which he would only later discover was important to many other people in Dundee. 'My uncle Charles O'Connell McHardy, who was in the Pelican Jazz Band in the 1950s, was the source of my original Maccaferi, the type of guitar used by Reinhardt through most of his life. He was also a best-selling novelist of *Send Down a Dove* [a tale of the submarine service during the Second World War].'

Before that iconic guitar was an Egmond, a gift from B.G. Forbes on Victoria Road for his fifteenth birthday in 1962. 'I was totally fixated on it,' he says. 'Guitar music had been making a much bigger impact at that time. It seemed everybody I knew were communists and aware of the folk revival in the US – people like Pete Seeger, Sonny Terry and Brownie McGhee.'

This interest in the world of folk and jazz came together in 1963 when Stuart and friends started the Dundee Modern Jazz Club in the Trad Café at the top of Rosefield Street.

'Ken Hyder and I were at Harris Academy together. We were in the Shakespeare Café with another friend when we had the idea. I didn't play there, but we ran it for about a year from 1963 into 1964. The Palais band would come up and have a jam on a Sunday night, because they could play stuff they couldn't play at work. Ken was obsessed with Dave Brubeck and sent him a membership card – he did write back to say thanks very much!'

Ken Hyder left Dundee in his late teens and became a respected drummer, with a particular talent for fusing musical styles. His band, Talisker, formed in the late 1960s and were together until the 1980s, blending jazz and Scottish traditional music.

Dundonian jazz talent had been making an impact at the highest levels for decades, however. Trumpeter John McLevy had left the city in 1937 at the tender age of ten to join George Elrick's band in London.

World-renowned jazz guitarist Martin Taylor has fond memories of working with John in the mid-1970s, and of hearing stories about McLevy's childhood. 'He lived in one of the lanes off the Perth Road,' says Martin, 'so when he was treated to a trip to Broughty Ferry for his fifth birthday, it was a pretty big deal and a long bus journey. Kids didn't pay until the age of five, so his mum told him that, when he was on the bus, he was four. As Dundee is just a huge village, as soon as they got on the conductor said, "Hello Mrs McLevy. And there's Johnny. How old are you now Johnny?" Of course he answered, "I'm five but I'm four on the bus!"'

John's father was a semi-professional drummer with his own band and he was keen to follow in his father's footsteps. 'John really wanted to be a drummer, but his dad's friend was a trumpet player so his dad pushed him in that direction,' adds Martin. 'He really wasn't physically built for the trumpet in that he had very bad teeth. His range was only a couple of octaves, but what he managed to do within those octaves was so musical and lyrical.'

George Elrick saw him play and convinced McLevy Snr to let the young-ster join at an age which seems inconceivable now. His only time spent working in Dundee was in 1949, initially with Joe Gibson's Band, and then Bernie Stanton at the Locarno. The 1950s took him back to London via Glasgow, working in Cyril Stapleton's BBC Show Band until 1954. A more settled period followed when he played with Francisco Cavez in the plush surroundings of the Savoy for many years.

As the young McLevy was leaving Dundee to play, John Lynch had a pupil who many jazz fans regard as perhaps the most important Scottish jazz musician.

Jimmy Deuchar was born in 1930 and learned the basics of the trumpet from Lynch, who had played bugle as a boy in the First World War and later became Director of Brass Music for Dundee. On demob from National Service, Jimmy joined the Johnny Dankworth Seven in 1951 and by the end of the 1950s, he was working and recording with the leading lights of the London bebop movement, including Jack Parnell. In the early 1960s, his reputation led to work with Ronnie Scott and Tubby Hayes and he was invited to join Kurt Edelhagen's Orchestra in West Germany – one of the most prestigious European orchestras. In 1966, his son Simon was born there, joining his three-year-old brother Stephen, his wife's son from a previous relationship with Italian recording star Piero Ciampi.

In Dundee, the East Coast Jazzmen were able to ride high on the success of 1960 for a while, but by 1962 the young Andy Lothian knew that a change was in the air.

TWIST AND STICK

'Our type of jazz just seemed to disappear between 1961 and 1962,' says Andy. 'Suddenly, we would be supporting the four-piece band rather than the other way around.'

By that time Andy was a full-time professional musician and as strange as it seems now, at twenty-two he felt too old to switch to the bass guitar. Having worked the circuit, he had strong contacts and had already started to promote acts through the jazz club, so a move into that area was relatively painless.

'He was always a good organiser,' said Andy Snr in the 1988 interview.

'He was forever running dances at school, much to the disgust of his mother, who wanted him to spend more time on his homework.'

The first act Andy Lothian booked was Vince Eager. This wasn't Eager's first visit to Dundee, however. He had suffered at the hands of impatient rock'n'roll fans when he opened for Gene Vincent and Eddie Cochran at the Caird Hall in February 1960.

'Vince Eager used to do the local circuit,' recalls musician Gus Foy. 'He was a tall, handsome English guy, always totally immaculate. That was all he had going for him though – when he opened his mouth, he was crap.'

'At the concert when the announcer said, "Vince Eager!" you could see the guys searching for pennies to throw at him,' laughs Gus. 'He was offering to fight the whole crowd! But when Gene Vincent came on – well, he was phenomenal.'

The Caird Hall had been the location of near riots from audiences of the most unlikely entertainers. Musician and memorabilia fiend Dave Burnett remembers a trip to the rather austere surroundings of the hall for a 1958 concert by Tommy Steel and his Steelmen. 'The support was The John Barry Seven. I also remember there being no stage lights – just the bright house lights.' All the better to see a riot with. 'In the second house mayhem descended.' Hundreds of girls had rushed the stage, overpowering security staff and in some cases leaping from the organ gallery above. The *Courier* reported that, 'The battle for Tommy between the mob and the stewards lasted several minutes.'

Whatever the rockers thought of him, the polished Eager was seen to be the ideal opening act for Andy Lothian Jnr's Top Ten Club at the Continental Ballroom in the Cowgate. 'This was early in 1963 and at that time you had to be a club – everyone had to register and show a membership card to get in. Licensing was easing, however, and I realised that in other cities, no licence was required for dancing on a Sunday.'

Andy Snr agreed to let his entrepreneurial son have the Palais on a Sunday evening (inadvertently allowing his band to chill out at the Dundee Modern Jazz Club).

When Andy Jnr was granted a licence to have an event that night, it began what a generation of Dundonians remember as a golden age of live music. For anyone hoping to meet a new lad or lass, however, there was a strange ritual that needed to be observed.

'It was a throwback from 1950s when you couldn't have dancing on a Sunday,' says Andy. 'At that time the Palais had a musical evening, which would start at 6.30pm and end at 9pm. There were tables on the dance-floor and everyone would sit at tables and drink orange squash.

'The only way to see if there were any good-looking lassies was to walk around the perimeter,' he explains. 'The Palais bandstand was a quarter of the way down the ballroom, so it was possible to walk right behind it and round to the other side. This talent hunt became known as the Monkey Parade.

'When the Top Ten Club opened at the Palais there was dancing, but we would fling the back doors open once the bands were done and people would flood out. The Monkey Parade would take place around the city centre until around 11pm.'

Not content with bringing new music to the Palais, Andy Jnr promoted some publicity-grabbing events. The first of these was a Twist Marathon in the West End Palais in 1960. This was a forerunner of the Scottish Twist Championship, held in 1962 at the JM Ballroom.

Twisters could have a five-minute break every hour, but these could be carried forward, most twisters taking a fifteen-minute break every three hours. 'They were twisting for about 100 hours. They looked like zombie penguins by the end,' recalls Andy. The event was won by Perth-born dancer Bobby Cannon, closely challenged by Dundee girl Cathie Connelly (who went on to become World Twisting Champion in 1964 at an event in Manchester). The twisters performed to records, but local bands also entertained.

Thirteen-year-old Donny Coutts was at the first night of the gruelling dance event. Already with his sights on playing drums, his attention was not on the gyrations of the teenage twisters, it was firmly on the band-stand.

'It was the first time I had seen The Staccato Five with Drew Larg – they were fantastic. I have to say I was also fascinated by the drummer who had one hand and was playing with a stick attached by a watch. I looked around and thought, "You lot better be twisting tomorrow: I want to see these guys again."'

The next night his face fell when he saw a different band. 'I was so disappointed, but when they started they were even better!' This was the Johnny Hudson Hi-Four, a band that Andy Lothian was now looking after, having also taken the step into band management. On bass was a young musician called Dougie Martin, who would be an important figure in Donny's musical future.

An important figure in his musical past was his mother, who was always encouraging when he sang as a small boy. 'Mum was a fantastic harmony singer and a huge Everly Brothers fan. She would teach me the third part of their songs and we would sing them at house parties.'

Donny met his first bandmate, Howie Wright, at elocution lessons. When Howie played a Lonnie Donegan tune on guitar, it was time for Donny to take up an instrument. 'We couldn't really afford a guitar but mum had a mandolin so I learned to play that. Howie and I would go to Castle Green on a Saturday morning and play, so that was officially the first gig,' he laughs.

By the time he was thirteen, the family had moved from the Hilltown to Thomson Street in the West End, not too far from Robie's. Donny now had his own record player and, having joined the pipe band and cadets, he was bringing 'any old drums' home to form some kind of kit.

Perhaps his mum wouldn't have been so keen to let her husband sign the Larg's hire purchase agreement for a drum kit if she knew her son's ulterior motives, as Donny believed 'it might be a good way to get girls'. In 1962, the Gigster kit was £22 and was almost immediately put to good use, playing at the school dance with The Spotlights.

'I was asked to join a band called The Wise Brothers and got the biggest gig of the day, St Aidan's Youth Club in Broughty Ferry. It was just before

The Beatles and bands were springing up everywhere.' With a fee of two shillings and sixpence, plus a rider of crisps and Coke, there were other benefits – the screaming girls.

It was well deserved. With no cars to chauffeur him around, Donny took two buses to the Ferry with a full drum kit. 'I didn't even think about it. I was in a band, it didn't matter.'

SOUP OPERA

The night Donny Coutts first saw the Johnny Hudson Hi-Four, he had no idea of the experience that the young bass player had already gained.

Born during wartime, in 1941, Dougie Martin was raised as one of five boys and two girls in the Fleming Gardens area. With nine mouths to feed and his father working as a bookie's runner, money was thin on the ground, but his mum Bella, a formidable woman, kept control of what could be a rowdy brood. For a young boy with ambitions to learn music, Stobswell Boys School seemed the right place to start.

'When I asked for music lessons, the teacher asked what class I was in,' Dougie remembers. 'When I told him, he refused. It turns out I wasn't stupid enough to learn an instrument – you had to be a daftie.'

In reality, he had been playing an instrument. With moothies around the house, by the age of seven he was a self-taught harmonica player and was performing in public at concert parties.

School was behind him by the age of fifteen, when he was working as a message boy at the Dundee Eastern Co-operative Society. 'I managed to get a tea chest there to make a bass. Alec McKillop had a guitar and Ronnie Davie played drums on old tins. So that was the first band in 1956, The Hep Cats.'

It was the height of skiffle and the trio with makeshift instruments would play in clubs. They also took it to the streets, mostly outside watering holes, and always keeping an eye out for the beat bobbies. With no cash to buy records, Dougie heard the hits of the day while hanging off the back of a dodgem car as he worked at Gussie Park Carnival.

'Alec McKillop went off to sea and gave me his guitar,' he says. 'I bought my first proper guitar, a Hofner, not long after that, but I didna know much about equipment, really.'

A band called the Mystery Men asked Dougie if he would join, and straight away he was playing at Perth City Hall. The lack of experience meant there were a few false starts as they didn't know how to switch the PA on – or the microphones. Masks came in handy to spare the blushes.

The band became a favourite in Dundee and found an appreciative audience at Saturday morning picture shows. Drummer Ronnie Jack remembers wondering who were behind the masks. At the age of twelve, he played with a band called The Castaways who had also approached the Gaumont to play. 'The Mystery Men had been on the week before us but I had no idea who they were at the time. When we played all the wee lassies wanted us to sign their arms. Then we sat down and watched the cartoons.'

The Odeon at Coldside also featured young bands as part of the entertainment. Guitarist and singer Brian (Lou) Lewis recalls how he was given his start at an early age. 'I had built a rudimentary guitar from Meccano and knicker elastic but my parents obviously thought, "we better buy him a real one, he might go oot in the street with that". We went to B.G. Forbes and got a Goldentone. The action of the strings was so high that my fingers actually went underneath. And of course, I started *Play in a Day with Bert Weedon*. Tried it for a day, couldn't play, chucked it . . .'

Lou was eleven when he first played at the Odeon. 'I think we went on during a break in *Dan Dare*. I tried to sing "Kisses Sweeter Than Wine" but I didn't really know the words. The guys I was playing with were a lot older than me, so shoved the wee laddie out front. I didn't mind. I was never lacking in nerve.'

Away from the Saturday morning shows, The Mystery Men discarded the masks to become the Johnny Hudson Hi-Four. 'John Moran had that Cliff Richard look – that's what was needed at the time,' says Dougie.

Hudson was deemed a more suitable name than Moran for a budding teen idol.

After agreeing management with Andy Lothian, the Hi-Four were soon heading off to the place where so many bands cut their teeth into fangs – Germany. The Hi-Four were the first band from Dundee asked to play there, although it wasn't Hamburg, it was Cologne. The band left in a blaze of publicity, carrying with them a gift from the Lord Provost for his opposite number.

Apart from playing their own shows, the Hi-Four were in demand as a backing band, and soon made their way to the meaner streets of Hamburg. Versatility was vital, backing artists as varied as Long John Baldry, Gene Vincent and Ricky Valance. 'That was the place to be,' recalls Dougie. 'All the big American stars were there. Being able to walk into a club and see Ray Charles was unbelievable.

'I became a good pal of Alex Harvey, who was out there at the time. One night I got a bit homesick and all I wanted was a plate of my mum's homemade soup. Alex looked after me and we trailed the back streets of Hamburg, trying to find me a decent plate of soup.'

Nothing is like your mum's homemade soup and Dougie enjoyed that when the Hi-Four returned to Dundee, becoming a resident band at Andy Lothian's Top Ten Club. In fact, if any band needed a plate of soup, they were whisked up to Fleming Gardens where the Martin home was renamed Bella's Roadhoose. Anyone calling at the door for Dougie would find Bella saying, 'No, he's no' here son. You wantin' a plate o' soup?' Donny Coutts remembers that you 'couldn't get your bum on the chair before having a plate of soup in your hand'.

Perhaps the best-known, now infamous, star to spend time at Fleming Gardens was a young rocker called Paul Raven, who had been backed by the Hi-Four. The young man contracted pleurisy and had an extended stay at the Roadhoose until Bella nursed him back to health (soup may have been involved). In the days of glam rock, the rocker changed his name to Gary Glitter.

When the Hi-Four decided to split, Dougie took a job with a Perth band called The Cyclones, who had a young female singer called Eve Graham, who subsequently if possible 'taught the world to sing' with The New Seekers.

'The first time I remember seeing Dougie Martin is with The Cyclones in Perth City Hall,' says Alan Gorrie of the Average White Band. 'He was singing Roy Orbison songs, and his voice was getting higher and higher and higher – I couldn't believe I was hearing anyone sing them that well.'

Dougie returned to Hamburg, this time with The Cyclones, but Andy Lothian was still in touch. In 1963, he convinced the Hi-Four to reform and prepare for what was to be their most high-profile concert.

WITH THE BEATLES

For Andy Lothian Jnr, that concert had been hard won. The Top Ten Club was in full swing and gaining a reputation for presenting acts when they were at the top of the 'hit parade'.

The key was predicting which records would be hits, then booking the acts well in advance. 'On some Saturdays I could be running up to twelve dances around Dundee – in Forfar, Blairgowrie, Kirriemuir and all points in between,' says Andy. 'I would get home late and listen to Radio Luxembourg – that's where I would hear new releases.'

Singles had a long lifespan and could take six weeks to reach their maximum chart position. If Andy thought a new release would be a hit, he would book the act then, rather than when they were climbing the chart.

'I would look at the Top Ten Club listings every week and think, "How does he do it?"' says Donny Coutts.

When Andy heard The Beatles' single 'Love Me Do' on its release in October 1962, he applied his usual thinking, and was keen to book the band. He had been working alongside Albert Bonici, who had the Two Red Shoes dancehall in Elgin and was the biggest promoter of bands in the north-east. 'Albert and I agreed to bring the band to Scotland at the beginning of January 1963. I was sure the record would be at the top of the charts by then, but for some reason, this time I lost my touch and the record got no higher than number seventeen.'

The relative indifference towards the first release, combined with the coldest January since 1740, meant that the good people of Elgin stayed at home on 3 January nursing New Year hangovers rather than going to the Two Red Shoes. The tour was scheduled to start in Keith, but the severity of the weather changed the travel plans of The Beatles, who had reluctantly been playing in Hamburg over Christmas. The next night in Dingwall, only nineteen hardy souls showed up to the Town Hall.

Andy was handling the next date, on 5 January at Bridge of Allan Burgh Museum Hall. 'I had been trying to get this venue for a while. It was a beautiful hall, and was generally used for dances and weddings by young farmers, but they agreed to give me a pilot night for The Beatles.'

Following the disastrous turnout at the Dingwall gig, Andy decided to keep staffing to a minimum, taking just one bouncer and his girlfriend Sheila to handle the cash desk. 'I really didn't think it was going to be a big night, even though it was Saturday.'

Andy's recollection is that about ninety-six people were there, the problem being that only four of them were women. 'This didn't please the guys and I was involved in making sure scuffles didn't break out. Some of the guys were throwing coins at the band and one hit Paul McCartney's bass and chipped it. I think I was more upset about it than he was.'

The crowd started to disperse in search of females, and as the evening drew to a close there were only a few people left, but they were well rewarded. 'I was pretty down by this time. I had been warned about protecting the chandelier and someone had tried to climb on it, so I was sure I'd blown my chance.'

He wandered up to the balcony and looked down at the band who announced they would play their next three releases. The man who, as a ten-year-old, had been fascinated by the reaction of crowds towards his father in the Palais, would now witness one of the first performances of songs that would make the four young men the biggest names in music history.

'They played "Please Please Me", "From Me to You" and "She Loves You". My jaw was on the floor. I hadn't heard anything like this before.

'I phoned Albert the next day and told him that we had to get them back. He wasn't convinced, probably due to the fact that we had lost money on them, paying a monumental £40 a night. But I had a feeling they were going to explode with those singles and I didn't want us to miss out.'

Before Albert Bonici knew it, he had been smooth-talked into taking a flight to London the next day, turning up uninvited at Brian Epstein's office to negotiate the return of a band which had bombed spectacularly.

Epstein agreed to see the Scottish promoters and sat back in his chair, saying that his boys found the trip 'quite interesting'. Quickly getting to the matter in hand, he asked what he could do for them.

'I did the talking,' says Andy, 'I'm good at that. So I said that we really liked them and would like to help them by having them back, but the £40 a night was too much and we would need them for at least ten days to promote them properly.'

Epstein paused, well aware that Andy had realised what was about to happen with the band, then replied.

'We could have them back – on three conditions,' says Andy. 'One, it was none of "your dancehalls", it was concerts. Two, it wasn't £40 a night, the price was now £500 a night. Three, the decision had to be made before our bums left the seats.'

There was another element to the negotiation, however. There was small print in the existing contract to say that if the band came back to Scotland, Albert would have first refusal on the shows. Without reneging on the contract, Epstein managed to make life difficult for two men used to running dances and shows in ballrooms.

'He left the room and Albert shrugged his shoulders saying, "Well that's that then. £500 a night? Concerts?" I said we had to have them as they were going to be massive. It was easy for me to say but Albert was the money man. He obviously had some faith in me, so agreed.'

Brian Epstein gave them three dates in October of that year. Andy was delighted. Three releases and three hit singles coming up, maybe more.

By the time tickets went on sale in April, there had been a number two and a number one hit. 'She Loves You' would be released in August of that year, a number one and the biggest hit up to that point.

'I placed a tiny ad in the *Courier* to say tickets would be on sale from Monday at my agency office in Gellatly Street, which was above the Labour Exchange. At 4am on Monday, I received a call from Dundee Police telling me in no uncertain terms to get my arse down there and open up, as 600 kids were "knocking hell oot the labour exchange". My secretary Cathie helped me out, and by the end of the day 1000 tickets had gone. We sold out both houses of the Caird Hall, and that was with the top prices at twelve shillings and sixpence! A few months before that, you couldn't have given the tickets away.'

There was no guarantee of a sell-out at the Caird Hall, even for the biggest acts. When Frank Sinatra appeared there on 12 July 1953, there were no more than a few hundred people there. Once the show was over he did visit the Palais, however, not far from his bunk for the night at the Queen's Hotel.

Before arriving in Dundee on 7 October, The Beatles would play Glasgow and Kirkcaldy. It wasn't a single bouncer this time, as Andy bussed through members of the Dudhope Boxing Club to Glasgow as front of stage security, including Dick McTaggart, who at that time held the 1963 ABA Light Welterweight title.

'The first house was always younger children and families so I had no problem there, but before the second house the noise was incredible. We were ready to open the curtains and these boxers hadn't shown up. The police inspector pointed to the balcony, where the kids were pounding on the plasterwork and it was chipping and falling on the heads below. He told me I'd better get this going or he'd close the place. To that I told him, "Good luck."'

After selecting a few of the biggest men in the audience to act as temporary security staff, Andy could announce The Beatles. 'It was a struggle to keep the girls away from the low stage – and they were strong! At last the doors opened and a load of drunk, Dundee boxers rolled in – the cavalry had arrived.'

With similar scenes in Kirkcaldy the next night, Andy was ready for the challenges of the Caird Hall.

This was the special gig that had tempted Dougie Martin back from Hamburg. Along with another Lothian agency act, The Caravelles, and local favourites Malcolm Clark and The Crestas, the Johnny Hudson Hi-Four warmed up the audience.

Backstage the bands mingled, but Dougie didn't get the greatest of reactions from John Lennon. 'I said something to him about the fact we had been in Hamburg at the same time, and I spoke about someone we both knew. He just cut me off, though. Nae wonder he wouldn't speak to me. You should've seen the tartan suits we were wearing! George sat quietly in a corner, but Paul and Ringo were great, they had a blether.'

'Those white tartan suits were pretty bizarre,' agrees Alan Gorrie. 'I remember the show being on a school night, so it was a bit of a treat to go.'

The local newspapers carried special supplements to welcome the band to the city. The *Evening Telegraph* of 7 October proclaimed in a caption, 'Here we see the renowned Beatles' jackets which have no collars. They have been likened to Quakers or space travellers.'

The next night the *Tele* gave a 'Pat On The Back For The Audience'. The Chief Constable said he would like to 'give a big hand to the public for keeping their heads. And long may they continue to do so.' Only six seats showed any sign of damage, something City Factor Charles McDonald described as 'about the normal amount of damage, say, after a wrestling tournament'.

Andy smuggled the band out through an exit that people barely knew existed and whisked them away to stay at the Salutation Hotel in Perth.

He believes that he was the first to use the term that has become a byword for fan hysteria. 'I am sure that when I was sitting next to a member of staff from the *Courier*, I said it was nothing to worry about, it was only Beatlemania.'

The Beatles phenomenon was to return a year later, promoted this time by Brian Epstein. 'He did it himself from then on,' shrugs Andy, 'but we were the first and we also made our money back from the disaster of January 1963 – and much more. Plus, we were part of musical history.'

Meanwhile, the publishing house that produced both local papers was in the process of putting together a magazine that would make the most of Beatlemania, and be ready for it when it returned.

TEEN DREAMS AND GIRLS FROM THE SCHEMES

In October 1963, while The Beatles packed the Caird Hall, a small team sat in an office a short stroll away, preparing the first edition of what would become a legend in magazine publishing.

It was an unlikely team, headed up by Gordon Small, who had been chief sub-editor of a D.C. Thomson girls' publication called *Romeo* – at that time the idea of a female in charge of any of the 'papers' was unthinkable.

However, technology was changing and a new building, complete with a state-of-the-art press hall, was being built on the Kingsway, far from the attractive red sandstone office building that had been standing in Albert Square since 1905.

'We had been printing *My Weekly* and *Bimbo* on a small press, but once the Kingsway was finished the new press allowed us to take the publications much further. They asked me to produce a one shot, something to show what the new machinery could do. We called this thing *Elvis Cliff and All* – desperate title I know, but it was to be the first time we could produce good colour pictures. We could now offer full page colour pinups, much bigger than anyone else.'

The problem at the time seems to have been that the men operating the swanky new machines hadn't quite grasped the technology as well as Gordon would have liked. 'The press manager told us we could have full colour pages, but some would have to be two-colour, meaning they could be black and one other colour.' Gordon chose blue, since he had pictures of the Everly Brothers in a swimming pool. That would at least make the water blue. 'When it was printed it was red – and they were diving into blood!'

It sold quite well, however, and Gordon was despatched to the corner of the third floor in spring 1963 to come up with a new title. The first task was deciding on what the feel of the publication should be. Gordon admits that, on paper, he was far from the ideal candidate.

'My interests were motorcycles and the hills – rock climbing and ice-climbing. I recruited Gavin McMillan who worked on *Red Star Weekly*. He was a very creative man, tremendous on story ideas. In design, we had Willie Gardner. He had been a cook in the RAF, I was an engine fitter and Gavin had been a rifleman in the Royal Scots, so we were a most unlikely crew. I needed kids around me who knew about pop music. By that time I was married and doing DIY – I had no interest in pop.'

Once a team had been recruited, the planning of the first issue was under way and the perfect name found. Although it has been reported that *Jackie* was named after children's author Jacqueline Wilson, Gordon says, 'Jackie was a popular girls' name at the time – as simple as that. She wasn't even on the staff at the time. However, when I met her in 2009, she still had a letter that I had sent her in 1964. It was very encouraging, offering her five guineas for one article but saying I couldn't use the other one!'

With a production schedule of sixteen weeks, it required more finely tuned powers of prediction than Andy Lothian's to tell who would be in the hit parade at the time. Cliff Richard graced the cover of the first issue which came with a free gift of a twin heart ring. The first issue sold a healthy 350,000 copies.

From the outset, its main competitors were *Fabulous*, *Valentine* and

Boyfriend, all London-based and able to turn things round much more quickly, but against those odds, *Jackie* started to beat them. There were smiles all round when the circulation figures came in on a Friday. There were also approaches to Gordon to head south. 'I had no interest in going to London – everything I wanted to do was here.'

One ex-D.C. Thomson employee who did make the journey south was Jack Hutton. During his time at the publisher, his enthusiasm for music grew, and in 1953 he secured a job with *Melody Maker*. He became editor in the early 1960s and toured with the biggest bands of the day, even joining The Rolling Stones for an American tour in 1964. He was also something of an entrepreneur and launched *Sounds*, among other music magazines, his run ending with the launch of *Kerrang!*.

Gordon firmly believes that the success of *Jackie* lay in recruiting the right type of staff member. 'The best people were girls from Dundee housing schemes, bright Dundee lassies who had their feet on the ground but were very creative. There was a mix with public schoolgirls, but the Dundee schoolgirl knew what life was about. They identified with readers in places like Blackburn, Leeds, Sheffield, Doncaster – they were our heartlands.'

There was no shortage of material to fill the pop pages of *Jackie*. With bands visiting the city every week to play the Top Ten Club, some were on the doorstep but occasionally the magazine would venture further afield.

'I remember going to Aberdeen to take pictures of Dusty Springfield. She said, "Don't take anything when I'm wearing spectacles or smoking." Unfortunately she did one or the other until 2am – at which point I left.'

Many of the exclusive pictures came from a Manchester bookies' son, Harry Goodwin, who had been recruited as official photographer for a new TV show called *Top of the Pops*, broadcast from a disused church in the city.

'He took the huge photographs that were on the walls, and he even had a dressing room of his own there. I managed to make contact and said, "When you've finished taking the black and whites, is there any chance of sticking in a colour film and taking some for us?" He would phone me on the morning of the show and tell me who was there. I would say, "Get me group shots of them and head and shoulders of him . . ." We got shots that no one else had. The film would arrive the next day and we would pick out what we wanted to use. I'm sorry to say the rest of the stuff was thrown away.'

Every opportunity to get exclusive shots was taken and all it took was a word with a bus driver to get bands where *Jackie* needed them to be. The Rolling Stones had been playing in Aberdeen and on the route south were passing through Dundee. A pre-arranged ten-minute stop in the rock garden of the Taypark Hotel was enough for the photographers to get what they needed. 'I don't know what they were all on, but they fell oot the tour bus. Brian Jones seemed the most sensible,' recalls Gordon.

When The Rolling Stones played Dundee in June 1965, they were whisked slightly out of town to the Invercarse Hotel (as were The Beatles the previous year) so *Jackie* could get some shots. They were staying in the Royal Hotel in the city centre, however, and offering Bill Wyman a lift back gave Gordon a small taste of their lives at that time.

'As we drew up, there was what seemed like hundreds of girls outside. He was terrified. Because I knew the territory, I tried to sneak him in a back way and find a pend. There was nothing suitable so he just shrugged and said he had to brave it . . . as he got out the car he seemed to just disappear into a sea of bodies and that was the last I saw of him.'

ROLLING WITH IT

A Rolling Stones show on 24 January 1964 taught Andy Lothian valuable negotiation skills. As well as running the Top Ten Club, managing the Hi-Four and an Aberdeen band called Tommy Dene and the Tremors, he was promoting high-profile package tours. These would come to the grand Caird Hall in the city centre. It had opened in 1923, the result of the philanthropy of jute baron Sir James Caird and, following his death, his sister Emma Marryat. It's unlikely that the city fathers could ever have envisaged aliens such as The Rolling Stones in these surroundings.

'Freddie and the Dreamers had a number one in 1963, but I had heard the next two releases so booked them six months ahead. They were to be supported by a group of young London lads called The Rolling Stones and in the intervening period things changed very quickly.'

There was more of an emphasis on the 'cool'. The coffee bar culture was thriving in Dundee, with the favourite Mod hangout The Hap Café on Arbroath Road. No problem that it was out of the city centre – they would get there on scooters anyway. Owned by the Soave family, it had a sweetie shop and a café downstairs, and the occasional band.

At the beginning of 1964, The Stones were the epitome of cool. The breakthrough EP *Rolling Stones* had been released and it was clear that the Caird Hall audience was much more inclined towards seeing them.

'As usual there were two houses,' Andy recalls. 'The crowd went nuts at The Rolling Stones, and when Freddie came on, there was nothing he could do to win them back – even dropping his trousers didn't work.'

A swift piece of negotiation between houses meant that Freddie was now supporting The Stones. In that six months and following the stratospheric rise of The Beatles, tastes had changed from pop to rock. 'That's when I realised that the Johnny Hudson Hi-Four would need to change.

'First, the name. I was talking to my mother and telling her I'd have to change their name and she said, "No you don't, they're just poor souls." And that was it. The Poor Souls. They were anything but – they were absolutely magnificent.'

CANNED HEAT

By 1965, Dougie Martin had a solid reputation in the music business. He was offered a job as vocalist with Morrissey Mullen and was also asked to join Manfred Mann, but he was happy being based in Dundee with his 'new' band The Poor Souls, an easy transition as it still had the same line-up of John Moran, Dougie, Chic Taylor and John Casey.

They were a main attraction at the Top Ten Club and visiting bands would often be reluctant to follow them. When Alan Gorrie moved to Dundee in 1965, his band The Vikings would also play the Sunday evening slot. 'We both used to rehearse in the Palais so we started swapping musical notes. Dougie was the only guy I admired in the flesh – he had the voice that I hero-worshipped.'

Andy Lothian was so sure that the band would take off, he put them out on the road, and together with a Norwich-based promoter called Bram Lowe (who later brought Jimi Hendrix to a tiny venue there) went about getting them a recording contract. As organised as the schedule was, there were occasional blips. 'We had to go to London for gigs,' recalls Dougie. 'Andy had found us nice digs in Swiss Cottage, but when we arrived and phoned the venue, it turned out we were there a week early. It was the same with every gig. So we were stuck in London with nae money, and when we opened the cupboards in the house, nothing to eat. We phoned Andy and he said, "Don't worry boys – I'll sort you out."'

Andy was always good at keeping contacts, and this was where connections in Smedley's cannery came in handy. Gus Kelly, who worked for Andy, was despatched from Dundee with a Mini full of tins, the only problem being there were no labels, so every meal was a surprise. Except it wasn't.

'Peas. Peas. Peas. Every time we opened a tin, it was bloody peas. For days we lived on nothing but peas. Eventually someone, I canna remember who, said, "I'm going to open a tin, boys, just on the off chance that it's no' peas." We heard this scream from the kitchen: "Carrots!" Well you couldn't see us for dust as we dived on him.'

It wasn't all penury, however, and spending time in London had its benefits. In February 1966, Dougie was having a pint in The Ship in Wardour Street and struck up a conversation with Steve Winwood. 'He asked what we were doing later and if we wanted to go to a gig at the Marquee. It was

Stevie Wonder. So, I was in the Marquee with Steve Winwood, watching Stevie Wonder and when I looked to the other side of the pillar, John Lennon was there.' Lesson learned in 1963, he didn't bother speaking to him.

The hunt for a record deal had also paid off and in 1965 The Poor Souls released a single on Decca, a Lesley Duncan song, 'When My Baby Cries'. The song was highlighted by Radio London in July 1965 and Jimmy Savile championed it on Luxembourg, but it failed to crack the charts. Andy Lothian is certain that it came down to the fact that it was ruined by an unsympathetic producer, who slowed the pace of the song.

As successful as The Poor Souls were as a live act, after a year in London and Norwich it felt that things weren't really happening. As Dougie puts it, we said, 'This is sh*te, let's go home.'

BLOWING THEIR OWN HORNS

'It really wasn't cheating,' says Donny Coutts. 'It was just giving them some ... encouragement.' The trend of teenage fans scrawling the name of a band on the van in lipstick was given something of a start by the bands, it seems. 'Once they saw it, it gave them permission, and they were away.'

In Dundee at this time, a fair amount of Max Factor was being sacrificed to the vans of The Poor Souls and The Vikings.

The Vikings were essentially a Perth band who consumed Dundonian members, swinging the balance in favour of its adopted home. 'I didn't come to Dundee for a band, I came to attend Duncan of Jordanstone art college,' says founding member Alan Gorrie. 'We were already fairly successful in Perth, but when Graeme Duncan and Roy Fleming quit, I was keen to recruit Donny Coutts and Mike Fraser from a band called The Syndicate, so I moved in for the kill. When Jock Taylor left, I asked Donny if there was any chance of getting Drew Larg away from The Honours and luckily he agreed. So that, along with Doug Wightman, was The Vikings' line-up.'

Mike Fraser is regarded as one of the most gifted keyboard players to come out of Dundee. His brother Kenny was similarly talented and a member of a jazz outfit, the Free Four, also a mix of Perth and Dundee musicians.

'And Donny. Well Donny is so talented as a singer and a player – he has one of those penetrating voices that you can spot miles away. Donny could have made it with his voice alone. Dougie Martin, Gary Clark, and Donny all have that in spades,' Alan adds.

There was a self-belief in The Vikings, something that Alan puts down to being at art college. If you were there in the first place you were good at something. Being good at music was a bonus. 'None of us were deep thinkers, we were free thinkers – who were getting a grant from the government,' he laughs. 'You started the term with Benson & Hedges and by the last few weeks, it was five Woodbine.'

(As a student in 1965, Alan may well have passed a lecturer in the halls called Mr Collins, who had just moved from Glasgow with his family, including young Edwyn. The future Orange Juice frontman spent his childhood in Dundee, but moved back to Glasgow in the middle of his secondary schooling at Morgan Academy.)

Donny Coutts believes a night in Strathpeffer was the key. Having previously played with The Wise Brothers, he joined The Syndicate, who were delayed that night because of heavy snow; leaving The Vikings to carry on until they arrived. He was asked to join them as singer when Jock Taylor left, but it wasn't possible at the time.

'I remember getting a phone call from Mike Fraser in December 1965 telling me we had both been asked to join The Vikings. I would be drumming this time as Jock Taylor had come back. This time we did, and our first gig was Christmas Eve at Kirriemuir Town Hall. The first number we played was The Beatles' 'We Can Work It Out'. Jock left again soon after and then Drew joined.'

Andy Rettie had been managing The Vikings and continued to look after the new line-up, although Andy Lothian was getting the band some of its work.

'It was a very exciting time to be involved – riveting from the moment The Beatles took off,' Alan recalls. 'That's certainly what inspired the Dundee bands. From an outsider's point of view it seemed that Dundee was like a microcosm of Liverpool. A seaport, a similar self-deprecating, lunatic sense of humour, everybody a wit and a lot of bands of varying quality, but all trying very hard to be as musically adept as they could be.'

During 1966, the band was playing the Top Ten Club, opening for acts like The Hollies, The Merseybeats and Chris Farlowe.

'It really was about the music. The Top Ten had some fantastic bands and the best were local. A few Glasgow bands came up but they couldn't hold a candle to the local guys. You could say they were "all frame and nae picture".

'The places we played didn't sell drink and apart from heading over to Laings Cellar for a pint, we didn't really drink. It was the same with drugs. If they were there, they weren't available to us, and you would think that an art college would have been the hotbed. There was plenty of hemp coming in on boats, but it must have gone off to Edinburgh and Glasgow on some nefarious transport.'

ARRAN JUMPING

Nefarious transport. Perhaps the best description of escaping to Arran for eight weeks during the summer. Andy Lothian's reach extended that far, and his bands would decamp there for the summer months, playing dances at Lamlash, Blackwaterfoot, Whiting Bay, and the big one, Brodick. They would also back the bigger artists who visited the island.

'Dougie Martin once borrowed a van from a guy for a day and took it back eight weeks later,' says Donny. 'Well, he had to get the gear to Arran somehow.'

'We were backing Gene Vincent,' says Dougie, 'but to be honest Gene had become more of a pal. One night he got absolutely blootered and we ended up carrying him across to the village hall where we were playing. We tried to get a fish supper in him to sober him up, but it was impossible. He was terrible that night.

'Then the next night Donny Coutts saw him play the Palais in Dundee and he was right as rain.'

Arran was a turning point for Dougie. He met his wife there and moved to Glasgow to set up home in 1967. The Poor Souls were over, although John Moran (Johnny Hudson) resurrected the name briefly when he moved to Canada in the late 1960s. Dougie wouldn't return to live in Dundee until 1976.

CLIMB EVERY MOUNTAIN

Donny Coutts wouldn't be in Dundee for a substantial period of time either, as The Vikings upped sticks and headed off to London in January 1967.

They had already recorded a single, a Paul Simon composition called 'Bad News Feeling', for ALP Records, the latest venture in Andy Lothian's expanding musical empire (ALP stood for Andy Lothian Productions). It became the eleventh and final release in late 1966. 'I had an arrangement with Polydor for ALP records, ALP being the pinnacle of sound perfection of course,' he laughs.

Listening to The Vikings' single again, Donny isn't so sure. 'Ach, it wasn't very good. No wonder Paul Simon never recorded it himself, it just doesn't go anywhere. The B-side's better. The proud moment though, was listening to it on Radio Luxembourg with my mum. It took me back to listening to the radio with her when I was a wee boy.'

ALP recorded eleven artists in studios in Birmingham or London, the first being a Fife band called the Red Hawkes. It also recorded Andy Lothian Snr and a groovy duo called Peter and Alison with their tribute to the new Tay Road Bridge, which opened in November 1966. This was not the first venture into recording for a Dundee promoter. In 1964, Murdoch Wallace of the JM Ballroom released a single called 'My Dream Came True' on what else but JM Records. The band Hammy and the Hamsters was made up entirely of players from Dundee Football Club, with the main man Alex 'Hammy' Hamilton.

For local bands, Andy Lothian's deal with Polydor reaped rewards, however. Dave Burnett, who played in a Top Ten Club band called The Phoenix, remembers visiting his offices one day. 'Andy had just received a new release from Polydor. We were blown away by it. It was "Hey Joe" and this was the first time we had heard Jimi Hendrix.'

Dundee also had its fair share of extraordinary musicians, and that included guitarists. Jim Kelly was a huge favourite and after a few years of gigging locally with The Durelles, Mark Dayton & the Honours, and The Honours he took the train south in 1967 to join Lulu's backing band. Destined for greater things, he joined Honeybus in 1968 for a successful couple of albums and the classic pop single 'I Can't Let Maggie Go'. He released a solo single in 1969, but headed back to Dundee in 1970.

When The Vikings headed to London, it was as a solid team, their previous disappointments put behind them. They had auditioned for The Hollies' producer Mike Mansfield at Parlophone the previous year at Abbey Road Studios, performing two original songs. Mansfield, although impressed by the band, wasn't sure if the songs were what he was looking for.

'We had driven down overnight,' says Donny. 'We arrived there about 4am and parked beside Regent's Park, changing in the van before heading off to the studios. I always remember the engineers wearing white lab coats.

'When we finished our songs, Mansfield said there was another hour and was there anything else we could let him hear. We did 'We're Doing Fine', a song recorded by Dee Dee Warwick (Dionne's sister) which hadn't been a hit. You could see something in his face change and when we had finished, he said, "It's a great song, but sorry boys, Billy J. Kramer has just recorded it." Aye right!'

Alan Gorrie remembers the moment well. 'These things happened. You went down with a lump of coal in your hand, they would polish it and give it to someone else.'

In London, The Vikings shared a house in Henry Road, Finsbury Park, with The Senate, a Glasgow soul band who had Alex Lidgerwood (later Santana) and The Wildflowers, who had Paul Rogers (Bad Company/ Free), Micky Moody (Whitesnake) and Bruce Thomas (an Elvis Costello Attraction) in the line-up.

They signed with the Peter Walsh Agency, which looked after Marmalade, Spencer Davis, The Tremeloes and the Love Affair, and were playing regularly at venues including the Marquee. During that time Donny was asked, on several occasions, to join Marmalade. 'I didn't want to do that. I thought we were going to be big anyway,' he says, but Mike Fraser subsequently played on many of their releases.

Auditioning for other bands was not uncommon, and a sense of innate Dundee fairness meant Donny didn't get a job he auditioned for at the Saville Theatre in 1967. 'I actually passed the audition and the manager said I would get £55 a week. That was a lot of money then, but I heard that the other three would be on £80. I told him that where I come from, no matter what, it's a fair split and I walked away.' He walked away from the Bee Gees.

The Vikings did record for Polydor in London, Donny singing a song called 'Take Me for a Little While'. Then the news came that it couldn't be released because Patti Labelle was releasing it on Atlantic (a Polydor affiliate) and Vanilla Fudge had also done a version.

There was also plenty of session work for good, solid bands. A performer called Wayne Gibson invited them to play on a record he was making. It was to be a Beatles song on one side and a Stones cover on the other. 'How original eh?' says Donny. 'Anyway, we do it in Advision Studios on Bond Street. We recorded both in an hour and a half and were asked if we wanted the session fee of two pounds four shillings or points on the record. We said we would take the money thanks very much – knowing it was dreadful. The record died a death at the time, and like all Stones covers felt the wrath of Jagger's tongue.

'Then it's 1974 and I'm watching *Top of the Pops*. Tony Blackburn comes on saying, "Here's a SUPER new sound from the northern soul scene – it's 'Under My Thumb' by Waaaaaaaaaaayne Gibson!!!"' Re-released on a Pye disco label it took hold on the dancefloors and sold in the region of 400,000 copies. 'Uch it's still rubbish,' says Donny. 'Alan Gorrie's not in tune and he's far too loud.'

WHEN CREAM TURNS

The Top Ten Club continued to pack the Palais every Sunday night throughout the mid-1960s. If it was important to the music fans, it held an ever greater significance for local musicians who had the chance to play on the famous bandstand.

The design of the Palais meant that musicians could stand behind and watch the band, a particularly good position for drummers. Ronnie Jack preferred to watch from the front, however, and distinctly remembers standing near the back, but feeling like he was being lifted off the floor by the thud of the bass drum when the Love Affair played.

Dave Burnett jumped in with both Cuban-heeled boots when the beat boom started in 1963, forging his dad's signature on a hire purchase form to buy an electric guitar from J.T. Forbes in the Nethergate.

The Destinies were his first band, playing local halls but also enjoying a residency at The Ponderosa on Clepington Road. When the blues boom followed, he wandered into Talking Walls with legendary Dundee drummer (Rebop) Tam Parks; but his longest musical relationship in the 1960s was with a bass player called Gerry McGrath in The Phoenix (the band, not the well-known Dundee hostelry), who later would play a large part in Donny Coutts and Dougie Martin's lives.

'We were very much a soul band,' remembers Dave. 'If Dundee had a reputation for being soul city then we fitted right into the groove.'

They supported The Kinks at the Palais in July 1966, when 'Sunny Afternoon' was number one. There was plenty of work for popular bands in the 1960s, and for some it was a case of combining business with pleasure.

The Kinloch Arms in Carnoustie was a popular 'just out of town' venue for Dundee bands. 'Gerry got me in affy trouble one night,' Dave recalls. 'It was the Glasgow holidays and there was a big crowd of women there.' In the 1960s, there was a good chance they had come to Angus to pick berries, then head out on the 'ran dan' of an evening. 'He convinced me to let the van go without us and we ended up walking back to Dundee. It was two and a half hours before we got a taxi in Broughty Ferry.'

Anyone who knew Gerry would go that wee bit further to accommodate. 'When we got a new record that we wanted to learn, we would play the 45rpm at the speed of a 78, so that he could hear the bass runs more quickly,' says Dave.

Things were slowing down elsewhere, however. Around 1967, Andy Lothian noticed a significant difference in numbers attending dances. Colour TV had arrived in Dundee and people were staying in rather than going out for entertainment.

'I was still running big concerts, but the business had also got wise,' he says. 'They would no longer allow a promoter to speculate whether a record was going to be a hit or not. Band managers would now build clauses into contracts saying that the money would automatically go up, depending on how successful the record was.'

Margins were getting tighter and it was becoming increasingly difficult for the company to finance concerts. 'There may have been a gradual decline, but one particular promotion meant the doors closed for good.

'Maybe I had lost my touch, I don't know,' says Andy. 'With Cream I thought, "These three guys coming together will be huge." It was more an intellectual knowledge rather than knowledge of how the public would react, however. I paid them far too much money a year in advance.

'They did nothing and fewer than 400 people turned up to two houses at the Caird Hall. That was the same in all three concerts I promoted. So that finished Andy Lothian Organisation Limited. It went into liquidation because it couldn't pay its debts. For band transport, I would hire buses from Napper Thomson in Lochee. We had a good working relationship and I hated the fact that I might not be able to pay my debts to him. The local guys were being paid first.'

On top of that, he had to return the band bus he hired for Cream in a rather unusual state. 'They had been in Newcastle the night before and thought it a jolly jape to visit a local bakery and buy boxes of cream cakes. They amused themselves on the journey to Dundee by throwing these cakes at one another. As the bus drew into the City Square in front of the Caird Hall, I couldn't quite make out what the white stuff covering the windows was.

'The three of them tumbled off the bus. Ginger Baker needed to get carried in, but as soon as he got into the dressing room, he was fine, like nothing had happened.'

The bill for Napper's bus came to £60, all the cash Andy had. He visited him in person to settle the bill and was touched that Napper never once mentioned cash. 'He was more concerned about me and gave me nothing but support. As I was going, I gave him his £60 – and he started to cry.'

CYMBAL OF BRILLIANCE

By the summer of 1967, The Vikings were not such a happy crew. Donny remembers feeling almost relieved that things were coming to an end. 'Drew and Dougie had fallen out and we had been playing as a four-piece without Dougie. Alan had the opportunity to join the Scots of St James and I was considering going back to college in Dundee, where I had a girlfriend.'

However, Donny's influence would be felt for a long time, introducing a young Dundee drummer to his first proper professional job in London.

'I knew a few guys who lived around the Perth Road and Mac Carnegie was one of them. Mac was a great friend of a young drummer called Robbie McIntosh, who would come to see me play with The Syndicate and generally hang about. I thought this was just another wee lad saying, "I want to be drummer" – they were ten a penny.'

When Robbie mentioned that he had a Ludwig kit (only Ringo Starr and Keith Moon had those), that grabbed Donny's attention. He accepted the invitation to visit Robbie's Kincardine Street flat and see it. Even though he was just fifteen or so, he lived in a flat, albeit with hardly a stick of furniture. 'I walked in and right enough, there was a Ludwig kit.'

It may have seemed unusual for a teenager to have such an impressive piece of gear, but Robbie had had an unusual upbringing. His father was the American actor Bonar Colleano, who had had a liaison with Robbie's mum while on location near Dundee. He was raised mainly by his Aunt Vi and his gran, who were also the source of the kit.

Donny remembers vividly what happened next.

Robbie: 'Want a shot?'

Donny: 'I'm left-handed.'

Robbie: 'Right enough, so you are. I'll have a shot, then we'll swap it around.'

'He started and it was utterly incredible,' says Donny. 'I said, "How did you learn to play like that?"'

Apart from being in the Boys' Brigade band, Robbie's education was jazz records. Philly Joe Jones, Buddy Rich, Joe Morello – these were his teachers. Mac Carnegie told Donny that one night when he went to collect Robbie to go out for a drink and on the pull, Robbie wouldn't move until he had absolutely nailed a Joe Morello lick he was trying to perfect.

Dave Burnett, at the time playing with The Phoenix, knew how good the young drummer was and visited Kincardine Street to try to convince him to join them. 'I always remember there was a tree on the Hawkhill that you could see from his window. The flat was two rooms – a drum kit in one and a bed in the other, but nothing else.'

When the drummer left The Senate, Donny knew that he was heading home to Dundee, but had no hesitation in recommending Robbie.

Alan Gorrie recalls that Donny had brought Robbie to a couple of the sessions of the Blue Workshop in Perth, a loose collective of musicians who would get together and have impromptu jazz sessions in front of an audience. Now he was charged with bringing Robbie to London for The Senate.

'I took Robbie down and he got the job instantly,' says Donny. 'They were off to play in Germany but at that time you had to be eighteen to do that and Robbie was still just seventeen. They got round it by dropping him off about half a mile from the border, where papers would be checked. He walked through at the crossing, long after they had driven through, and they met up another half a mile away!'

Alan describes him as having 'all of the Dundee humour in him. He was a phenomenally funny guy. He could say anything to anyone without getting a smack. That's quite a talent.'

Playing as a backing band in The Senate didn't always work out for Robbie. Backing the likes of Garnet Mimms or Lee Dorsey suited his style, but playing with Duane Eddy, well that took discipline and that's something that he wasn't always blessed with. 'Robbie and Duane didn't get on,' says Donny. 'One night Duane came off and said, "I didn't think you played well tonight." Robbie answered, "What a coincidence, Duane – I was just thinking that about you."'

He was fearless, or maybe just had plenty of Dundee front, but he once approached Micky Dolenz of The Monkees and proceeded to pick through his hair, like a chimpanzee grooming.

Robbie's most glorious moment may have come one night in Tramps nightclub, where the great and good of the London music scene were trying to be über cool and ignore Freddie Mercury. Not Robbie. As bold as a guy speaking to his mate in a Hilltown boozer, he approached the flamboyant rocker and said, 'I think you're great, I watch you every week . . .' Mercury looked puzzled and said, 'What do you mean?' Robbie replied, '*The Freddie Starr Show*. I watch it every week!'

Donny found himself at the mercy of Robbie and Arthur Brown's humour in the tranquil surroundings of a London park. 'It was a sunny day and we saw a guy selling ice-cream. Arthur said to Robbie, "Take my hand, son," and with no hesitation at all, he gets down on his hunkers and they go to get an ice-cream. When Robbie gets his cone, he takes it and sticks it in the middle of his forehead. The guy isn't happy and starts shouting at them. Robbie's still on his hunkers with a cone on his napper and Arthur Brown says to the guy, "Do you know who I am?" The guy says, "No. Should I?" So Arthur Brown – and I can't quite believe I'm saying this – shouts, "I AM THE GOD OF HELLFIRE," and starts going into the full "Fire" routine. I tell you, I was glad I was standing at a distance . . .'

Robbie made two live albums with The Senate and spent time working at The Piper Club in Rome, where Mike Fraser joined the band. For a short time, there was a third Dundonian when Jim McAra came in to replace Alex Lidgerwood.

As the decade came to an end, Robbie was working with Brian Augur's Oblivion Express. Alan Gorrie had been working with Onnie McIntyre in Scots of St James (Hamish Stuart joined briefly before leaving to form Dream Police) which became Forever More, while Roger Ball and Molly Duncan (dubbed the Dundee Horns by Maggie Bell) were in demand as a horn section. The pieces that made up the first line-up of the Average White Band were in place.

Donny was back in Dundee, studying but still playing, initially with The Right Time, and then a college band called The Sleepy People. In the time he had been away, new faces were appearing at live venues and reflecting the changing tastes in music of the late 1960s.

ORIGINAL LINE-UP

'I can't write a note of music,' says Gordon Douglas. 'I can't play chords in a way that another guitarist would understand and I can only remember what I should be playing through a strange form of hieroglyphics.'

This apparent lack of conventional ability hasn't stopped the songwriting. Mention the name Gordon Douglas to any of the better-known Dundee musicians and they'll be forthcoming about how influential he has been. 'Gordon Douglas always was very encouraging,' says Michael Marra. 'It was the absolute opposite of the competitive thing – a talented man and always very kind to me.'

This unassuming man was brought up in a home that resounded to the Great American Songbook. It was always busy as his father, then boss of the huge National Cash Registers (NCR) factory, entertained guests from the American side of the business. 'My dad also brought records back from his American trips, music that was pretty exotic to me.'

When the family moved into Greywalls on the Perth Road, there was even more room to entertain. 'It was a very big house. We had a huge music room with a piano, so I could record songs, very badly, with a makey-up tape machine.'

Like any schoolboy interested in music in the mid-1960s, he rounded up like-minded pals to form a band. His friends at Harris Academy were John Fitzgerald, Wayne Hutton and Bert Donaldson. 'We would rehearse in John's house in Menzieshill, with Bert on bass, John on lead guitar and Wayne on a big bass drum. I took vocals. There was a tape machine and a mic hung over the wardrobe door, so I'd have to sing into the wardrobe.'

As a school band, the main claim to fame was playing at the Harris dance in the main hall of the school. As 'a proven chicken', Gordon says the appearance helped him manoeuvre more easily among the genuine bullies of the school. 'I soon found them nodding to me with a certain grudging respect in the corridor, an early lesson in the awesome power of music.'

The earliest gigs were at Wallacetown Church Hall, St Aidan's Church Hall, and St Andrews Town Hall. He says every gig, no matter how small, was a learning experience, and not all good – faulty equipment, huffy musicians, agents who sent you to the wrong place, being double-booked, venues going bust, and the constant risk of running out of petrol.

However, it was the music that mattered and the songwriting prowess of The Beatles, followed by the harmonies of Crosby, Stills and Nash were the inspiration for his bands, including the first line-up of Wells Fargo.

'John, Bert and I, along with Jeff Clark, were the first line-up,' he says. 'John had introduced me to Jeff, and that was a life-changing event. He was writing original material and it was great. It was what I wanted to do.'

Gordon was also recording bands at Greywalls. One of these was Grizel Jaffray, a folk outfit named after the last witch to be burned in Dundee in the seventeenth century. 'That line-up was Christine Stewart, Allan Barty, Lou Lewis, Berend Versluis and Tony van der Kuyl. Tony was writing a lot of material at that point about Dundee. That was the first time it dawned on me that you could write about your own environment.'

THE BOTHY WELCOME

Lou and Tony were part of the folk scene that was thriving at The Bothy, upstairs at The Bread (Breadalbane Arms). Tony had had been playing with Jim Reid and the Shifters and Lou had formed a duo with his friend Tam Corness.

'Tam and Lou, we were called; incredibly imaginative,' says Lou. Following his early triumphs on Saturdays at the Odeon, Lou had become a respected guitarist but started 'mucking about' with his friend Tam, leading to a residency in The Bothy. Like Dougie Martin, he had a job at Gussie Park Carnival, which exposed him to the current hits, but he was drawn towards playing the country rock coming out of America's West Coast in the late 1960s. 'Very few people had heard this stuff and they probably thought we wrote it. We didn't ever tell them any different,' he laughs.

Jeff Clark had been going to The Bothy for some time. 'It had a reputation for traditional folk music,' says Gordon, 'but Tam and Lou were a breath of fresh air, playing what I would call modern folk music. In 1969, when I had just started art college, Jeff had managed to talk the owner, Jim Stirling, into giving him a night every week. After a few weeks he asked if I wanted to join him. This I did in flash: two vocals, two acoustic guitars, *amplified*, and original material. The amplifiers alone raised more than a few disapproving eyebrows from some of the more established folkies, and there were a few charges of cheating levelled at me for my open tuning.'

The folkies were far from the narrow-minded, Aran-jumpered, hand-over-the-ear stereotypes, but they did have strong opinions on what they liked. Dave Burnett remembers Tony van der Kuyl booking his blues band Talking Walls into the St Aidan's Youth Club and ordering them to play nothing but John Lee Hooker and Bo Diddley numbers. 'I paid the price for the gig when I had to sit through him and Lou playing at a Hamish Imlach folk concert at the Caird Hall,' says Dave. 'I was only there to see Billy Connolly and Gerry Rafferty (The Humblebums) who were on after them.'

INTO THE WOODLANDS

Although he moved to university in Edinburgh in the mid-1960s, Stuart McHardy made regular trips back to Dundee, and was a contemporary of Tony, Lou and Tam at The Bothy. He remembers the beginnings of what became the city's best known folk club, in the Royal British Hotel at the top of Castle Street. 'That was the first time I ever played in a jug band, but I remember it was big news as it had attracted folk like Bert Jansch and Archie Fisher.'

That night, in March 1963, was the first night of the Dundee Folksong Club, later called the Dundee Folk Club, which moved around various locations until finding a permanent home in the Woodlands Hotel in Broughty Ferry in 1965.

Russ Paterson and Willie Whyte were the club's founders, having met through a mutual love of music while working at D.C. Thomson in 1962.

'Willie just poked his head around the screen one day and said, "You play guitar, don't you? Come round to my house on Thursday night."'

Russ had been playing guitar since he was a boy. There was only one guitar teacher in town at the time, Violet Burns, and she sure as shootin' wasn't playing the kind of guitar that Russ was hearing on Hank Williams records.

Originally from St Cyrus, the family moved to Dundee, where Russ tried to find records he could learn guitar from – he had a guitar which his father said he had found floating in the dock.

'I was called up to do my National Service in Cyprus and took the guitar with me. It was the time of the skiffle explosion so that's what we played, in a band called The Sinners. My sister would send tapes from the UK to keep me up to date with the latest music.'

From that first night at Willie's house came the idea to start a folk club. It started with an ad in the local paper (employee discounted of course) asking for anyone who was interested to get in touch. About twenty people turned up at the first meeting in Ann Street School on 9 January 1963. 'The janny got in touch to say we could meet there for a few hours,' says Russ.

There was an ambition to bring the best current folk artists to the town, but that meant saving up. Once the original members had saved enough to bring Archie Fisher, the first night in the Royal British Hotel was arranged. 'We got much more than we paid for that night, with Archie bringing along Bert Jansch, Jill Guest, Josh MacRae, Maurice Frankel and Pete Shepherd, along with our local singers.'

Venues through 1963 and 1964 went from The Stag to Bain Square, the Craigtay Hotel, the Taypark Hotel, and then from September 1965, the Woodlands Hotel, hidden behind trees in a residential area.

Apart from booking some of the biggest names in folk at that time, Russ and Willie performed as The Inn Folk, joined initially by Ally Lowden on bass and latterly Allan Barty on fiddle and mandolin (who played with Barty's Bow and later with The Lowland Folk). 'That let us tap into a wider circuit for the group and we got some good gigs, supporting the likes of Tom Paxton.'

Performers liked the Woodlands: it was an appreciative audience who kept quiet. This was as much to do with Willie's technique as good manners. 'One night after Christmas, Allan Barty had come in with a new jersey that his mum had knitted him for Christmas. You should've seen this thing. It was a shame – he was just a laddie. Somebody was being a bit rowdy until Willie shouted, "You. At the back. Keep quiet or I'll get Allan's mither to knit you a jersey!"'

A young Fife songwriter was making an impression on the folk scene at the time when the Woodlands was at its height of its popularity. 'My main connection to Dundee was Robin McKidd,' says Rab Noakes. (Robin was one of those who showed up at that first Ann Street meeting.) 'I grew up in Cupar and we really didn't come to Dundee much. The big nights out were Kirkcaldy and when the big package tours came, we would go to Glasgow.'

When he left school, Rab didn't go to university but remembers what he describes as 'interfacing' with that life in the back room of the Hawkhill Tavern, which was very amenable to musicians. 'It wasn't just music. There were conversations about many other things, including what books you were reading. It was a voyage of discovery.'

He had already had two fairly major voyages of discovery, in London in 1966 and again, along with Robin McKidd, from 1967 to the end of 1968.

At the time there was a real hierarchy of folk clubs and the Woodlands was regarded as being a very good one. Few people were booked as a headline act straight away. 'It was commendable quality control,' says Rab. 'It wasn't being snobbish, it was just looking after the audience. Willie and Russ were great themselves, so it was quality from the word go. Once you had been there, maybe next time or the time after, then you would get a booking to yourself.'

The Woodlands was regarded as a club where the audience would be entertained. 'Not just getting up to sing with a hand over one ear,' as Russ says. Rab, however, feels that the stereotype of the Aran jumpers and po-faced folkie was a myth. 'These people were real raconteurs – they had the songs, but their stories had a real association with the songs. This was very genuine, not reverential at all.'

The club ran until 1971, closing because the increased price of artists meant that they would have to charge five shillings on the door to cover the costs. The last night was 11 April 1971, but it wasn't long before one of their floor singers, Gus Foy, took over the running in conjunction with a promoter called Norrie Maiden.

'Simple songs, that's what I liked,' says Gus. 'You wouldn't think it, with my first record being the soundtrack to [Biblical epic] *The Robe*, but hearing Burl Ives was a turning point. After that, when Bob Dylan came on the scene, I went straight out and bought a harmonica.'

His friends had started playing in skiffle groups, and after playing a washboard, Gus learned a couple of chords on guitar. After a couple of years in folk clubs, he became a Woodlands floor singer.

As well as taking up the baton at the club, Gus acquired a guitar that had belonged to Russ. 'I went into Forbes' one day and saw this beautiful Epiphone. I said, "Is that Russ Paterson's?" He had traded it in because it wasn't working for him, so I pushed the boat out and bought it. Michael Marra bought it from me, but I've no idea where it is now. He says it was stolen but I think he left it in the back of a taxi . . .'

The Seventies

The Seventies

A LIFE IN BRACKETS

Long before the second exchange of that legendary Epiphone, Gus Foy was intrigued by a guitar in a plastic carrier-bag, or certainly by the slender, shy-looking young man carrying it, as he made his way up the aisle at the Woodlands.

'He comes wandering in, looking like a miniature Wild Bill Hickok, with long hair and beard, and this guitar in a carrier bag. He says, "Are you Gus Foy? Can I maybe sing a couple of numbers?"'

Carrying on the Woodlands tradition of quality control, Gus had to audition any new acts who came in. 'I said, "I don't want to be rude, but I need to hear you first. Can you give me a couple of tunes?"

'When he started I thought, "OK, what have we got here then?" I said I didn't recognise the song and he told me it was his own. He did another song, same thing again. I asked how many he had, and he said, "Hundreds."'

It was Michael Marra, who had been persuaded by his friend Arlene Gowans from Lochee to go to the club.

'The first time I saw Angus Foy was at Shore Terrace, waiting to get a bus to Broughty Ferry,' says Michael. 'I saw he had a guitar case; he was an enigmatic-looking man. I wasn't keen to go to the Woodlands, but Arlene said it would be OK if I just did a couple of songs. Gus was significant, because he saw how nervous I was and was very good to me. He took me under his wing and explained a few things.'

The men struck up a friendship almost immediately. 'I would go to the club every Sunday and afterwards we would go to Gus's house in Whitfield and rehearse a few numbers. We formed a duet and would play locally – Fife and Angus mainly.'

The nerves weren't caused by a first public appearance. Michael had performed at an NCR Christmas party as a child in the 1950s and at the Saturday-morning picture shows in the Gaumont as a teenager, inspired by his piano-playing brother Eddie, who was in a band.

It had been a musically inclined household in Lochee, where Michael was one of five. Dad was a jazz enthusiast, but also favoured the Irish tenors and some Beethoven, while Mum was a singer and played a rather fine Bluthner piano.

He was shown a few things by Eddie before he went to piano lessons in Lochee, but a reluctance to deal with written music led him to develop his own way of working.

'I love the shape of written music, but it looks like an adventure with Neptune rather than what they're supposed to convey. To me, the piano is all lying in front of you. It's difficult to make a mistake as everything leads to something else. I wanted to be a songwriter, so the piano was a good place to be sitting.'

Songwriting was the aim, once he realised he would never play for Dundee Football Club, of course. As he told Phil Cunningham on Radio Scotland's *My Life in Five Songs*, 'I never wanted to see my name in lights, I wanted to see it in brackets.'

Influences were broad, from the music of Charlie Parker (that introduction coming from Eddie) through to The Beatles. 'We all loved them. They wrote their own stuff and that was a big thing.' Being brought up in a Catholic household, hymns were also an influence. 'My song "Mother Glasgow" begins with a section of "Soul of My Saviour" – that was always a hit to me – and in "All Will Be Well" (on the album *Posted Sober*), I used the line "flowers of the rarest". To me they were great tunes and immediate hits. I'm an atheist, but hymns are tuneful and have substance. They're trying to convey a message and use really bonny words. It's that affection we have for something we were brought up with – "the hair of the Dogma", if you like – I stole that from Flann O'Brien, but it's in a different context.'

For Michael, Bob Dylan changed everything. 'He used metaphor and blew the whole thing open lyrically. He wrote political songs that weren't just openly greetin' about something. When I heard him, I thought he was an elderly man so when I saw how young he was, that was a big excitement.'

He also remembers seeing Cat Stevens playing at the Top Ten Club. Having only read about him, Michael now saw this young, handsome, talented songwriter. 'It seekened my erse, I have to say. I also saw The Vikings play there – they were a great group. Alan Gorrie would sing like Ray Charles and then, of course, he was part of a band that conquered America and that lifted the bar for everyone.'

Expelled from Lawside Academy, he had various jobs, first as a printer's message boy at fifteen, then apprenticeships to a baker and an electrician. At the age of seventeen, he took off with a guitar and a copy of the new Humblebums album and spent time in London and Amsterdam.

It was on his return that this first spot at the Woodlands occurred and his partnership with the enigmatic-looking man began. The duo evolved into a band called Hen's Teeth, which recruited Dougie McLean, Arlene Gowans and Michael's younger brother Christopher.

KNIGHT IN SHINING BROGUES

'Michael and I were rehearsing around at the Marra house when he said, "Mind if my young brother comes through and sits in? He's been learning guitar,"' says Gus Foy. 'So Chris comes through, still dressed in his Lawside uniform, and says, "What key are we in?" He was incredible, putting in what we call the "lemonade". I couldn't say anything else except, "Can you play on Sunday?"'

Chris got ten bob for that Woodlands debut, playing second guitar.

'Michael had hauled me through and said, "Play something for Gus,"' Chris recalls. 'He ran the club with Norrie Maiden (also known as Dean Eastwood), but Gus programmed it. Apart from the music being great, I felt protected playing there, being fourteen.'

Hearing much of the same music as his older siblings, Chris believes the seminal records for him as a boy were *Peter and the Wolf* by Prokofiev, The Beatles' *Rubber Soul*, the *West Side Story* soundtrack, Duke Ellington, and Josh White. 'It was always The Beatles for me and particularly the *White Album*. You could really hear what they were doing in the studio. You felt like you were in the room. I found it more interesting that people made this music happen, rather than it being a magical thing that appeared from nowhere.'

'To Michael's music contemporaries, it seemed that Chris had appeared from nowhere. Stewart Ivins, who had come to Dundee from Galashiels to attend Duncan of Jordanstone art college, remembers hearing Chris for the first time: 'It must have been 1972 so he would be fifteen or so. Louie O'Neill and I were doing a little thing in the back room of the Hawkhill Tavern and Michael says, "My young brother plays. I'll bring him along." He just seemed to arrive fully formed.'

Of course, he didn't. 'I starting learning guitar and piano. Eddie and Michael had guitars and I played one chord, D if I recall, for about two years. I think it was about the age of twelve when it clicked in and I started putting the time in. It was about five or six hours a day – that sounds a lot, but it was nothing at that age. You get completely focused on it.

'That Tavern back room was pretty wild. Everything was plugged into the light socket and there were no mics, so we would sing into a speaker turned the other way round. They managed to sneak me in, but it wasn't too obvious. I just piled in with the art college students.'

Chris wasn't just impressing his brother's pals though. He had a significant effect on an acquaintance at Lawside.

'I always loved fads,' says musician and songwriter Steve Knight. 'I was a skinhead and then got into the suedehead thing, but it all changed when I met Chris in 1971. I didn't particularly like him, but we had a mutual pal called Eric, who I was supposed to meet up at Chris's place one night.'

Steve's priorities at the time are obvious. 'I was wearing a dress blazer, a brown checked Ben Sherman shirt, Wranglers, red socks and black brogues. When the door opened, I saw him bouncing down the stairs with his wifie's hair – you know, that horrible 1960s long hair. He was wearing a teardrop collar shirt, a tank top, flares and white sannies, Dunlop red flash actually.'

The boys went upstairs but Eric didn't show up, so Chris picked up a guitar and started playing. 'I was mesmerised – it was a totally life-changing evening. When I went home, I started thinking about music more seriously.'

Steve was a music fan, enjoying Mass for the singing. Just as well – as an altar boy he was at St Joseph's practically every day. 'There were usually three wifies and a very hungover priest – he did the fastest Mass in Scotland, just wanting to get off.'

Within a couple of weeks Steve decided that he would be a bass player, even though he hadn't really grasped what the role of the bass was. An out-and-out mooch to a granny in Australia resulted in a donation of £5, which was put towards a £12 Jensen bass from Westport Supplies. The rest came from a paper round. 'Not long after that I practically moved into the Marra house. Chris shared a room with Mick, but he was at his girlfriend Peggy's in Wellbank Street a lot, so we had that room to ourselves, really.'

Chris introduced Steve to the student culture that he was experiencing while playing with Michael. 'Mick and his pals all had great parties, with guys like Dougie McLean, where they would play guitars and sing. Chris and I would plunk and hang out with these guys – we'd be in our Lawside uniforms and watch as a joint was passed around the room. I really got into the lifestyle – grew my hair, started wearing flares and even cheese-cloth shirts.'

Steve would watch Chris playing with Michael while still working on his bass playing. He started playing in bands at about seventeen, and by the age of nineteen was in demand.

By this point Chris had joined Hen's Teeth, whose music he describes as 'folk rock', giving him an excuse to play electric. The songs were a combination of Michael's own material and covers from the likes of John Prine and the Incredible String Band.

Around the same time, Stewart Ivins had brought a rather different outfit together. His influences came from a peripatetic childhood, having lived in Africa, 'I made up Grundig reel-to-reel tapes of rock'n'roll before we went out,' he recalls. Then, when his parents moved out to Singapore, he went to boarding school, visiting them in the holidays.

At college in Galashiels, there was an increased interest in music. 'I think it was the John Mayall and the Bluesbreakers album with Eric Clapton – the one where he's reading *The Beano* on the cover – that started me playing seriously. I was really precious about it. I wasn't inter-ested in anything else.'

Ironic, given Clapton's choice of reading material, that Stewart should arrive in Dundee. 'It was 1970 and, of course, at art college the first thing is to get a band together. I met Louie O'Neill, who was a great rock'n'roll piano-player and we recruited Jonathan Ogilvie (Jog) as drummer. That was Mort Wriggle and the Panthers. It was pure rock'n'roll classics, just fantastic fun – we never really rehearsed and anyone could come along and sing or dance. Jog was also playing for Hen's Teeth, so that linked us into Mick, Gus and Chris.'

When Dougie McLean left Hen's Teeth to go off and concentrate on more traditional material, eventually joining the Tannahill Weavers, the rest of the band wondered what their next step would be.

TRUE BREAD HEADS

At the beginning of the 1970s, The Bothy was gaining a reputation as the place to hear a much wider range of folk and country rock.

'It was the coolest pub in the world. Full stop. No question,' says Stuart McHardy, who had returned from university in Edinburgh. 'Previously we had been going to a session at the Tavern, which Bruce Millar had kicked off – this was earlier than the period when it became the real art college hang out.

'Jimmy Stirling, who ran The Bread, was open to having a range of nights upstairs. At that time Tam and Lou were pretty much the house band but you would see Jim Reid doing his stuff, and of course Gordon Douglas and Jeff Clark were playing as Wells Fargo. At that time I also remember seeing Phil and Clark Robertson, the brothers from The Sleaz Band.'

It's no exaggeration to say that in the early 1970s, The Sleaz Band were one of the UK's hardest-working live bands. They had formed in 1968, when the art college revels booked them as Rock Tonsils and the Sleaz Band, sharing the stage with a new outfit called Pink Floyd. With Jim Bodie on vocals, Clark on lead guitar, Phil on bass and Frank Kosiba on drums, 1969 was a busy year, with sixty gigs, including support to Peter Green's Fleetwood Mac in Glasgow.

By 1971, Jim Ross had replaced Frank on drums. The band were now professional and did 163 gigs that year. There were almost as many gigs the next year, but on better bills with the likes of Alex Harvey (before the Sensational Alex Harvey Band), Nazareth, Slade and the Edgar Broughton Band.

In August 1972 Phil left the band for a few months, but he was convinced to rejoin later that year, when a rejuvenated line-up including Jim Kelly (ex-Honeybus) and Robbie Stewart on drums looked to move the band on.

There were better tours and recording sessions, but the only release came in June 1974: the single 'All I Want is You' on the Fontana label. Jim Kelly left shortly afterwards and it wasn't long before the band broke up.

If the Robertson brothers were regarded as the Bothy guys who 'made it', there were plenty of opportunities for emerging artists to try out.

Michael Marra says, 'I took Stuart McHardy's spot one week when he couldn't do it and I tell you, I had to develop a solo act very quickly. Lou Lewis also helped me with that.' While Michael was playing, Lou realised there was something missing. After the second song, he whispered in Michael's ear that he should tell the audience he was having a ten-minute break. 'Lou reappeared ten minutes later with a PA and set it up for me. You can't repay that sort of thing.

'That night showed me that musicians should have a solo act, something that can stand up on its own, even if it's for economic purposes. It's also good for writing. There's less chance of getting away with a duff number on your own than in a group that can make a bit of noise and be entertaining. So, thank you, Stuart McHardy, for that.'

Stuart recalls that the first performance of Michael's he saw at The Bothy initially left him cold. 'His brother Eddie was a pal of mine and said his wee brother was going to come down to the pub, so could he get a turn? He did James Taylor's "Fire and Rain", and at first I wasn't sure as it was such a perfect version – spot on. That really wasn't what I was into, doing straight covers. But as I listened more, I realised that it was SO perfect and beautifully done, no one could fail to be impressed.'

For the music fan, this was a time when several gigs could be seen in one night. Folk musician Helen Forbes remembers coming into town with friends and going from gig to gig. 'We would go to The Bothy, but could also go to the Bowling Alley (the union for the Bell Street Tech, now Abertay University), and of course the New Dines at Dundee University.'

Helen's dad was a piper, which led her into playing folk, even though she would seek out more blues rock. 'We just lived to see live bands.' Of course getting back to Broughty Ferry was always the problem. 'Once or twice we managed to swing a lift in a panda car with the "lost handbag" trick, though!'

The diversity of music in Dundee at the time welcomed those who showed an interest, and when Frenchman Alan Breitenbach arrived in 1971, he was embraced as not only a like-minded musician, but a bit of a character. Dundee likes that.

'I used to hang about at flea markets in northern Paris,' says Alan. 'All my friends were gypsy swing players, and that's where I learned to play Django Reinhardt stuff. I was fascinated by the rhythm of it. I would also play with people like Alan Stivell, the Breton pipe and harp player in the 14th arrondissement.'

He had completed a nursing course in Edinburgh before finding kindred spirits in Dundee. 'I was interested in rock'n'roll but was more of a jazz swing player. I was looking at a guitar in Larg's and was strumming away on "Sweet Georgia Brown", when a guy said, "I do that as well – fancy a tune?" John Dunn at Larg's was always OK with that. That was Willie Clark and we became good friends.'

He soon became part of a group of musicians who seemed to live at The Bothy. 'There were great bands but one I loved to play with was Gypsy Joe and The High Cheekers. In fact, practically everybody played in the band at some point – John Adam was the only member who was always there.'

Alan recalls that there was a loft in The Bothy where musicians would keep gear. 'It saved humping it back and forward. You had to remember and no' walk between the joists of course. One night, I was half p*shed – in fact I could have been completely p*shed – and my foot when straight through the ceiling. Everybody was looking up, saying, "There's a leg – where did that come from?!" Of course, the way I fell, I'd caught and trapped my balls – I was screaming! The pain was unbelievable!' That's a long way from the glitterballs of the Palais de Danse.

TEX EDUCATION

Andy Lothian Snr said goodbye to his beloved dancehall in 1973 when it was sold to Murdoch Wallace Jnr, who wanted to decant the JM while the ballroom was transformed into the Barracuda, a Flintstones-inspired pleasure palace, complete with tree house.

There were opportunities for local bands to get decent support slots, even if they had to create a band to do it. Stuart McHardy remembers the plot hatched by Tony van der Kuyl to support Fairport Convention when they were booked to play the New Dines in 1971.

'Tony decided that we should support them, no question. We got a band together with Alan Easson on drums and a guy called Tex Toomey on bass. We had met Tex in the Tavern when he sat in on some sessions.'

The band would play Tony's original material, even though Stuart was also a songwriter. His experiences with record companies had not been particularly encouraging, however. 'I had given a tape of my songs to a producer called John Smith at Apple. We shook hands, he agreed to listen to it and as far as I was concerned, that's a deal. After three months he hadn't got back to me, so I phoned up and no one would put me through – again and again and again.'

The solution was simple: get drunk, rip-snortingly drunk actually, and pay Apple a visit to get the tape back. 'I was p*shed and I was angry, and I can fleg fowk when I'm like that. "Where's John Smith? Where's my f*cking tape?" They looked petrified and went away to scramble through a pile of cassettes. I shouted, "You'll no' see me again!" Bet they were heartbroken at that eh?'

Tony and Stuart had the songs but not the name. 'I remember us falling about laughing thinking about names, but in the end one of us came up with Tayport Convulsion. Fairport loved it.'

The band had all rehearsed with one another, but the four of them never quite managed to get in a room at the same time. 'We got on stage, and Tex froze. Absolutely could not move, couldn't play a note. It was a big crowd for Fairport Convention and he had never played in front of that many people. So Tony covers his mic and he's shouting at ME, "What the f*ck's he doing? Get him to move!"'

The gig may have been a disaster but they went back to the Angus Hotel with the band and chatted until the early hours. 'Shame about the gig though,' Stuart says. 'There was some good stuff in that set.'

SHADES OF GRAZE

The crowd witnessing the implosion of Tayport Convulsion that night did miss out on hearing Tony's material, according to Gordon Douglas. 'I was inspired by the direction that Tony took in his songwriting – it showed me that I should be looking around me for subject matter.'

It was something he would put into practice soon after. In 1970, Lou Lewis and Berlend Versluis approached Gordon and Jeff to ask if they had considered making Wells Fargo a four-piece band. 'I was pretty much against it,' says Gordon. 'I thought the volume would be too much for that room upstairs. I couldn't have been more wrong. The nights we were playing quietly it was pretty flat and when we played loudly it was jumping. They were queuing on stairs at six to get in.'

The room was tiny. It would take sixty seated, but 200 people would be packed in on some nights. The round windows with small panes would be the first victim to the heat when someone would put an elbow through one to get some air.

'We played there from about 1970 to 1973, the last year I was at art college,' says Gordon, 'and we were playing four nights a week. Allegedly somebody did a streak one night and no one noticed him, it was so packed.'

Outside of The Bothy, the band was popular enough to merit the protection of Dundee's gangs, who guarded their territories fiercely. 'When we walked down Reform Street, one gang walked us halfway and then we were picked up by another gang to walk the rest. Again, the power of music eh?'

Wells Fargo only played original material, apart from The Beatles' 'I've Just Seen a Face' and the first couple of lines of 'Blue Moon'. 'We never had any problems playing original material,' says Gordon. 'We would hear from the back, "Play something wi ken!" but it was always Bert Donaldson winding us up.'

Late in 1972, Jeff and Gordon started to make calls to record companies to organise appointments. Young bands trying to get record companies to notice them today may find that unbelievable, but as a result of those calls they were given times to come in.

'We made two appointments: one at Air London, George Martin's label, and another at Island,' says Gordon. 'At Air we played a song to two "suits", but before we could start the second they left and brought another two "suits" in. Whether they were there to throw us out we weren't sure, but they asked us to play the first one again, then another and another. We could tell they were keen, but how keen we weren't sure. Then they asked where we were going next and said we shouldn't sign for anyone else before they had a chance to talk to us again. The rest of the day was a bit of a blur. It really couldn't have got any better.'

The band were asked to arrange a London gig and at short notice they could only secure a Sunday afternoon jam session at the Marquee. One of the stipulations was that they would provide the equipment for anyone who wanted to play, all for a fee of £16. The van was loaded and they were off, apart from a quick stop on the Perth Road to lay in supplies. When the van screeched to a halt outside the favoured purveyor of pies, the gear shunted forward and there was an audible crunch, but that was put to the back of their minds until – well, until it needed to be at the front.

One of the amps had a broken Bakelite socket, and even in London there was no chance of finding a replacement on a Sunday in 1973. As luck would have it, most of the acts were solo and others managed to cope with the hasty repair. 'What they couldn't get their heads around was the lack of bass gear. Well, we didn't have a bass player until John Fitzgerald joined later.'

The change from Wells Fargo to The Cows came after this gig, ironically during a visit to an Indian restaurant with the men from the label. It may have seemed to come out of thin air, but Gordon remembers that after a failed attempt by Wells Fargo to secure an *Opportunity Knocks* slot at the Dundee auditions, he had drawn two cows on chairs playing guitars with no strings and captioned it 'Opportunity Knocks for the Cows'.

The men from Air flew to Dundee with a contract. 'My dad's lawyer had taken a look at it and pointed out one thing in particular,' says Gordon. 'If the company no longer wanted us, they were within their rights to stop us playing, and not pay us. I discussed this with one of the directors and he said something along the lines of, "Gordon, trust in me. That's never going to happen. I signed you. I'm a director of the company. I love your music . . ."'

When the contract appeared, the first band argument happened. With separate recording and publishing deals, Jeff and Gordon would be the beneficiaries of the publishing deal as they had written the songs. 'I just had to say that if they wanted to write songs they could be included in the publishing. It wasn't nice though, not a good feeling at all.'

A few months later came the news that was 'never going to happen'. The director who had given Gordon such assurances was off, to join an organisation which shared the building with Air. 'It was Cookaway – Roger Cook and Roger Greenaway's company. These were the guys behind Blue Mink's success and they had written "I'd Like to Teach the World to Sing". We had walked past the offices on several occasions and wondered what all the silver Coke bottles were for.'

The single choice was a song called 'Palais de Danse' – it's clear that Gordon was inspired to write about his surroundings. Apart from that the band also had songs about Greasy Pete's (a chipper in Kincardine Street) and the Wellgate Steps. Other songs were the exotically named 'Vietnam Can-Can', 'Be-Bop'n-Bop' and 'Nightmare Tango'.

'I thought "Palais de Danse" was starting to show its age by that point to be honest,' says Gordon. 'However, that was the choice and the plan, ironically, was for Roger Greenaway to produce. We weren't sure he was the right man for the job, but he was having huge success with The Drifters.'

The band were based in London, finding sanctuary in the one-bedroom Hampstead flat of *Sounds* journalist Ray Telford, who was something of a champion of their music. One of his live reviews said: 'The Cows' music embraced many aspects of what goes in to make the best rock music ... something like the Flying Burrito Brothers but with a wider range of ideas.'

Apart from musical chairs at Air, in 1973 plastic was in short supply, due to the coal strikes. The band was struggling to make ends meet and the release of the single became crucial. In a last-ditch meeting with Air's John Burges, Gordon was left in no doubt that they were no longer interested in promoting the band, but as they had spent five days in studios in London and Worthing, they would not be released until someone paid that bill. 'We were, because of the bad contract, unable to play in London without their say so, and they were saying no,' recalls Gordon.

The band couldn't play in London and now the van had died on the way back from a gig in Bristol. 'We couldn't afford to have it fixed so left it outside our manager's house for months until, at the instigation of our roadie Charlie Wright, Willy Wong bought it and brought it back to Dundee to use as part of his Hong Kong restaurant business.'

The last straw for Gordon was hearing that the situation was affecting his family in Dundee. 'My wife was dealing with the Larg's man, who was coming round every Friday to collect payments for the drum kit and PA we had bought from them on tick. I had no option but to come back. Jeff and John stayed but the rest of us moved back.'

Although John Sherry, owner of the Greyhound in Fulham Palace Road, had offered to buy out the contract, Air was asking too high a price, 'proving that a bad contract is much worse than no contract at all,' says Gordon. Air London eventually released the band in May 1975.

Back to reality in Dundee, Gordon got a job as a plant hire manager, but the next band, Seconds, again with Lou Lewis, followed pretty much immediately. This time Sandy Robertson was on drums and George Boyter, an old art college pal, was on bass. All Cows tunes now consigned to history. Gordon and George shared songwriting responsibilities on a new set, which was performed at a regular Sunday gig in Laings.

The band recorded some of the tracks at Castle Sounds in Edinburgh, but when Lou and George took it to London and came back with the 'good news' that they had a serious nibble, Gordon bowed out. He had no desire to go back to London and 'put my head back in the lion's mouth and smell its bad breath'.

As Lou and George went off to explore the new possibilities, an offer from Dundee Rep Young People's Theatre to work on a rock musical came at exactly the right time for Gordon.

BLACK DAY FOR THE WHITE BAND

In 1970, the template first created by the Blue Workshop in Perth in the mid-1960s was on the brink of producing the Average White Band. 'We were all working in London,' says Alan Gorrie. 'We got Onnie away from the Roy Young Band. Molly and Roger were with Stone the Crows, and Robbie had been with Brian Augur's Oblivion Express, so basically everyone was sprung from other bands. Mike Rosen was also with us at that time on trumpet.'

They became the studio band of choice and played on Island sessions of the time, including Johnny Nash's 'I Can See Clearly Now'. However, only two of the band, Robbie and Onnie, had the distinction of playing on Chuck Berry's novelty hit 'My Ding-a-Ling'.

The band's first gig was in 1972 – not so good for Mike Rosen, who was out, but good for Hamish Stuart, who got the call. Alan believed that the band needed another vocalist, one with a strong falsetto sound.

At the time Bonnie Bramlett (of Delaney and Bonnie) was planning a solo album and heard the Average White Band play in a North London club. 'I think they figured that if they flew a whole ready-made band over who could play like this, it was going to be a lot cheaper than hiring session musicians in Los Angeles,' says Alan. 'All they had to do was put us up in a hotel for six weeks, which in outer LA is not expensive, and pay us pocket money. I don't recall getting paid for it but we didn't really care – it was a way of getting to the States. That changed our lives completely – in six weeks in LA you get exposed to all the stuff that is going to thrill you forever.'

It was the pivotal time in the band's direction, being exposed to the Isley Brothers and Sly Stone, meeting people from Stax, and being in the studio with Bobby Womack and Sly Stone's brother. 'And nicking licks and bits and pieces from all these guys,' admits Alan. 'We came back at the end of six weeks with an armful of records that you wouldn't get in the UK. We had been going to the Whisky [a Go Go], watching people like Stevie Wonder in clubs – all experiences that were life-changing. At that point our sights were firmly focused on getting back to the States in our own right.'

That happened in late 1973, with their first album for MCA, *Show Your Hand*. During a two-week run at the Whisky, they realised that the American version of the album was receiving no promotion at all. 'We knew that the next record had to be done right,' says Alan, 'and that's why we came to LA in 1974 to record *AWB* – what became known as the White Album.'

At the end of 1973, they had made a version of the album that was rejected by MCA, allowing them to walk over to Atlantic Records with it. 'They got what we were about and Jerry Wexler signed us pretty much immediately. By April 1974, we were on our way to Miami to work with Arif Mardin – it all happened in a blur.'

In Miami, after working on two tracks, Mardin realised he wasn't going to get the right drum sound for Robbie McIntosh. So the band moved to New York and finished the album in two and a half weeks. By the end of May 1974 the record was in the can. 'They sent us back to Scotland for the summer while they mixed and got it ready for release in August.'

During that break Robbie caught up with his friend Donny Coutts. 'I had been playing and we were in the car afterwards,' he recalls. 'Robbie says, "You shouldna be playing here. You should be getting yourself to America. I'll get you a job. I'll speak to Bonnie Bramlett. I'll get you a job." He spotted a full half-bottle of whisky and said, "Is that yours?" I turned away for a minute and when I turned back, pretty much the whole bottle was gone. I said, "So, about this job . . ." and he says, "What job?" He was an incredible boy.'

Following the summer break, the Average White Band had a week at the Bottom Line in New York, then went straight on to the Troubadour in LA for a triumphant run of shows.

'And that was the end of the beginning,' says Alan. At a party to celebrate the Troubadour gigs, on 22 September, Robbie and Alan both took strychnine-laced heroin that they believed to be cocaine. Robbie lost his life – he was twenty-four years old and left a wife and child. Alan was only saved by the intervention of Cher, who managed to keep him conscious until help arrived. 'There's a lot of untruths been written about the event,' says Donny. 'One in particular that Robbie was such a hardened drinker that he refused to be sick and that killed him. Robbie was a hardened drinker but that wasn't the case at all.'

Donny found out about the event through a phone call. 'I was in bed with flu when the phone rang about 11am. It was a reporter from the *Daily Record*, who immediately launched into questions about Robbie, asking me what he was like. I was completely confused AND they were also saying that Alan might be dead as well. I was in total shock but managed to say I didn't know anything about it and put the phone down. The phone rang again and it was Mac Carnegie, to break the news.

'Robbie was buried in Barnhill Cemetery and it's the first time I can remember being in distress at a funeral. To this day I can't bear to hear anyone say uncomplimentary things about Cher – it's very possible that she saved my pal's life.'

Circumstances meant that no one from the Average White Band could be at the funeral. 'Robbie's remains were being flown back to Dundee and we couldn't afford to come back with him,' says Alan. 'We also had to stay on and fulfil some gigs with sit-in drummers and dig ourselves out of the biggest hole in the world – that's what it felt like.

'The influence never goes away. It's still there. There's never a situation when there's a groove problem that I don't immediately think, "What would McIntosh do here?" and we always apply that, the McIntosh rule of thumb.'

Robbie's friend Steve Ferrone replaced Robbie on drums and only one album, *Soul Searching,* was more successful than the White Album in terms of sales. 'The flawless album was the White Album so his legacy is intact.'

Even today as the Average White Band tour and 'try to fit some quality life in' they still retain that spirit of the jazz workshop in the mid-1960s.

JAZZ IN DUNDEE – MORE THAN A FILM ABOUT SHARKS

Dundee's most famous jazz musicians were in demand in the mid-1970s. Jimmy Deuchar had returned to Dundee with his family, setting up home in Broughty Ferry, but was still involved with top-flight orchestras throughout Europe. He joined fellow Scots saxophonist Gary Cox and his friend Jack Parnell on the 1979 recording *The Scots Connection,* but when he was at home, local jazz fans couldn't believe their luck when he would play at his Sunday afternoon jazz sessions at The Sands, Broughty Ferry's nightspot.

Martin Taylor met Dundee's other jazz trumpet star, John McLevy, in the mid-1970s. 'I first met him in the old BBC building in Bond Street, where he worked in a big band. I knew that he was also in the Benny Goodman Orchestra. Goodman had a US orchestra and a European orchestra. The European [one] was all London-based musicians and almost one-third were Scots, John being one.'

He also introduced Martin to one of his most valued collaborators, an accordionist called Jack Emblow, whose most famous appearance is surely in The Beatles' 'All You Need is Love' broadcast. 'I met Jack through John in Glasgow in 1976 so I have a lot to thank him for.'

In Benny Goodman's European orchestra, John was often a featured player, particularly on 'Baubles, Bangles and Beads'. Martin recalls, 'He was once asked, "Why do you always feature John?" He looked at the players and said, "Well, in the States I have one of him, one of him, ten of him, twenty of him . . ." He came to John and said, "But we don't have one of him."'

BOLIVER'S ARMY

The country rock of Hen's Teeth and classic rock'n'roll of Mort Wriggle were drifting closer, primarily through sharing a drummer in Jonathan Ogilvie. 'He was the link between us,' says Michael Marra. 'When's Hen's Teeth came to an end, it seemed natural that we would all get together. It was a broad-minded group musically, with no one leading from the front, but every band needs someone to move things along, and for us that was Stewart Ivins. Without Stewart the group would never have existed – he went out and found our work. He was the only one capable of holding it together.'

The line-up of what became Skeets Boliver was pretty settled, the only irony being that Jonathan Ogilvie, the drummer who linked them, decided to leave. The seat was filled eventually by the eighteen-year-old Brian McDermott. He also remembers the energy that Stewart brought. 'He almost had to be the manager as well. He worked incredibly hard. We all worked hard in some ways, though. We'd arrive at St Mark's Church on the Perth Road every day at 9am and treat rehearsing like a proper day job.'

Brian had first picked up drumsticks at the age of twelve, primarily because his best pal Tam Murphy had been sent to the NCR pipe band for drumming lessons, and he tagged along. 'Uch, I had nobody to play with, so went along with him, but I was the one that got completely hooked. I had always liked music. My brother Joe and I had these plastic Beatles wigs that just clamped on your napper. I think they came from Woolies. They were pretty cool.'

Drum lessons at St John's High got him into the school band, which involved, 'a lot of skiving, learning how to smoke, and some music as well'. He was recruited to local orchestras, but by the age of fifteen it was timpani out, T. Rex in. 'I still didn't have a kit, but when I listened to records I knew exactly what I should be doing. The first full kit I played belonged to Sandy Robertson, who played in a band called Elegy.' Brian auditioned for Elegy, a band in which future bandmate Peter McGlone was playing. 'He said he couldn't believe I didn't get it, but they thought I was a bit too young. It was probably only four or five years, but it probably seemed like a lot at the time.'

Peter McGlone started playing trumpet at Harris Academy and was also an orchestral player for a while. While teachers felt he could have a career in music, his parents weren't as keen, even though (or maybe because) his dad had musician friends.

'My dad was pally with some of the guys who played in the Palais band. There was a cobbler's on Hawkhill, where the brass players would hang out in the back shop and have a drink. That's where I got my trumpet. I remember the smell of leather and shoe polish and whisky and cigarettes. I liked the look of that lifestyle . . .'

He had a good start in the life of a musician, being expelled from school at fourteen. An apprenticeship at NCR followed, but when he thought about playing with a band, the trumpet didn't seem an ideal instrument. 'I considered the guitar but thought, nah, everybody's playing guitar. I'd have to be really good. Then I thought about the sax – it's pretty cool *and* it might help me get a girlfriend,' he laughs. 'My dad knew a guy who was selling a sax, so we went up to the house. In fact he wasn't, his *wife* was selling it. The guy walked in when the deal was being done and went mental.

'Eventually he came through to speak to me and asked me what I wanted to do with it. When I told him I really wanted to get out and play, he let me have it cheap. The guy had emphysema and could hardly breathe, but when he handed it over he looked at me and said, "Remember, that's a ticket to anywhere." '

Peter found a band and, with access to electronic effects put together by NCR engineering pals, created a distinctive sound. 'I got a phone call from some guy saying, "Are you Pete McGlone? Do you own a sax?" Note they didn't say, "Are you a sax player?" ' He was taken to a rehearsal room at the back of Dens Park to see how he fitted into a band called Elegy. 'I had to raise my game, these guys could really play.'

Elegy wrote their own material and had a residency at the jazz club in the Queen's Hotel. As a four-piece they had reached the Scottish finals of a *Melody Maker* competition. Now, as a six-piece, they won that heat and headed to the Roundhouse in London for the final.

They came third, and although Peter was still working in NCR at the time, he took the opportunity to go to Germany with the band to play air bases. 'Playing to American forces in Fulda – I stuck it for about six weeks and came back, but Steve was really keen to go down that route.'

Guitarist Steve McDonald went back to Germany once Elegy had split, this time with a band called McDonald's Farm. 'The American forces were very well looked after,' he says. 'We played at Spangdahlem base – they would also be getting major acts like Ben E. King in there every week. Some of the bases were in secret locations and we were taken there blindfolded. We played at other US bases – one in Greenland was completely under the ice.'

Peter and Steve worked together again when an American manager was looking for a band to back his singer Sharon Tabor. 'At the time the Average White Band were big in the US, as were Bay City Rollers, so he thought he would find her a Scottish band. Steve got the gig then brought in all his pals to form the band. We checked the manager out as much as we possibly could and he seemed sound.'

There were personal hairdressers and choreographers. New clothes were provided, as were chauffeur-driven cars. The band were based in The Pleasance in Edinburgh during rehearsals, and then had a week's residency before heading off to America. A record deal had been signed, they had been in the studio and the news of their departure for the US was on the front page of the *Daily Express*. And then Sharon, along with the manager, vanished. 'It seems that he was borrowing money right, left and centre, and from the kind of guys that you *really* need to pay back. So it was back to the drawing board.'

A few months later, Peter took a call from Steve, who told him to turn on the TV. Frank Sinatra and Sammy Davis Jnr were descending the steps of an aeroplane, and just behind them was the disappearing manager.

Steve went on to become one of the founding members of a Beatles tribute band called Ringer with Ian Murdoch. He now plays with Tripper and has played with Denny Laine over the years.

Peter was back in cabaret, playing residencies in Perth. 'I was enjoying getting a good wage, but I got a call from Stewart Ivins to sit in at a gig. I didn't know who they were, but I went down and did it anyway – it was maybe 1975. I liked the mix of rock and country and it was clear that this was the real deal. We had a residency in Laings, but I was still doing the cabaret stuff. Eventually there was an ultimatum and I decided to go with them full time. My younger brother Allan, also a sax player, completed that Skeets line-up.'

Brian McDermott had also been a stand-in, but when he didn't get the Elegy seat, he played with a band called Badge. He had spoken with

Chris Marra over a pint in The Scout and, after standing in with Skeets a few times, he was asked to join.

Like many bands at the time there was a period when they thought moving to London was the thing to do. 'We wanted to test the water,' says Brian 'so one of the Marra cousins put us up at their place in Shepherd's Bush – all of us and the roadies, sleeping on mattresses. Also, they were proper vegan. This was the mid-1970s and we were boys from Dundee who had never heard the word "macrobiotic". They were kind enough to make this meal for about ten boys and we all looked at it and wondered "What is it?" I think everybody ate the sprouts – they didna LIKE them but at least they recognised them. The rest was a kind of brown mush. Everybody pushed it about the plate, hoping it would magically disappear – except the roadie Bob Barty. He hoovered it up and started on somebody else's!'

In 1976, the proactive Stewart Ivins entered the band in a competition called Popscot 76, run by the *Sunday Mail*. 'I did it, but I didna really like it – I dinna like competitions,' says Michael Marra. They reached the final, which was held in Glasgow in September and although they didn't win (that honour went to a Glenrothes band called Paris) they won a recording contract with Thunderbird Records. 'Imagine what kind of recording contract you *win*,' says Chris Marra.

The contract came through just days after the competition and the first recording was a song called 'Shithouse Door'. With no possibility of radio play, the name was changed to 'Streethouse Door' (although the record made no such concessions) and backed by a song called 'I Can't See the Light'. The review in *Record Mirror* read: 'Vulgar fun-filled blue-beater, huge in Dundee.' The second single for Thunderbird was 'Moonlight in Jeopardy', reviewed as a 'Mexican-flavoured happy pop shuffler'. The *People's Journal* applauded its 'listenable quality'.

The band was constantly on the road, something which certainly made them gig-ready when they received a frantic phone call in February 1977. Steve Gibbons (Steve Gibbons Band) had been involved in an accident in Aberdeen and now couldn't support Bebop Deluxe at the Caird Hall that night. Stewart received the call at 5.30pm but the band went on. The reviewer in the *People's Journal* of 12 February was obviously caught out not watching the support band – and admitted it, saying: 'I heard sufficient comments from members of the audience to suggest that they had played their usual driving set.' The gig was a particular highlight for Brian McDermott who was celebrating his nineteenth birthday that day.

Come the summer it was time to get back in the studio. 'We had recorded two singles and were back to do something else,' says Gus Foy. 'Elvis had just died [in August 1977] and the producer asked if we would do a tribute to Elvis. Michael says, "No." The producer asks why and Michael replies, "He didna sing any of our songs so I'm no' singing his." '

The summer of 1977 also saw the band recording a TV documentary for the BBC *Everyman* series. Filmed in July at rehearsals at Dudhope Arts Centre and at Laings, the band was paid a decent fee of £300. When the programme was shown on BBC1 in January 1978, they had named it *I Can't See the Light* – B-sides can come back to haunt you. The listing from *Radio Times* said that the show 'looks at the music and lifestyle of Dundee pop group Skeets Boliver'.

What the band didn't realise was that *Everyman* covered religious, spiritual and moral matters. There is absolute agreement that they didn't sign up for the God slot, but, in the end, it was national television. 'At the end of the day though, the pounds, shillings and pence were good,' says Gus, 'but it didn't do us a lot of good subsequently. A couple of places, including the Hope and Anchor in London, cancelled bookings thinking we were religious freaks.'

What the religious programmers would have thought of Michael as Enid – The Duchess of Newtyle, teetering around Laings in platform shoes and a frock we'll never know. His inability to handle 'heh heels' led to the postponement of a farewell gig to Laings in November 1977 when he dislocated his knee walking downstairs.

Soon it would be a farewell gig to Skeets Boliver itself. Michael believes that, 'Wales did us in. We had a run of gigs there and on the way back it was a sorrowful van, full of guys thinking about their future.'

In mid-April 1978, Skeets played Fishguard, Abertillery, Port Talbot, Pontypridd, Carmarthen, Tonypandy and to end it all, the Skewen British Legion. 'I remember sitting in digs in Wales, at the very top of this horrible boarding house and almost greetin' – wondering what I was doing there,' says Chris.

The writing was on the wall, with Michael clearly keen to develop his songwriting. 'It was a great group, a brilliant bunch of guys and fantastic at coming up with ideas, but there was competition with three writers in the band. That didn't really suit me.'

Stewart also recognised that Skeets, by 1978, were perhaps a band out of time. 'It really was time to call it a day,' he says. 'We did a gig with Magazine at the 100 Club and the place was full of folk in bin-liners. I knew the punk thing was happening as I was helping out in Groucho's record shop, but the punk thing was so strong that we were being faced with at best indifference and at worst open hostility. You just think, "I'm no' doing this anymore."'

A sorrowful Poparound in the *People's Journal* reported on the farewell gig, in Bloomers (the last incarnation of the Palais) on Boxing Day, 1978. 'I don't think we've heard the last of the members of the band. It might not be too long before some, or all, are back in another form.'

'Let's go and play the clubbies. That was my plan,' says Gus. 'I did that, then Eddie Marra and Stewart came in. We were Marra, Foy and Ivins – MFI. For an encore, we'll build you a wardrobe.'

MAKING HIS MARX

The fourth of July 1976 was a Sunday. With television coverage of the US bicentennial celebrations to watch on one of three channels, it would be a relatively easy day for a house move, even if it was from Edinburgh to Dundee.

'Everything was packed into a Sunblest van, but it broke down around South Queensferry,' recalls Alastair (Breeks) Brodie. 'It wasn't the greatest of starts but at least we weren't alone.'

Apart from Annie, his wife at that time, the van also contained assorted hippies who were making the move to introduce the people of Dundee to healthy eating. 'We felt that we were in a bit of a rut and had this idealistic view of moving out to the country. One of our neighbours in Edinburgh was from the Dundee area and was opening a wholefood co-operative there called Beanos.'

In the mid-1970s there was the first real sign of what Breeks calls 'hip capitalism', where hippies went down the route of going into business rather than getting an office job. 'There were four of them and they would take two of three joined cottages at Kingennie. Did we want one? We thought, "Why not?" Was it reckless? I suppose. Throw up good jobs and move somewhere you've only been twice in your life, and only on fleeting visits.'

The plan was to open a record shop in Dundee – that was something that he had a little more experience of.

Growing up, Breeks had a love of music and football. The music edged ahead as he got into his teens, when he says he became the 'annoying wee laddie asking for posters in record shops. 'I would be the guy who would have a list of records for sale on the notice board on the High School in Edinburgh. I always had a bag of records with me.'

The name Breeks came from a proper childhood gang. 'There were three of us who would sit together, eat our lunches, and read *Broons* and *Oor Wullie* books. I was Brodie Breeks, Mark Steel was Steel Breeks, and Neil Booth was Boothie Breeks – we were the Breeks gang. After a while the other two dropped their Breeks and I kept mine. Now people can address something to Breeks, Groucho's, Dundee and it gets to me.'

At the age of seventeen, he had a Saturday job in the Varsity Record

Shop on Edinburgh's Nicolson Street. 'I remember spending one morning in 1971 wrapping up fifty copies of "Chirpy Chirpy Cheep Cheep" – every person who came in asked for it. I tried to convince the owner to order stuff by bands like Medicine Head. I was definitely a hippy in waiting.'

Despite the fact that he wasn't destined to play, it was obvious that the passion would push him into working with music. An attempt at studying civil engineering was quickly abandoned as gig-going got in the way. 'The first band I paid to go to see was Jethro Tull at the Usher Hall in 1969 – the Chrysalis Tour, with Savoy Brown and Stone the Crows. We didn't have much money but I also managed to get three of us in to see John Mayall with two tickets. I had good draughtsman skills, so I did a replica and fanned them out as we went in. The guy just took them and tore a strip off the side.'

There was another half-hearted attempt at a 'proper job' as a trainee structural engineer and technician, but the day-release at Telford College turned into cruising record shops, which turned into getting kicked out and a year on the Broo.

'That was great. Bed all day and going to gigs at night. I was in Greyfriars Market one day, though, and a friend told me someone was needed to run the record stall in Cockburn Street Market. Now that was more like it. The guys who owned it had the Great Western Trading Company – but also had a stall selling second-hand records, tatty jewellery, cheese-cloth shirts, joss sticks, all that stuff. They asked me a few questions, then asked if I could start that afternoon.'

Don't get excited – he started the next day. It was 1 April 1974 and he went in as manager. He may not have had management training but he certainly knew about the records he was selling. After a few days, with the nod to employ staff, an unemployed flatmate came on board. It was only a year and a half later that he thought about moving, when a new market in Leith Walk was due to open. 'I was offered the record stall and took it, going into partnership with a guy from Cockburn Street. It showed that the best thing I ever did at school was an O Grade in woodwork, as I was able to draw and build the stall. We did really well, but it didn't last, as the guy who owned the market took the rent money and buggered off.'

Back at Cockburn Street, his old job had gone to the assistant, who had bought the job. 'Ronnie had wandered up to the stall one day and said, "Any jobs going?" Davie, the assistant at the time said, "I'll sell you mine." So Ronnie, who was from Kirriemuir, bought the job for £20. I was lucky when I got back as I was offered the job of assistant manager of the whole market.'

The Dundee move came not too long after that. Annie suggested that going into partnership with Ronnie, who knew the area, might be a good idea. Having decided to make the move, there were a few trips to Dundee to see where the second-hand record shops were. 'There was The Record Exchange up the Hilltown and Rock of Ages at the bottom of Victoria Road, but apart from stalls in Dens Road and Lorne Street Markets, that was it.'

(Among the shops selling new records at the time were Bruce's in Reform Street, Cathie McCabe, which had originally been in the city arcade but moved to the Murraygate, and B.G. Forbes in Commercial Street, where drummer Ronnie Jack had to call on some customer service. 'I bought the cassette of Steely Dan's *Pretzel Logic* there, but when I played it, it was *Ken Dodd's Greatest Hits*. Now, I've nothing against Ken Dodd, but everything said it was Steely Dan. When I took it back to the shop, they looked at me like I was daft – until they tried it out and "Tears" blasted all over the shop. They believed me and turned it off pretty quick.')

When looking for a site, the system couldn't have been simpler. 'We looked at a map and drew a triangle,' says Breeks. 'One thing you don't do is step on other people's toes, so our point of the triangle gave us the West End. The shop we found had been a fruit and veg seller at 89 Perth Road. It was called Garthley's, but had no "To Let" sign, so we ended up going through all the Garthleys in the Dundee phone book to find out which agent was handling the let. It was a small shop, very basic and with no toilet, but it was £5 a week, the same as the cottage, so we decided to take it. We gave them a cheque for six months' rent, they gave us the keys, and we were in the next day.'

The name Groucho came from an idea, never realised, to open up a jeans shop in Edinburgh. There was a women's clothes shop called Garbo, which had a striking image on the front of the shop, so the thought was Groucho would be the same.

The shopfitting was a DIY job, with carpets nailed to the floor, but woodwork skills again came in handy for building clothes rails and racks. 'The beat bobby was a guy called Dave. He would come in and ask how we were getting on. Then it was off with the jacket and sawing wood for us.'

Opening day was 16 August 1976, with takings of more than £70. The shop had been financed by a loan against Breeks's Edinburgh flat (they didn't know it was scheduled for demolition) and stocked with Ronnie's record collection. Apart from the mainstay of second-hand records, it sold joss sticks, leather pouches, printed mirrors, cheesecloth shirts, Afghan coats, second-hand American baseball shirts and a full range of smoking paraphernalia.

'Within the first week, we got to know Stewart Ivins. He came in, chatted about music and became our introduction to anyone in the Dundee music scene.' By the time the shop celebrated its first anniversary with a party, Skeets Boliver was the band and the Brodies had a daughter. They had also moved from Kingennie into a flat in Seafield Road near the shop. 'That was much handier, me having Crohn's Disease and working in a shop without a toilet!' Crohn's affects the digestive system and can be incredibly debilitating.

At the second party, the legendary local performer St Andrew made his first appearance, but Breeks was given much more than he bargained for. 'Bob Anderson, who managed Mafia, was looking after another band called Street Level. All of a sudden this other band came on and Bob wanted them to play. I wasn't too happy, but he says, "Just let them have a shot. . ." They had a female singer called Jackie McPherson (now BBC Scotland newsreader Jackie Bird) and all the band were stripped to the waist – apart from Jackie, of course.'

By the time of that first party, punk had arrived in Dundee, and although hippy and punk were uneasy bedfellows, this was a business and the demand for singles was there. 'We managed to get in some punk singles, but we also had the T-shirts, bondage trousers and bum flaps. That started the Saturday pilgrimages up the Perth Road. Kids would come in from places like Forfar, Brechin and Carnoustie. They would get off at the Seagate bus station and take a thirty-minute walk to the Perth Road shop to get a couple of punk singles . . . You wouldn't get kids crossing the road for something they wanted now.'

It was the age of the badge, and rummaging in butter tubs made it easy for light-fingered scallywags to pocket a few when backs were turned. 'Keeping the DIY punk ethos in mind, on Thursday you'd get the *NME* and find out what new bands had sprung up. On Friday night we would make up badges using a handheld machine. I would tear things out of *NME*, slap them on a bit of backing with a bit of cochineal and bit of razor blade – if you were really lucky you would have a bit of wart or a scab. Stick all that in with a picture of Ian Dury – they loved the one-offs.'

Groucho's was not alone in rampant badge theft, as music writer Tom Doyle recalls. 'We were real heavy metal kids so would go into Rockpile, which reeked of patchouli.' Rockpile had started life in the late 1970s off the Blackness Road and moved to the more central Westport location in the early 1980s. 'We would say to Ian [Walker], "What's that record up there behind you?" and as soon as he turned round we had badges in the back pocket.' Musician Kit Clark always felt that the smell made going to Rockpile feel like 'somewhere illegal'.

Breeks still has a badge in the back shop with a John Peel quote, saying, 'The Bay City Rollers would be vastly improved by sudden death' and it's an ethic that the shop has maintained with its Bay City Rollers amnesty box. 'When I was working in Varsity Record Shop, they opened a disco above it and I was asked to work for them on the opening night. The Rollers were opening the disco, this was at the time of "Keep on Dancing", before Les. My job was to hand out these 10 x 8 photos to girls ... they were everything I hated musically.

'I made a decision that Groucho's would never EVER sell one of their records, and then I decided to take it a bit further. If anyone offered to sell them, I said I wouldn't buy them but would destroy them for free. When Eric Faulkner was in town, he dropped in to see the amnesty box, but I don't know if he quite got what it was.'

Dundee bands were always supported, however. The first release on Groucho's Records was a version by local favourites Mafia of the Fontella Bass hit 'Rescue Me'.

'Groucho's record shop was really helpful and hugely influential,' says Alan Gorrie. 'Supporting local bands to put out records is a great thing to do.' The record wasn't to be the last.

In the early 1980s, there was a move to the Marketgait, to a shop beside the Angus Hotel, when the Perth Road agent wouldn't renew the lease. 'To be honest, we were scared stiff of moving away from the West End into the town,' says Breeks. 'We thought it was far too expensive and wondered if people would still come to us.'

There was nothing to fear, as business improved at the city-centre location, something that Breeks puts down to being in the right place at the right time. 'The indie scene was booming and we weren't doing nearly as much in second-hand singles. We started getting indie albums in – the more mainstream shops didn't really do that and we didn't need to do any deals with record companies. Takings trebled practically overnight.'

The close proximity to the hotel, where bands would stay after Dundee gigs, certainly contributed to the star-spotting potential. 'The Smiths had played the university when "This Charming Man" had just been released and I can't say I really knew who they were, apart from Morrissey. Alan Matheson, who worked here at the time, had been in touch with Johnny

Marr. They came in and Alan went out on the shop floor to talk to him. I do remember that Marr bought a Rickenbacker guitar badge, Morrissey bought a Dusty Springfield single and Mick Joyce bought a packet of Rizla King Size and some hair gel.'

Style and music were running in parallel throughout much of that time and clothes were selling well, but with a tiny back office there were no facilities for trying on clothes or shoes. 'There was no option but to vacate my chair in the office if someone wanted to try a pair of shoes. We ended up with a huge shop in the Overgate.' The new shop opened in November 1984 and was called Breeks. 'Not an ego thing,' insists Breeks. 'We just couldn't think of what else to call it. The Mods came in for the tonic suits and target T-shirts. Some liked the zoot suits and the baggy Bowie trousers. The flat tops went for American jackets and baseball shirts and the punk bondage stuff was still selling.'

Ronnie had now been bought out completely, having been a sleeping partner since the move from the Perth Road. 'He would probably admit that he wasn't as into the music side of thing as I was. It was a great partnership, but like many, it just ran its course.'

The Breeks clothing store also ran its course and after three good years, it sold everything off to close in 1987. 'The casuals had appeared and there was nothing in an alternative clothing shop for them.'

There was also a concert ticket agency, set up in conjunction with local promoter Stuart Clumpas. This was a help through quieter times, but come 1997, the rumours surrounding the demolition of the Overgate were substantiated – with the wrecking ball starting on Groucho's doorstep. 'Most shops could be given three months' notice to move, but thanks to my brother-in-law we had a watertight lease. They were obliged to relocate us but all they could offer were shops that cost five or six times our annual rent.' Eventually the ball was swinging and the developers had to offer Groucho's a store six times the size of the one that was about to be pulverised, for the same rent – and then fit it out.

The next two years saw the bulldozers edging closer. Three moves were aborted, through no fault of the shop's management, and when the demolition was at the front door, heaven and earth was moved to get Groucho's into the Nethergate location, where they have been since 1999. 'We can see the site of the old shop from the front door,' says Breeks. 'They gave us a blank canvas and fitted it out as we wanted. I subsequently worked out that moving us from beside the Angus Hotel to a shop diagonally across the road must have cost the better part of £250,000, when you take into consideration the cheap rent at the large unit, all the legal fees for the moves and the aborted moves, plus the shopfitting of both stores.'

Now Breeks finds that customers are generally older, but although downloading is having a serious effect, there appears to be a new generation of kids who are rejecting it. They can see that they don't have what their parents have – a collection of music that they can look back on.

Certainly the younger bands in Dundee – such as The Hazey Janes – have found inspiration flicking the racks of vinyl at Groucho's. Band member Andrew Mitchell bought his first record there. 'It was Buddy Holly, "That'll Be The Day". I thought, "The smell in here, it's so ... pungent," ' he laughs. 'When I was a bit older I would sell records at the weekend to buy beer and hope they would still be there later to buy back. It was more like pawning.'

Matthew Marra, son of Michael and fellow member of The Hazey Janes, bought The Beatles' *Blue* album. He remembers Breeks taking it and saying, 'Good choice.'

'That was a real seal of approval.'

The band's drummer, Liam Brennan, is ashamed to say that he bought a CD 'but it was King Crimson'.

Guitarist Stevie Anderson is appreciative of the knowledge that Groucho's staff can bring when he's looking for something specific. 'They know what you like and if something comes in that they think you'll appreciate, then they keep it aside and play it to you the next time you're in.

'I was gutted one day, though. A band I was in had supported Peter

Green at Fat Sams and it was the first time I had ever considered asking for an autograph, so I brought down a guitar. He was kicking about and I asked him if he would sign it, but he refused and even when I said I was the support he pretty much told me to f*ck off. A couple of days later I was in the shop and Breeks says, "Oh, Peter Green was in. He came through the back for a cup of tea and signed a few things for me!"'

The affection that record-buyers hold for Groucho's was repaid when The View recorded the anthem for Record Store Day 2011, changing the lyrics to include Groucho's and filming the video in the store itself. 'The shop was also the cover of the single,' say Breeks, 'and it put a huge smile on my face when someone sent me a picture of the window of the Rough Trade store in London, and there was a huge poster of Groucho's.

'I think we've done the Dundee public proud by not changing things too much and keeping things pretty traditional. Partly that's down to me having Crohn's Disease. I thought about branching out, but the lesson I learned from the clothes shop was: don't spread yourself too thin. I'm very fortunate to have the team I have in Frank, Moog, Andy and Cara.

'It wasn't until twenty-five years in that I had to sack someone and it was twenty-eight years before I interviewed someone. It was always that I knew someone who fitted the job. Now it's my friends' kids. I'll give up when it's their grandchildren wanting jobs.'

BLAST OF THE MOHICANS

As Groucho's was adapting to the arrival of punk, Gordon Walker remembers it as just 'clusters of daft fowk' springing up around the city. Few would disagree, but it has to be said that the stink bomb that punk lobbed into the Dundee scene always came with a wicked sense of humour.

The Sex Pistols played the Bowling Alley in October 1976, just days after signing a record deal, but their return in December of that year was pulled by the Caird Hall following the infamous *Today* interview with Bill Grundy.

Punk polarised music fans, as Steve Knight remembers. 'When punk happened and Chris Marra didn't get into it, there was a separation of the ways, musically. Jog [Jonathan Ogilvie], who had been with Skeets Boliver, was finding their stuff a bit smooth, so left to get together with me, Steve Reid and Steve Falconer, but we also had Allan McGlone from Skeets on sax.' The band was charmingly named Bread Poultice and the Running Sores. 'We wrote the whole set in one night,' says Steve. 'The first gig was Pete McGlone's girlfriend's twenty-first birthday party – she was horrified at all the swearing and everything.'

No record remains of the Bread Poultice set, but lost classics include a punchy little number called 'Love Me Like a Joob Joob' and they were adopted by Edinburgh art-school punk band The Rezillos as a favourite support act. 'It was a fantastic year – we played three or four times at Nicky Tams in Edinburgh, and had a huge reputation there because Steve Falconer had set off a fire extinguisher one night.'

Steve Falconer embraced the daftness of punk in its extreme, telling the audience he would play the guitar with his teeth like Jimi Hendrix, and then strumming the strings with his dentures. When Bread Poultice supported The Rezillos at the Bowling Alley they were asked by the band to play in Edinburgh the next night. 'They said, "We'll come and see you. There are guys from the American record company in town. We'll bring them as well." That day for some reason, maybe I was the most sensible, I had to go and meet another record company guy in somewhere like Strathaven. I didn't drive so had to get the bus there – and he was a d*ckhead anyway. I had said to the band that I would meet them in Edinburgh; they just had to bring the gear through. I got to the gig about 6pm and the manager was delighted. We had sold out. It got to 7pm, the place is heaving, and there's no band . . .

'I think I had a pound on me, so went to a phone box. Eventually I got Steve Reid and he said, "The boy winna drive us through 'cos Falconer called him a pr*ck." I phoned everybody I knew who could drive but nobody could do it. The Rezillos came in and brought the record company with them, but eventually I had to say the rest of the band weren't coming – the manager went mental.'

To compound the misery, Steve had no money to get home. His dad refused to go to the station and pay his fare and it was several hours before he could get someone in to cover the journey. The relationship with The Rezillos was strong, however, and they asked him to audition for the bass job. He went back for a second audition but Simon Templar got the job.

Once Bread Poultice had split, it was back to occasionally playing with Chris in McDonald's Farm and in another band called Tivvy. 'It was OK and it was good money but it wasn't me really.'

Gordon Walker and his band The Quick Spurts weren't too happy with Bread Poultice. 'Nobody said that you had to actually play to be in a band.' For a year Gordon and other daft fowk had been calling themselves a band and getting badges made at Groucho's with the name on it, but they didn't own an instrument between them. When Bread Poultice played, Gordon says they were 'shamed into it'. The Quick Spurts' first gig was also a birthday party and it was three weeks away.

'We had to buy instruments, then Forrey Rosscraig and I wrote the set. Oh, we were sh*te – simply headlining at this party because we had been so good at being deceitful. There were another band called The Trendies and they were proficient. So we were in Dairsie Village Hall on a rainy night in January and sh*tting ourselves. We enjoyed it though – got the appetite for showing off. We played the Jimmy Shand, the art college, Ardler Community Centre, and St Andrews University. I think someone who was vaguely musical joined us but nobody liked us. We weren't popular. There was nothing to recommend us at all.

'I started another band in summer of 1978 with Al Hendrickx. From the outset I was the most talented, having played for about five months. I missed out on joining The Junkies, who formed in 1979 when I was in

London. But when I came back, it was just band after band – they were all keech.'

The Quick Spurts may not fly to the lips when old punks get nostalgic, but The Scrotum Poles certainly do. Formed in 1978, the line-up settled into Craig Methven (Smeg Pole), Colin Smith (Stripey Sleep), Steve Grimmond (Sid Gripple) and Glen Connell (Burt Spurt). If any of the punk bands could be described as professional, then The Scrotum Poles were, releasing a limited edition cassette *Auchmithie Calling* the next year and raising enough money to release a single, 'Revelations', recorded in Edinburgh. The song was mixed in London, and Colin Smith drove down with the tapes, aided by a guy who could be regarded as an unlikely champion of the punk scene, Ricky Ross, long before Deacon Blue and still in Dundee at the time.

A friend of the band was the man who put the Crank(y) in *Cranked Up*, the short-lived but influential fanzine which burned brightly and gave the great and good a few verbal Chinese burns along the way.

'There were about eighteen issues in total,' says Jock Ferguson. 'It was a huge amount of work as I was also working for British Telecom. It reviewed bands but there was a lot of nonsense as well. A few people wrote for it, but if anyone sent us stuff we would use it – it was very open.'

Jock was left cold by the soul that was widely regarded as Dundee's musical strength at the time. 'I'm not aware of the soul thing – my pals and I didn't like it. We liked guitar-based rock with a good front man who put on a bit of a show.'

As a young boy, he was drawn to the radio, picking berries at Longforgan to buy a transistor from a pawn shop in the Westport. 'It was three pounds ten shillings and it became the love of my life. I remember my dad bought a Perdio radio from Larg's. He worked at Post Office telephones, so rather than buying a battery that would go inside the radio he would purloin a massive battery that worked on the same voltage. He'd tape it to the radio but it was bigger than the radio itself.'

When Jock was about fifteen, the music of Alex Harvey came into his life – he had been listening to Emerson Lake and Palmer, but by the age of nineteen that was binned. 'Cut your hair, wear tight breeks, and like bands that barely play, please. I started DJing because no one was playing the kind of music I wanted to hear. Places like Tiffany's and Teazers weren't for guys like me but I wasn't a student so I couldn't go to the union and see The Ruts, The Jam, The Skids – bands like that were all on the college circuit.'

He started DJing for Dundee Football Club at Dens, where he managed to slip in some punk singles (he says he loved to see some pogoing on the terraces), but with Joe Lamb he recorded 'Johnny Scobie' to raise money for the club.

'I started going to see bands at the Tayside Bar and befriended Craig Methven from The Scrotum Poles. I would DJ when they were playing and apart from punk it was the Postcard label stuff and alternative rock. The Tayside Bar was a dump but it became something of a wee scene. That's where we could be ourselves. There was incredible camaraderie.'

The cheek of punk was alive and kicking with a small label called N-R-G. There were only two releases and one by The Drive, called 'Jerkin', managed to stir up some welcome publicity. It could be said that The Drive wasn't strictly a band. Working Dundee musicians including Ronnie Jack and Bruce Money were asked to go through to a studio in Edinburgh and record the track, written by Gus McFarlane.

The band put together for the single did one gig on the back of the horrified publicity that the record received ('Banned punks cut own sex single') but musicians like Ronnie were more used to appreciative audiences than being sprayed with lager. This being Dundee, a reviewer from the *People's Journal* did think it was about a coat.

AN OFFER NO ONE COULD REFUSE

Despite what Jock considered the pseudo-soul reputation of Dundee, the punks wouldn't have it all their own way in the mid-1970s. Dougie Martin had been in Glasgow since 1967, but was considering a move back to Dundee with his band Cosa Nostra.

'My agent phoned me, which was a shock,' says Dougie. 'He never phoned me because the band had a residency; he didn't really need to get us work. He said, "What are you calling yourselves just now?" I told him, "Cosa Nostra," and he said, "Cosa Nostra? What the f*ck does that mean?" I told him it was the Mafia and he said, "Mafia – that's a good name."'

Donny Coutts hadn't played for several years. When he was in his fourth year at art college, Roger Ball had asked him to join the Average White Band on percussion and vocals, but with just a year to get his degree, he turned him down. 'I didn't play for a good while, but when I saw Dougie's band he told me that he was coming back to Dundee and the drummer Robert Ryan didn't want to do the commute. Did I fancy it?'

He did, but at that point he didn't even have a drum kit. No problem for Dougie, with his legendary reputation for being the great arranger. 'He got a kit from somewhere, and I ended up playing with the band, which had become Mafia.'

Duly signed with a local agent, the band turned up to a wedding booking in Forfar, only to be told, 'You're not a steel band!'

Dougie says, 'We looked at one another and said, "Jimmy Smart!" Smart was an infamous Dundee agent and it only took the mention of his name to make Dougie's old English sheepdog bark loudly.

'He sent us there as a steel band, and we turn up wearing white zoot suits with brown pinstripe and spats. It was some wedding though,' says Dougie. 'We had to start with "You Are the Sunshine of My Life" – as the guy rode a horse up the aisle. We're on stage ready to go and his wife comes down the corridor dressed as the Queen of Sheba. Then they came up and asked if we would like white or red wine. We all said white – and were waiting for glasses to appear when out comes individual ice buckets, placed beside us on stage. And they just kept coming.'

'By the end of the night Dougie was in the kitchen dookin' for chips

– while they were cooking . . .' says Donny, 'Alan Sheridan had thrown his suit jacket on the floor while he's juggling eggs, and someone starts playing the spoons . . . I have no idea how I got home but I woke up in my hallway stark naked and surrounded by nude books. I honestly have no idea where they came from.'

Alan Sheridan decided to move away to Jersey and Gerry McGrath (from The Phoenix) was recruited on bass. The addition of Gerry was a musical bonus and gave Mafia a third excellent soul singer. It also ramped up the madness. A favourite line of Gerry's is recalled by Keith McIntosh of Rainbow Music: 'Somebody would go to the bar and shout, "Gerry, you want ice?" and he'd say, "Eh, but mind and get fresh stuff, nane o' that frozen sh*te."'

There was plenty of work for the band and they also had a residency in the Ambassador on Clepington Road, formerly the Ponderosa coffee bar in the 1960s.

Donny was still in regular touch with Alan Gorrie, even though the Average White Band was, in 1976, promoting the platinum-selling album *Soul Searching*. Alan was keen to send record companies to see Mafia, and on a trip to the UK, he went into Craighall Studios with the band to record some songs. Mafia had a dual existence: one night they were in the studio with the bass player of a globally successful band, the next backing a magician at the Ambassador.

The band was always on the hunt for good players, however, leading Peter McGlone to feel a sense of déjà vu. 'I got a call from Dougie: "You Pete McGlone? You got a sax?" Again, "Have you got a sax?" not "Are you a sax player?" I was pretty dismissive and told him I was busy, which I don't think he was used to. I didn't know it at that point, but people usually said yes to Dougie. A wee while later my brother Allan told me he had a new gig, saying I had to come and hear them play. So I went down to rehearsal and I realise this is the gig I turned down. I thought to myself, "I have to get into this band."'

Peter went to a gig in Fife and without invitation, joined his brother on stage to bolster the horn section. No one said anything. In the car on the way back, Dougie asked if he was free the following Thursday for another gig. 'It turned out that everyone in the band thought someone else had hired me.'

Most of the band had full-time jobs. With a three-night residency in Carlisle, that meant going back to Dundee after every gig, getting up for work, and then heading straight back to Carlisle. That included Donny. 'I think we had car trouble, so we borrowed Dougie's uncle's taxi. Just before we got there, we switched the light on to kid on that we had got a taxi all the way. You should have seen the faces. They saw the gig money disappearing before their eyes.'

Roadies were as important as any of the players in the Mafia set-up, and none more so than Pitso. 'He was *the* roadie in Dundee,' says Peter. 'He was called The Bear, so you can imagine the size of him. He was a shop steward in the Caledon boatyard, but also the roadie that everybody wanted. When he worked with Mafia, he was an equal.'

Pitso and another Dundee roadie called Peem McGovern did the Simon and Garfunkel world tour. 'Peem sent for his mum and dad, who live in the multis in St Mary's Place,' says Donny, 'and by that time Peem had struck up a friendship with Steve Gadd. [Gadd is a god among drummers, having played with everyone from Chet Baker to Steely Dan to James Taylor to George Benson – it goes on.] In those days Steve had to have his girlfriend sitting on the side of the stage for reassurance, but Steve and Peem got on really well. At an aftershow party, he made the introductions. "Mum, Dad, this is Steve . . ." and after a pause had to say, "Sorry, Steve, what's your second name again?"'

Pitso's bearlike stature was helpful when the band was playing in London. Alex Harvey guested on a couple of songs, but as Donny describes it, 'He was blootered. He picks up a guitar and tries to start "Boston Tea Party" and he's falling all over the place. I see Pitso out the corner of my eye ready to move. Somebody takes the guitar off Alex and Pitso wheechs him under his arm and gets him off the stage. Roger Ball from the Average

White Band was there that night, so he jumps up to start playing something to divert the audience's attention and all I can hear from the wings is Alex Harvey screaming, "Who the f*ck is he?!!!"'

The Glasgow promoter Alan Mawn was a supporter of the band and during a meeting with American music executive Larry Uttal, he recommended that he should catch Mafia. Uttal wasn't keen. He just wanted somewhere to have a quiet drink before his flight, having just finished a trip where he had watched countless bands. However, when Mawn played him a demo, Uttal changed his mind.

'He came to see us and immediately wanted to sign us. So we make an arrangement for him to come and visit us in Dundee,' says Donny. 'So here's Larry Uttal in my living room in the Ferry, and he produces a contract. He was working for Bell Records, so the contract had obviously been written for the Bay City Rollers. Every time it had their name, it had been scored out and Mafia written in! It also said he had the rights to our scarves and T-shirts and dolls!

'I could feel Dougie looking at me and I know what he's thinking: "What about the advance?" It's left to me to ask, but Uttal says there would be no advance but, "You guys can keep on working and then, when the album's done, you have to be ready to drop everything and come to America."

'There's a silence that seems to last an eternity, only broken by Dougie saying, "I canna sign that. I've been promising Jennifer a new washing machine for months now."'

Some opportunities were too good to turn down, however. At a restaurant in Dunfermline, the changing area was next to the kitchen store. 'Of course, when Dougie spotted the frozen steaks, he helped himself, but when we packed up after the gig there was a puncture on the trailer and no spare. Dougie said he would send a mechanic from work to pick it up the next morning. It was all locked up so the gear would be safe,' says Donny.

The next day Willie arrived, ready to change the wheel and hitch up

What's on at the Palais? No address is given in this ad from the local press, everyone knew where the Palais was.

Dance away the Blues at

"THE PALAIS"

to the Swinging Strict Tempo Tunes of
ANDY LOTHIAN'S ORCHESTRA

TUESDAY : 9 p.m. - Midnite, 4/-.

WEDNESDAY : CLUB NIGHT
8.45 p.m. - 12, 4/-; Members 3/-.

FRIDAY : 9.30 p.m. - 1 a.m., 6/6.

SATURDAY : 9 p.m. - 12, 6/-.

No Jiving   No Teenagers

SUNDAY NITE —

TOP TEN — TEEN TIME at "The Palais"
7.30 - 10.30 p.m.

© DC THOMSON

Andy Lothian Snr gives Andy Jnr some guidance on the Palais bandstand.

The Hep Cats with bridies. From left: Jim Kelly (not of Honeybus), Dougie Martin, Lewis Grier, Ronnie Davie.

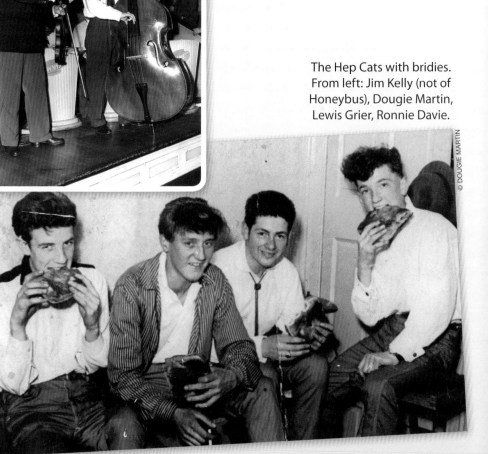

© DOUGIE MARTIN

Who are those masked men? The Mystery Men. From left, back: Benny Esposito, Dougie Martin. Front: Ronnie Davie, Jim Smith.

The Beatles meet Hugh Robertson and George Ryden of Dundee FC backstage at the Caird Hall in 1963.

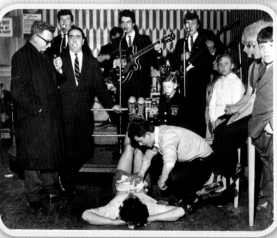

A dancer at the Twist Marathon in the West End Palais takes a break while the Johnny Hudson Hi-Four look on.

Dreamy. The first issue of *Jackie*, from January 1964.

Every Thursday, 1964 6d

Jackie
for go-ahead teens

FREE TWIN HEART RING

SUPER FULL COLOUR PIN-UPS OF CLIFF, ELVIS, BILLY FURY and The Beatles

PERFUME TIPS FOR A MORE KISSABLE YOU

DREAMY PICTURE LOVE STORIES

COLOUR PICTURES OF OUTFITS TO MAKE YOU PRETTY IN THE RAIN 'N' SNOW

PHOTO FEATURES AND WAY-OUT EXCLUSIVES ON ALL THE POPSTERS

The Poor Souls, from left: Dougie Martin, Chic Taylor, John Casey and Johnny Hudson, embrace flower power in *Pop Weekly*.

The Inn Folk, from left: Ally Lowden, Willie Whyte and Russ Paterson.

The Vikings' 'Bad News Feeling' on ALP Records.

TOP TEN CLUB

PALAIS, Tay Street

SUNDAY at 7 p.m.

THE VIKINGS

who have just recorded their first single for ALP Records— and it's a knock-out!! Look-out for news of its Release Date.

And don't forget our latest release—"FRIDAY NIGHT," by the RED HAWKES, already edging in the charts!!

New Sound Spot.

THE PHOENIX

Admis...

New Members ...

Who's on this week? *Evening Telegraph* ad for the Top Ten Club at the Palais.

Taking it to the bridge with The Vikings. From left: Donny Coutts, Dougie Wightman, Alan Gorrie, Drew Larg, Roy Fleming.

© MAC CARNEGIE

Robbie McIntosh behind the kit at the Marquee.

The Average White Band finally comes together in 1972. From left: Robbie McIntosh, Malcolm 'Molly' Duncan, Roger Ball, Hamish Stuart, Onnie McIntyre, Alan Gorrie.

© AVERAGE WHITE BAND ARCHIVE

Gordon Douglas takes a break from writing new songs at the piano.

© GORDON DOUGLAS

SKEETS BOLIVER

NEW SINGLE
'SHEETHOUSE DOOR'
(c/w I Can't See the Light)
Thunderbird Records
THE 116

THUNDERBIRD

Censored. The Skeets flyer for the first single, 'Shithouse Door'.

Rare picture of all of Skeets Boliver live. From left: Chris Marra, Brian McDermott, Michael Marra, Gus Foy, Peter McGlone, Allan McGlone, Stewart Ivins.

Rokotto ready to go on the road, with manager Murdie Wallace Jnr. Howard McLeod is in the hat.

The end of an era as Andy Lothian Snr sells the Palais to Murdie Wallace Jnr.

Summer of '76 and the first day for Groucho at 89 Perth Road.

Adding colour to the music scene, Rainbow offered something different to Dundee's musicians.

The first Bread Poultice gig at Nikky Stewart's twenty-first birthday party. From left: Bob Carrol, Peter McGlone, Mr and Mrs Falconer, Steve Knight, Steve Reid and Chris Marra. Front are Steve Falconer and Jonathan Ogilvie (Jog).

Breeks behind the counter at the Marketgait shop.

Shiny new wave from The
Headboys. From left: Lou Lewis,
George Boyter, Davie Ross and
Calum Malcolm.

Steve Knight and Billy
Mackenzie at Gussie
Park Carnival.

The Associates' first
publicity session in 1978.
From left: Steve Knight,
Billy Mackenzie, Alan
Rankine and John Murphy.

the trailer. The restaurant owner bolted out and demanded to see inside but, genuinely ignorant of the previous night's events, Willie said he was only there to change the wheel and take it away.

'The guy insisted it was going nowhere,' adds Donny, 'saying there were stolen goods in there! Willie got to a phone box and told Dougie the story, who then told him to wait twenty minutes, go back, change the wheel and drive away – the guy wouldn't do anything to stop him.' Sure enough, Willie changed the wheel and drove off, all the time being watched from the window. 'Dougie had called the guy and said, "I'm from Fife police. I believe you had a band there last night. Did you have any problems?" When the guy related the whole story, "the police" said they had been watching them for a while and this is a lucky break. Let the trailer go, and they would catch them at the first roundabout!'

Some things did catch up with them, however. 'We were soundchecking for a support at a university gig and the main act walks across the hall,' says Dougie. 'He shouts, "Good god! Dougie Martin! How's Bella?"' It was Gary Glitter, who as Paul Raven had been nursed back to health at Bella's Roadhoose. 'At the time we thought, "What a nice bloke for remembering,"' laughs Dougie.

BORN INTO FUNK

With the Palais sold to Murdoch Wallace Jnr, dancers in the mid-1970s were flocking to Tiffany's and the JM, where a young musician from the West Indies was making his mark. Howard McLeod had arrived in Scotland from the Caribbean in 1966, having learned to play drums in the West Indies at a small community centre. 'I was there every day from 10am to 6pm,' Howard says. 'It's all I wanted to do. When you're raised in the Caribbean, you hear music all the time at the beach and I started off with steel drum and percussion.'

Along with a group of other West Indian musicians, he made the journey to Scotland and found himself in Stonehaven. 'We also played in Aberdeen, but then Murdie Wallace asked if we wanted a residency at the JM Ballroom.' So the band, Ray King and the Flamingos, arrived in Dundee in the early 1970s. As well as Ray and Shirley King, the band were Cleveland Walker, Lloyd Owen Wisdom, Calvert Ward, Jerry Bartholomew, and of course Howard, later to be known as 'Bongo'.

In 1972, a new female singer joined the line-up, a young girl who was working at the Timex factory, but had shown that she could more than handle the vocals. Yvonne Jenkins (stage name Susan Childe) had sung with the band when Shirley was ill. Following a break working in London, she joined the band when there was something of a split in the Flamingos' ranks. 'A few of us had secretly been rehearsing a soul and funk set. We had to do it without Murdie knowing – he wouldn't have been pleased. So we left to form Rokotto and the JM band became Susan Childe and the Flamingos.'

Perhaps Wallace wasn't pleased at first, but he saw the potential in Rokotto and decided to manage them, now joined by the teenage singer Lorna Bannon, known as Sister B. 'We started touring, doing our funky disco thing,' says Howard, 'and one night in Aberdeen we were offered a record deal.' It was September 1976 and the label was State Records, owned by two former members of The Rubettes and already successful with acts like The Real Thing and Mac and Katie Kissoon.

They would have more success with Rokotto, who had two hits with 'Boogie On Up' and 'Funk Theory'. 'We played so much, but should have probably spent more time recording,' says Howard. 'We had the hits, but there could have been more.'

In a *Blues and Soul* article, published in January 1979, a journalist travelled to Paris with the band and seemed rather taken with Bongo: 'Always with an eye for a lovely lady (he claims any lovely lady) he is probably the most flamboyant of the group when it comes to dress. He has got past the days of coloured wigs but his clothes are to say the very least SHOWY.'

Away from that, Howard was a solid funk drummer who was the back-bone of the Rokotto sound until they split in 1981. Lorna Bannon went on to join Shakatak, and now lives in Brighton, having become one of the country's most successful session singers.

Meanwhile, the Flamingos continued to entertain Wallace's customers at the newly opened Barracuda. They had a succession of drummers, including Ronnie Jack, who had just got married and was also holding down a job. 'One night the air conditioning was blowing hot and cold,' remembers Ronnie. 'It must have gone off and I was falling asleep at the kit. It was "Rainy Night in Georgia" and I was getting slower and slower . . . it must have sounded like the record winding down. Suddenly I hear Lenny Sylvester shouting, "Ronnie, wake up!" I hadn't quite gone to sleep but it was close.'

Susan Childe was a familiar name in Dundee pubs and clubs for ten years or so but now lives in the US, where she still sings under the name Yvonne J.

Brian McDermott also fell into a residency when Skeets folded. 'When Mick decided to go off solo, it was very odd for me. It had been my exis-tence, so it seemed really strange not to be doing it. I knew my mate was leaving Susan Childe and the Flamingos, so I marched in and spoke to the manager, who did the deal there and then. He showed me the dressing room, where there were all these horrible, multi-coloured satin shirts with ruffly sleeves. He said, "That's what you'll be wearing." I did it for a few months but it was just a job. It was kinda disco-ish for me. And I never wore the shirt!'

THE NEXT STAGE

Gordon Douglas had put London behind him. He was now working with Pat Joyce, having been approached by Dundee Rep for write some-thing for the Young People's Theatre. This also involved putting a band together, so it was back to The Bread to recruit Colin Warnock, Bruce Money, Louie O'Neill and Wayne Hutton.

The band needed to work with the cast closely to get the songs right, so Juliet Cadzow, Maureen Beattie and Tony Roper were at every rehearsal.

The Devil's Rock opened in January 1976, when the theatre was still on the Lochee Road and was well reviewed (although Gordon discovered years later that Tony Roper had called it the 'Lochee Horror Show').

Gordon says, 'I always remember getting a telegram from Mick Marra saying, "Break a leg," and not understanding that meant good luck!' The band had gelled so well that they decided to go out and play together as Stan and De Liver, Gordon writing a new set of songs.

If Gordon was happy to be taking another direction, then Lou Lewis and George Boyter were determined that their songs were worthy of vinyl.

'George and I had gone back to London and had a meeting with EMI publishing,' says Lou. 'They said they liked the band but couldn't really see anything they could use. We asked if we could come back in a couple of days and he agreed. I bought a £10 guitar, we locked ourselves away for a couple of days and emerged with some new songs to take back to the next meeting.'

Lou and George went back to record in Castle Sound Studios in Edinburgh, owned by Calum Malcolm. Davie Ross worked in the studio but if anyone needed a drummer, he would do it. 'We did demos of the song to send for a publishing deal, but MCA wanted to sign us as a band. We didn't even have a name so we ended up being called Badger – I just couldn't escape the animal thing!'

Signed in late 1976, the band put out a single called 'Bidin' My Time' in early 1977, but it failed to make an impression. 'They were looking for us to do these big orchestrated ballads and the next thing they were sending us to record in Abbey Road. That was a great experience. We put the tracks down and then they added a thirty-two-piece orchestra. They were cheesy ballads. I just couldn't sing that stuff *and* I sing in a Dundee accent, which didn't help.'

The band decided to hand back the advance and walk away. 'It was time to write as a band and not with publishing in mind,' says Lou. 'I had been going to the 100 Club when we were in London and watching punk and new-wave bands – I was getting more interested in stripping everything back.'

Once new demos were done, there was support again at EMI publishing, where younger employees, liking what they heard, were distributing the tapes to A&R (artists and repertoire) men. 'Suddenly we heard we'd been offered a deal again. It was £15,000. Then another company offered £20,000, then another put in £30,000. They were bidding blind. They had never seen us play.'

In the end two companies were in the running, EMI and RSO. 'To be honest we looked at both labels and thought RSO might be more fun.' So in 1978, on the strength of demos alone, the band, again with no name, signed to RSO for £100,000.

'At that time it was important to construct an image,' says Lou. 'I got a pretty severe haircut and went to the schoolwear shop on Commercial Street. I bought a school shirt, tie, and blazer, and wore them with white Kickers and skintight jeans. I was due to meet the guys at a pub in Edinburgh and I turned up like that. The next thing I knew they were off to do the same. I had also gone to the Army and Navy in Union Street because they sold enamel school badges. I had bought one for Calum, saying Head Girl. So that's how we became The Headboys.'

The band still hadn't played live. They could create what they needed in the studio, but it was time to decamp to Shepperton Studios to create a live sound – from the bass drum up.

The album had been put together from demos and some new recordings, but there wasn't a single. 'We needed something anthemic, so we wrote "The Shape of Things to Come". We weren't alone – a lot of bands worked like that at the time, only writing a single because they had to.'

A European tour followed with Wishbone Ash and headlining gigs, one at the Rock Garden where they were supported by a little Irish band called U2. 'The Shape of Things to Come' was a minor hit but achieved almost cult status and was followed by 'Stepping Stones', which had been the B-side of the Badger single. The album, *The Headboys*, received good reviews but the experience of being 'pop stars' didn't sit well with Lou. 'Things like the TV programmes, *Top of the Pops* and all that, it just didn't interest me. There are things we did for foreign TV stations that I've never seen and it should probably stay that way.'

A Dutch TV station was particularly interested in the band recording an album track, rather than the single. 'We were driven out to a school and had to perform in a classroom, then suddenly all these blonde five-foot-ten models in schoolgirl uniforms appeared to dance around us. That was long before Britney Spears thought of it . . .'

The Headboys were also the first rock band to sign to the German classical label Deutsche Gramophon. 'We were really well treated there – well fed and taken to the best dos, but after a wee while it's difficult to fake enthusiasm for more sausage.'

The best of all experiences was making the video for 'The Shape of Things to Come'. It is New Wave 101, filmed in a dark, abandoned power station. Lou was asked to get in the car and drive a few yards across the shot. 'But I don't drive, do I?' So, with the handbrake off, crew members pushed the car. 'Then they said, just climb up there and pretend to play. But I've got vertigo, haven't I? I did it, but there was no way I was taking the Gibson up, I took up an old Telecaster instead.'

By 1981, they had had enough. 'We were in our thirties so the fame thing wasn't what we were after. My only regret is not going to America with the band, but I'm still proud that we stood together and handed that advance back so we could start from scratch.'

While Gordon was writing *The Devil's Rock* he didn't see anything of George and Lou. 'The next time I saw them, they were on *Top of the Pops*, and genuinely I didn't envy them at all. I was happy to see them enjoy success. Anyone who knows me would agree that what they were doing just wasn't me.'

There was always Stan and De Liver of course, wasn't there? 'I had taken a rare holiday to Penzance, and when I came back found out that I had been removed and they had a new singer, but these things happen in bands. I could fully understand it when I saw who I'd been replaced with – a young man called Billy Mackenzie.

'I bumped into Billy in Albert Street, not long after. He apologised and it was obvious he couldn't really understand what had gone on. I just said, "That's bands for you!"'

CRYPTIC BLUES

Billy Mackenzie's voice had been a point of pride for his parents since his childhood, when he was wheeled out to perform for aunts, uncles and friends of the family. When that happens, it can feel that whatever talent you possess isn't really your own.

A failed apprenticeship behind him, Billy reached out to his relatives around the globe and spent time living in London, New Zealand and the US – all relatively short spells, despite the fact that he had married in Las Vegas in 1975.

He was later to say that any wanderlust had been satisfied in his teens, so the hills around Dundee were enough escape for him – providing there were whippets by his side.

'I clearly remember hearing him for the first time in 1976, when Louie O'Neill said I had to come to The Rep and hear the new singer in Stan and De Liver,' says Stuart McHardy. 'I wasn't convinced until my wife Sandra, who was stage manager at the time, said, "No – you *really* do." So I went along to rehearsals and thought, "Holy sh*t, this boy is ridiculously good."'

Stan and De Liver would play the occasional gig in Laings, a venue more associated with Skeets Boliver at the time. 'I went down to see Skeets one night,' says Ricky Ross [Deacon Blue], but they weren't playing.

'I didn't know who the band was, but when the guy started singing everyone paid attention. It was quite amazing – I think I also remember him wearing dungarees.'

Louie O'Neill had spoken to Billy about Stuart McHardy, saying he knew something about jazz and had experience of dealing with record companies – even if they weren't good experiences.

'He came down to the flat and he sang me this thing he had written – "Blue Soap", it was called. The boy had four octaves and every note – I mean every note – was bang in the middle. I was gobsmacked at the talent. He asked for some advice about what to do – I was ten years older so he probably thought I knew.'

Stuart and Sandra moved to Edinburgh the next month, and when a band asked if they could recommend a singer, Stuart called Louie to get a number for Billy, who came through to try out.

Edinburgh was also the meeting point for Billy and Alan Rankine, then playing with a band called Caspian. The two proceeded to tour the pubs and clubs with the typical covers set of the day. There was money to be made and equipment was required for whatever they were going to do.

Not everyone who experienced Billy's unique vocal talent was instantly impressed, however. 'I met Billy at a party on Benvie Road,' says Steve Knight. 'He wasn't part of our crowd – actually I thought he was really strange. I was in the living room being pensive and thoughtful, obviously nobody to get off with … and Billy stands up and starts singing some jazz classic. It might have been "God Bless the Child". I'm talking full pelt. Everybody else in the room got up and left, saying, "F*ckin' weirdo …" but I loved all that stuff so I thought, "That's brilliant." When he finished, I asked him to give me a shout if he ever formed a band.'

About a year later, Steve bumped into Billy again. 'He said, "I've got this duo with this really ugly guy from Edinburgh called Alan Rankine," and I became involved at that point,' says Steve. 'What a laugh we had.'

The band, Mental Torture at that point, meant Alan was spending time in Dundee to rehearse in a warehouse on Dens Road belonging to one of Billy's uncles. 'We were always looking for drummers,' says Steve.

A musician who almost joined at that point is Steve Aungle, who had taken up drumming at the age of nine. He had already started taking piano lessons but didn't have the same passion.

'I was pretty young when I was thinking I would be in a band, get girls, take drugs – that kind of dream,' he says. He started living the dream at the age of sixteen in the Charleston Bar in what he remembers as a 'sh*tey clubby band. I had already started on that cabaret-type circuit and did that for two or three years while I was still at school. In 1978, when I was eighteen, I put an ad in the *Courier* looking for a new band. I didn't have any work but wanted to save up for a new drum kit. I had heard that doing weddings and country and western nights could earn you much more money.'

Steve received two replies. One was from a band in Kirriemuir called Tangles, and the other was from Billy Mackenzie. Billy invited him down to his clothes shop, The Crypt, for a chat.

The Crypt, with its *Addams Family* vibe and coffin-shaped changing rooms was completely alien to Dundee in the 1970s, and combined Billy's innate creativity with an inherited sense of retail nous.

Steve felt decidedly out of place when he showed up, in what he remembers as thick specs and a donkey jacket. 'He was a really slick, groovy-looking guy, with a white shirt, and really white teeth. He asked what bands I was listening to and I said Talking Heads and Devo. He seemed to like that answer and asked if I could play like a drum machine. I said no bother, so he said come along to a rehearsal. They were going to be rehearsing in Edinburgh and at that point I had just started university and didn't have a car so I had to say, "Sorry. Good luck." So I went off and joined Tangles and played the clubbies.

'I didn't put two and two together until years later, when I became pals with his brother John. I didn't know he was Billy's brother, but when he started talking about The Crypt, I realised it was the same guy.'

Another Dundee drummer who made it as far as an audition was Lloyd Anderson. Son of the Dundee entertainer Bud Anderson, Lloyd got his first kit when his father noticed that when Lloyd was drumming along to something on the TV (usually with knives on the sofa) he was able to pick up on the more intricate accents. 'I would ask my sister to get empty sweetie jars from the Linlathen shops, and I could use them as toms.' It was a friend called Eddie Robertson and the boys' shared love for David Bowie that ignited the spark about performing. 'He played "Ziggy [Stardust]" on guitar one night and that was it for me.'

The Edge was his first band, with the Kellyfield Hotel resembling a Wild West saloon on some nights. 'The band was cocooned, even though chairs were flying. When it was finished, everybody sat down and had a pint.

'I can't really remember why that band broke up. It might have been something to do with the taxman,' he laughs.

Lloyd was playing on the pub and club circuit when he had the chance to audition for Billy, Alan and Steve. 'I remember having to haul all my gear up to the top of a Mackenzie warehouse. I went in and they were all sitting on chairs, looking incredibly cool . . . you should've seen the state of me.

'Billy comes up and says, "Ken that kinda Rod Stewart "Do Ya Think I'm Sexy?" drumming, can you dae that?' They still hadn't found their drummer.

The band was a picture of elegance compared to others in the late 1970s and, as Steve Knight remembers, Billy used it to his full advantage. 'Billy was brilliant at getting off with women. He'd say, "They twa are up for it. I'll go and get them." Right enough, they would come back with him. Some nights we wouldn't go home and stay in the shop overnight. Great times.' The music was being worked on, however. 'We rehearsed and sent away demos, but we had never played live.'

Chris Parry from Fiction Records loved the demos and invited the band to come to London. He also convinced them that a name change from Mental Torture was advisable, and The Associates came into being.

By that time, Ricky Ross was working in a youth project at the City Churches. 'There was a Saturday-night club with local bands, usually punk bands, so there would sometimes be a bit of a rammy. There were a lot of kids from the Hilltown and I remember this guy standing on a table. He was different to anyone else there – much more stylish. He would be shouting, "They've no' even heard of The Associates." It was John Mackenzie, who would bring Billy's tapes down. I never actually saw them play in Dundee, though. I was shocked when I came across the news that John had died in 2010. He was a lovely boy, John, he definitely had a spark of what his big brother had.'

In London, The Associates stayed at Chris Parry's house. 'We must have only been about twenty,' says Steve Knight. 'The Cure were there as well. They must have only been about seventeen, but his wife was used to having bands to look after.

'Chris really wanted us to play live, so the three of us moved to Edinburgh and did some gigs there. They weren't great – we still couldn't get a really good drummer. We went on tour with Siouxsie and the Banshees and The Cure for a few gigs. At one we turned up and ate all Siouxsie's food, thinking it was our dressing room. We got chucked out and into our toilet!

'The Cure had a success with "Killing an Arab", so we were put back on the road with them and The Passions ["I'm In Love With A German Film Star"].

'Halfway through, Chris took the band off tour to make an album and that's when I left. I was having girlfriend problems [Steve was going out with a girl that Billy had previously been involved with] and we had a huge scrap in Bradford. The album, *The Affectionate Punch*, was finished without me and I do regret that. I love that album would loved to have been on it.

'They really were a duo and I was in the middle, getting on with both of them really well. I do think that if I'd stayed things might have been different and he might not have ruined Alan's career.'

COLOURFUL CHARACTERS

The music shop is the lifeblood of a scene. It's the source of new gear, from a capo to a new amp or a place simply to gaze upon a forbidden Stratocaster like an exhibit in a museum. A music shop can be something of a dream palace and a place where musicians come to meet, to find out who's looking for new players, or where the new gigs are.

Although shops such as Larg's in Whitehall Street and B.G. Forbes on the Victoria Road served the trumpet-playing schoolboy and the wannabe Beatle well, there was always an opportunity to do something different.

Keith McIntosh spotted that opportunity at the end of the 1970s while he was working in an architect's office, where he admits that he was about to be 'found out' as he approached his final exams. He was playing in bands and realised there was space for a shop that served a different kind of musician. He had no idea how 'different' they would turn out to be.

Keith, along with Alan Roy, opened Rainbow Music on the Hawkhill at its junction with Peddie Street in 1979. It was an entirely different proposition from Larg's, where musicians' favourite John Dunn wore a suit to work every day and was the epitome of politeness to everyone who came through his department. Musician Greg McCaffrey once heard him say to a well-known character, 'Ah Alex, we haven't seen you for a while. Are you taking your bad debt elsewhere?'

Rainbow ('a sh*t name, no idea where it came from but we were stuck with it') was far from being impolite but had a more relaxed approach.

'I was walking up Hawkhill one day and looked into the window at Rainbow Music,' says musician Ged Grimes, who had a part-time job in Larg's. 'Keith saw me standing outside and invited me in for a cuppa. There were so many guitars. I had never seen that kind of music shop before.'

The prospect of a sale was almost too much for Keith at the beginning. 'A guy came in with his wife and their newborn baby. She sat in a chair and he was looking at amps and in particular a Music Man, which was quite an expensive bit of gear. He decided he was going to buy it and said, "It's a lot of money but I'm going to take it and I'll pay now. You get it boxed up. I'll get the car." '

Keith was on his hands and knees packaging the amp when the customer left the shop. 'This was the first sale and a really good one, so I jumped what felt like six feet in the air and shouted "Yesssssss!" I turned round and the wife was still sitting there.'

Learning the retail trade was a difficult process at times. Saxophone player Peter Benedetti came into the shop when it first opened and Keith was desperate to do business. 'He was looking to buy an effects pedal, and asked if we did trade-ins. I wasn't really experienced and asked what he had. He told me he was willing to trade in "a convex mirror, a Victorian pelmet and a diver's suit." '

The shop was in that location for five years and continued to attract characters when it moved, first to Bell Street for ten years, and then to the Cowgate, where it is today. 'A guy came in and asked if we would give him £20 for his white anorak. I told him it was a music shop but all he said was, "So?" Greg McCaffrey was in the shop at the time and he offered him £2 for his tanktop.' Another customer came in, pointed at a set of bongos and said, "See they bongos – is that the sehz o' thum?" '

Rainbow had a reputation for being staffed by musicians who could provide additional advice. When digital entrepreneur Chris van der Kuyl became interested in music at school, he had been hanging around Larg's. It took a cooler school friend, Stewart Clark, to introduce him to Rainbow. 'I started hanging out there – and remember a seminal Rainbow experience. They organised a demo day in the Marquee nightclub and pulled in the best musicians – Brian McDermott for the drum clinic, Ged Grimes on bass, Derek Thomson on keyboards and Chris Marra on guitar. Lloyd Anderson did a song with them. This was the first time I had met these guys and I geekily hung about them, probably bothering them by asking too many questions.'

The staff may have been experienced but they didn't always have great business sense. 'We had a customer order for the sheet music of the theme from *Lovejoy*,' says Keith. 'Someone thought they were using their initiative and decided to order ten copies at once. Nine copies gathered dust on the shelf for years to come.'

The shop would also employ the services of their customers when they needed work to be done. 'I phoned Gerry McGrath from Mafia when I needed the outside of the shop painted. He answered the phone, "Gerry McGrath – half man, half brush" for a start!' laughs Keith. 'I was watching him paint, using gloss paint and a roller. I said, "Gerry, I didn't know you could use a roller with gloss paint." He assured me you could, but it wasn't as simple as that. He ran the roller up the wall and there were hundreds of little bubbles. He said, "See that. If you get a cowboy painter to dae that, all the bubbles would still be there at the end." I went out later and right enough, no bubbles. I asked him what special technique he had to get rid of the bubbles. He shrugged and said, "F*ck knows. They just a' seem to burst . . ." '

THE EIGHTIES

The Eighties

THE PATRON SAINT OF PURE CHEEK

It had been eighteen months or so since the farewell Skeets Boliver gig. Michael Marra was pursuing a solo writing career, Brian McDermott was playing with Gordon Douglas in a band called Spies, and the McGlone brothers were with Mafia.

Chris Marra was newly married with a child on the way around the time that Skeets split. He admits it wasn't his most artistically satisfying time.

'A job came up with a band that had a residency in Aviemore over the winter at a five-star hotel, but it was good money and we got to eat in the restaurant. I had been playing in Tiffany's five nights a week but was also working in a factory during the day, so it seemed like a good option. There was a lot of drinking up there, though, and I caught a wee bit of it. I would be home on Monday and Tuesday and would meet Brian McDermott on the Tuesday for a drink. I got into that habit of ordering a pint for yourself while you're waiting, and finishing it by the time the round is ready. I was lucky, though – it didn't really affect me that much.'

Chris decided that session work in London was the next move for him. 'One thing it did was really tighten up my playing. I did loads of auditions and realised I had to get faster, smarter and more tasteful – it was the first time that taste had come into the equation.'

Meanwhile Eddie Marra, Gus Foy and Stewart Ivins were still doing it for themselves around the Dundee pubs and clubs as MFI.

'And then Andy Pelc appeared,' says Gus.

Stewart knew Andy from art college. They bonded over *The World's Worst Record Show*, an album that Kenny Everett had put together and released on K-tel. This offered such classics as 'Paralysed' by the Legendary Stardust Cowboy and 'My Feet Start Tapping' by Adolph Babel. 'We absolutely loved it,' says Stewart, 'but Andy was always a very unusual guy.'

Andy Pelc had been raised in Fintry, with a Polish father and Irish mother. The heritage was reflected in a small but eclectic family record collection. 'We had a Bush radiogram but only three records,' says Andy. 'Mine was The Beatles' *Twist and Shout* EP, Dad's was a 78 of the Polish Red Army Orchestra performing "The Volga Boat Song" and Mum's was *Irish Anthems of the IRA*.

'I would play them in various rotations at different speeds to give the illusion that I had a much wider record collection. And if you stuck a thruppeny bit on the stylus with a bit of chewing gum, it made it heavier and gave it a deeper, bassier sound. Early drum and bass, I think.'

Young Andy was able to make his own entertainment. Saturday was pocket-money day and the ritual trip to the 'shops beside the Powrie [bar]' to buy 'a joobly – orange, always orange – a copy of a song words magazine and some keps [caps – small explosive charges on a paper reel, fired in toy guns]. I collected them but rarely fired them, enjoying the wee cardboard thing that kept them in tight little circles too much to spoil it.

'I remember on one occasion, walking along Fincraig Street, belting out the New Vaudeville Band's "Winchester Cathedral", which must have been in that week's magazine. A guy shouted, "Oi! Son. Brilliant." '

When Andy left art college, he had little experience of anything musical but had that shared sense of humour with Stewart. At the 1980 Groucho's party in Laings, a few members of Skeets Boliver played together and welcomed a newcomer on to the stage. 'I always belted it out after a couple of beers, so Stewart suggested that I do a few numbers.'

The first performance of Andy Pelc in front of an audience consisted of a kazoo rendition of 'Also Sprach Zarathustra' [by Richard Strauss but best-known as the theme from *2001: A Space Odyssey*] 'Runaround Sue' and 'Fireball XL5'. There was a different dimension to the performance, however: a character that had developed through nights spent with his friend Chris Taylor.

'Chris and I did a couple of wee things when we were laddies,' recalls Andy. 'When we were at the commercial college, a guy called Nigel Simpson heard us mucking about in the canteen, and asked if we wanted a turn at the Forfar Folk Club. We did two weeks on the trot. That was it, though. We were seek walking home from Forfar when we missed the bus.'

This short-lived career would have coincided with the period when Michael Marra and Gus Foy were playing the folk club circuit as a duo, being billed on one occasion as 'Mike Marro and Guf Foy'.

Andy and Chris had, for their own amusement, started speaking in a half-Dundonian, half-American accent and this was the basis of the character that became known as St Andrew, and first took to the stage of Laings that night. MFI were playing a Labour Club the next night and asked Andy if he wanted to come along and repeat the performance.

'I was there that night,' says Peter McGlone. 'I had met Andy previously at his house in Fintry when I was giving his brother sax lessons. He was just the daft brother, annoying his brother like all families do. At the Labour club, he was sitting there really quietly.' Andy has a stammer, so Peter was surprised when he got up to join MFI on stage. 'It was incredible. There was no hint of the stammer and this guy just transformed as soon as he got on stage. He was hilarious.'

Andy says he found that the different accent of the character helped to keep the stammer under control. 'The big, big voice helped to get things out. It also added confidence.'

For about a year, Andy would join MFI at gigs. 'Eventually I was also getting paid,' he laughs. 'It started with a couple of pints and I was happy with that but it became five, six or seven pints – it was getting unhealthy.'

His part in the proceedings was also growing as the character became more rounded. 'We thought we could create a wee band here. When we were thinking of a name, we looked at the papers for inspiration. At that time the St Andrews Woollen Mill were advertising, and we thought we could do something with that.'

The band called and checked that there would be no problem calling itself St Andrew and the Woollen Mill. 'Not at all,' they said, and took the endorsement further by asking the band to do a gig in the shop. 'We took a wee band and set up. They made an announcement: "Attention shoppers. Today we are delighted to have the St Andrew and the Woollen Mill band with us. Take it away, boys." There were maybe ten, fifteen punters at most in the shop. I'm six feet away from a guy who's been fitted for a jersey by his missus. It kinda set the tone for the band.'

The songs St Andrew performed were covers initially, a few being culled from that Kenny Everett album. The character was a Dundonian who had spent many years performing in America in a hellish version of the White Heather Club. Now he was back in his hometown and bringing the cheesy glamour of the Vegas showroom to the pubs and clubs of Dundee – he treated every pub backroom and social club function suite as if it was the most glittering room in Caesar's Palace.

As with Skeets Boliver, Stewart was the driving force behind the Woollen Mill as 'Lonesome Guitar'. There was Gorgeous Guf Foy, Eddie 'Lil' Chopin' Marra and a parade of drummers including Jog, Glen Jones, Sid Brand and Tam Parks. 'We had a lot of serious drummers and they must have thought, "What sh*te is this we're playing?"' says Gus.

Donny Coutts became the Woollen Mill drummer of choice, christened as Hector O'Sexual. 'People really wanted that gig,' says Donny. 'Amazing players were lining up to get a place if anyone left. They all wanted to play with St Andrew.'

There was another addition in Peter 'Wild Man' McGlone. 'Sometimes, I couldn't play for laughing – you couldn't help yourself. Often you were the target of the joke, but it didn't matter. The crowds just loved this persona

– punters either half believed it or wanted to. And he totally committed to that character of being a huge star playing a pub in the Hilltown. You know what the gag is but you still fall for it. His delivery was fantastic.'

There are many reasons why audiences bought into the character. Not only was it original and genuinely funny, it gave some credibility to the Dundonian accent. After years of being told to speak properly at school ('It's "yes", not "eh"') here was a 'superstar' using the local lingo and describing experiences that would hardly be recognised outside the city limits. Later, that would develop into a wider Scots vocabulary, but at the time it gave Dundonians the permission to be perfectly plazed beh the wiy they spoke.

It didn't have to be spot-on musically, and as Andy says, 'I don't have a technically brilliant singing voice, but it's distinctive.' Stewart believes that their apparent lack of competency was in the band's favour. 'There were still remnants of the punk thing around and we played the Tayside Bar a lot, so it wasn't an idea to be that good,' he laughs.

Gus Foy was constantly surprised at the following. 'I couldn't believe it. The places were always packed and a lot of the time it was crap.'

There were support gigs to the likes of John Cooper Clarke and Gary Glitter, but when Tam Parks called to say that a band was needed on Skye for the festive season, Andy rose to the challenge. 'It seemed the Mafia boys couldn't do it, but we could borrow their van and PA. I would sing, Tam on drums, Chris Marra would play guitar and we'd get this young guy called Gary Clark to play bass.'

Come 23 December, the Mafia van was on the A9 heading to Skye. They had a band, they had a PA, what they didn't have were any songs prepared. 'We were going to get that sorted in the van on the way up,' says Andy. 'Of course that never happened. We arrived at Portree Village Hall with nothing ready. Plus, the guy started battering us with nips.'

The band thought there would be a few hours to sort out whatever it was they were going to do, but it was not to be. 'The guy then says, "You're on."' The memory is of thick velvet curtains and the band standing on stage with not a clue what they were doing. 'The place was heaving.

There was livestock in that crowd. I just looked around at the guys and started singing "Wake up in the morning, slaving for bread, sir . . ." I knew they could join in with "The Israelites" easily and we proceeded to busk "Twist and Shout" and anything else that they could remember. We pulled it off, though. Four gigs and we weren't a bad wee band by the end of them. What did call ourselves? The Together Guys . . .'

'Yes, I was in the Together Guys,' says songwriter and musician Gary Clark. 'On Christmas Eve, the power was pulled on the hall so it plunged into darkness. We went outside in the pitch black and it was snowing – it was really magical. Apart from that it was debauchery and mayhem.'

The appetite for St Andrew led to the release of a cassette called *The Woollen Mill Story*, a combination of recordings, live material and an 'interview' with a local radio DJ. 'We took Andy up to Radio Tay and blagged our way in,' says Stewart. 'We told them nonsense about Andy having just returned from working with The Corries in Tampa, Florida. I don't know whether they just went along with it or they really believed it, but it turned out well anyway.'

They found a great supporter in Breeks Brodie from Groucho's, who offered to finance a single release. 'Eddie Marra came up with an idea of doing a Jimmy Shand version of "Pinball Wizard",' says Andy, 'and we had also come up with the idea of giving "The Skye Boat Song" special treatment.'

Breeks remembers that, 'On stage, Andy would say, "The next song is from our fourteenth album on the Dark Side of the Haggis label . . . it will be released about the same time as Peter Sutcliffe [the Yorkshire Ripper]." Anyway, we had a falling out, it was about two years, but everyone's had a fall-out with Andy at some point, so no big deal. After that we used to play snooker every Tuesday night and one night I said, "Let's bring out a record on the Dark Side of the Haggis label. I'll pay for it." That was "Pinball Wizard"/"The Skye Boat Song".' It found an unlikely champion.

'When "Pinball Wizard" came out, Tom Robinson was doing a World Service show every morning from 3am to 5am. He made it his record of the week,' says Andy. 'I just loved the thought of tribesmen in deepest Africa listening to this.'

When technology moved on, *The Woollen Mill Story* was transferred to CD with the addition of six recorded songs, two written by Michael Marra.

Tom Robinson wasn't the only one spreading the word about the Saint. When Jethro Tull visited the Caird Hall they sent word that they wanted to meet St Andrew. (He didn't go – they wouldn't send a taxi.) *The Woollen Mill Story* was also being played on the Average White Band tour bus. Years later, Andy was introduced to Alan Gorrie in the corridors of Duncan of Jordanstone, where Andy works and Alan was revisiting for old times. 'He told me that he managed to get the American band and crew to pronounce "You seeken meh erse" properly . . . I was proud of that.' The Woollen Mill was also joined by AWB member Molly Duncan on stage in The Windmill Bar on the Hilltown.

There was a bit more to not accepting Jethro Tull's offer. Andy had started work on a variety show with Michael Marra, and they were locked away in Andy's flat. *That's Lightweight Entertainment* was to be a mix of *Seaside Special* and *The Monte Carlo Show.*

'I was one of the dance troupe, the Young Idea, but I was a female dancer,' says Peter McGlone. 'The whole idea was that no one was allowed to do what they usually did. Gary Clark got to sing, though, but I suppose it was "Mother of Mine" and he did sing it in short trousers.'

One of the highlights of the evening was a classical guitar recital. Bob Quinn was a classical player as well as a well-known bass player and teacher. He was asked to play 'Cavatina' (the theme from *The Deerhunter*), which he duly did. Introduced as The Man across the Pletty, what he didn't know was that the recital would accompany a wrestling match between Michael Marra and sax player Peter Benedetti.

This venture into the ring gave Michael a great opener when he was interviewing actor Brian Glover for a radio show. 'He was in the Manchester studio and I'm in Glasgow. I said to him, "I believe you did a bit of wresting – did a bit of that myself . . ." He said, "Oh aye, what name do you fight under?" I said, "Tiny Tim O'Rourke," and he said, "Big lad are yi?" and I replied, "Oh eh."' This from a man who doesn't scare six foot, even in the Duchess of Newtyle's treacherous high heels.

The Woollen Mill was looking for other outlets for its particular talents, when Stewart came up with the idea of a musical. 'In the 1930s and '40s, radio would do half-hour adaptations of films, using the same actors. There was a version of *Stagecoach* and I really thought the part of The Ringo Kid was perfect for Andy.'

Stewart applied for the rights and was asked how much he expected to earn from the production. 'I said, quite honestly, that I expected to lose money on this. The guy said, "Send me 100 of your English pounds and you can do it."'

With no females in the Woollen Mill they had to find a suitable love interest, and cast Jackie McPherson. She was working with teenage magazine *Jackie* at the time but also singing in various bands including Street Level, and she agreed to take on the role of Dallas the saloon girl. 'She was a good singer and great performer,' recalls Stewart. 'It took a lot to handle Andy too.'

Jackie says that most nights, after finishing work at D.C. Thomson, she would be off singing with a band. 'At that time in Dundee, it seemed everyone I knew was in at least one band. Street Level had a certain amount of success, but at one point I was in about four bands. One night, it was a synth-pop band that supported Echo and the Bunnymen, one night it was the New Romantic stuff, and the next night I was getting into my leathers for a rock band. There were nights when we would go to Aberdeen, do the gig, party afterwards and go pretty much straight into work the next day.'

Jackie loved playing Dallas, being particularly fond of her song 'Payday Lady'. 'I really believe the songs have stood the test of time. It was an unbelievably fun time.'

Following the original production, *Stagecoach* toured and is simply described by Andy as 'the best game of Cowboys and Indians ever. Gus was the only one who put any great effort into learning his lines for rehearsal.' Where Andy is concerned, the term rehearsal is used loosely. 'We just let him do his stuff really,' says Stewart, 'He was the only one that didn't stick to the script.'

Michael Marra's take on how to handle Andy's particular talent is that, 'You have to make allowances for a guy like him. He's like me in that he really needs to psyche himself up before he goes on stage. He's pacing and pacing – it's really not easy. When the two of us are in a room waiting to go on, it must be murder for everybody else.'

When gigs were over he would be offstage and away before the applause ended, usually in a car with his fishing gear, heading away to the quiet of Perthshire.

MEETING OF MINDS

In 1980, Mafia's 'Rescue Me' was Single of the Week in the *NME*. Yes it was. And they were as surprised as anyone else. 'We were in London,' says Peter McGlone. 'Donny and I went and bought some music papers. And there it was.'

The single had been produced by David Balfe, who had a recording studio but had written the pop hit 'Beautiful Sunday'. (Balfe's son Lorne is now a soundtrack composer and has worked on major Hollywood movies – and also wrote the theme tune to the BBC Scotland soap *River City*.)

However, at the time there was also an indie producer called David Balfe who worked with Teardrop Explodes and Echo and The Bunnymen – and that's where the confusion may have arisen. 'It's not that we didn't do a good version of the song, it just really wasn't *NME* material,' says Peter.

Meanwhile, his former Skeets bandmate, Michael Marra, had been following his ambition as a songwriter. 'When the group broke up and we were still speaking to each other, I considered that a victory,' he says. 'At that time, I was influenced by a songwriter called Rab Noakes who came from Cupar. He was singing about here, about where we come from.

There was a song on his first album called "East Neuk Misfortune", where he says, "I wandered into the east on early closing day." I was excited about that – I knew that was Wednesday.

'He was called a folk singer but those doing folk clubs were a much wider breed than that. It was an individual who turned up with a song. Gerry Rafferty was another in that mould.'

For Michael, whose ambition was to write rather than perform, the changing landscape of music was not entirely welcome. 'Isaac Guillory, an American guitar player I worked with, said that when Carole King made *Tapestry*, for those songwriters who wanted to live within brackets and remain relatively anonymous it was all over. She was the shining example of professional songwriting, so if she went out and did it, then it was over for anyone else. I would have preferred to sit in my studio and knock the hits out,' he laughs.

He recorded an album for Polydor called *The Midas Touch* on which, he says, 'I got to work with a lot of great people, but it fell on its face. I was contracted to do two, but I ran into problems with the company and the second album never got finished. I fell out with the manager, headed back here and I've never really had a manager since then.'

Back in Dundee, he found that not only were there the musicians he had worked with previously; there was also new blood coming through.

Gary Clark and Ged Grimes had been friends and musical kindred spirits since the mid-1970s at St Saviour's High. For Gary, music was the only option. 'My dad has tapes of me singing at parties when I was about three years old. It was an absolute obsession from day one and nothing else was ever considered as a way of making a living. If I even entertained the idea of doing something else, I considered that a failure. The only reason I went to art college was to meet other musicians.'

Like many first guitars, Gary's was an acoustic from Woolworth's. 'I think I was about eleven and my mum didn't want me to have an electric – she thought I'd electrocute myself. I figured out how to take the microphone from a portable cassette recorder and use the machine as an amplifier, so

I managed to electrocute myself anyway. She gave in a couple of years later and I got an electric. No amp though – I had to borrow that.'

Gary taught himself to play but had no idea how to tune a guitar until he was ill and used the time practically, by asking his mum to buy a book on tuning from Larg's. 'That was the first time I was playing proper chords, until then I tried to play Slade songs on a tuning I made up myself!'

Gary started writing songs at about the age of thirteen and had a school band, mixing his own songs with covers. 'All the bands I liked wrote their own stuff, and then when I got into sophisticated stuff like Steely Dan I always knew that if I was going to make this work I'd have to write songs.'

When Gary saw Ged Grimes, or rather the quality of gear that Ged was bringing into school, the friendship blossomed. 'I had been in a band since I was about nine or ten,' says Ged. 'My dad put us out as the Grimes Folk Four to perform in old folks' homes and with concert parties. It was my sister Jane, brothers Peter and Sean and me. Peter wasn't much more than a toddler so he did the Little Jimmy Osmond bit, which the grannies loved.'

When he was fourteen, Ged started playing with a band called The Blue Macs at weddings and the occasional club. It was two accordion players, a drummer and Ged playing guitar and singing. 'I think I was the one getting the sympathy vote at that point. Apart from country dance stuff, we did a bit of Smokie, bit of Bellamy Brothers, you get the idea . . .'

Ged also worked in Larg's in his spare time, so between that and the band, he was making decent enough money to buy good equipment. 'I'm sure Gary clocked the fact that I had nice guitars. That was the start of the most pivotal musical relationship. We would get together in each other's houses and work things out. Then we got a band together and that's the point I switched to bass.'

The band, Dirty Work, performed lunchtime concerts at St Saviour's, with the school magazine for 1978 devoting several pages to an interview and photographs. When they are asked what they would say to people who think their music is too obscure, they say: 'Obviously we play the type of music that we like and if we play our music often enough, the audience will identify with our music and gradually appreciate it.' That was to prove all too prophetic.

Gus Foy remembers meeting Gary at this stage. 'Gary's girlfriend lived across the road from me, and I think her dad said he should come over and see me. I was happy to talk to him and show him the kind of picking style that I do. I had a gig with Eddie Marra that weekend at the Ferry Inn, so I asked if he wanted to come down and play guitar for me. He seemed like quite a shy young fella but he was dead keen and came down to do it.'

By the time he had started art college, Gary's school band had already recorded a few tracks in the SLR studios in the Seagate. Grant McDonald, who had the studios at the time, was sufficiently impressed to let Michael Marra hear the tracks. 'I got a call from Mick Marra and that blew my mind,' says Gary. 'He became a real mentor. He took me to London, introduced me to his management at the time and I was put in a studio with great musicians.'

Stewart Ivins remembers sitting in the studios when Michael was playing the tapes. 'I was amazed and asked who it was. Mick pointed at Gary sitting in the corner. He was so shy.'

Once Gary had started college, he would have to pass Forbes music shop every morning, and even though on a student grant he couldn't afford any of the guitars, he liked to look. He also met keyboard player Derek Thomson in there, who was to join Gary and Ged's band, Clark's Commandos, shortly after that.

He was getting a taste of what it was like to gig with different musicians, however. In Mick McCluskey's DVD, *The Rock 'n' Soul of Dundee*, Gary remembers playing with Mafia for a short while. 'I got a call from Dougie Martin saying Gerry McGrath was on holiday and would I stand in playing bass? I didn't play bass at that time but Dougie says, "Ach, you'll be all right." We met at his place and in an afternoon I got a rundown of the history of soul and Stax. I think it was Inverness that night and I still had to keep watching his hands to see what I was doing.' Gary also says of that time: 'Everybody thought the rock stars were having a good time – it was the boys in the clubby bands that were really living.'

At art college Gary felt he was treading water and he couldn't imagine getting a record deal in Dundee. Then he was introduced to Brian McDermott. 'I was definitely playing with Gordon Douglas in Spies when Mick Marra first mentioned the name Gary Clark and gave me a cassette. He said he thought they needed a drummer,' says Brian. 'I listened to the tape with three songs on it and thought they were just brilliant.'

Brian had worked at Contact printers so they could use the loft to rehearse with Clark's Commandos, but he was planning to leave for London. Pete Lawton, who had managed Skeets for a while and was working for Chrysalis Records, was going to make some introductions.

Ged remembers being star struck by the fact that one of the Skeets Boliver guys would be playing in the band. He had started a degree in hotel management and catering and, while on secondment to the Queen's Hotel, told them he had booked a holiday. In reality, he headed off to play with Michael Marra on Skye. 'After a year of college we told Duncan of Jordanstone that we were finished. We were heading off to London to be in a band.'

UNION CITY BLUES

The Palais, in its last incarnation as Bloomers, had been destroyed by fire in 1980, taking with it the glorious history of the Top Ten Club and the acts that came to Dundee week in, week out. The live scene had stagnated and needed an individual to shake the city out of its musical torpor.

When Stuart Clumpas arrived in Dundee from Glasgow in 1978, he encountered a city that didn't look too welcoming. 'I remember the old Hawkhill, the tenements and pubs that should have been knocked down years before.' He was in Dundee to attend university, and apart from studying accountancy, he began to lay the foundations for the career that he had always wanted to follow. 'Even at the age of fourteen, when I would go to gigs at the Glasgow Apollo, I'd look around and say, "I'm going to put on gigs in here one day."'

With a year at Strathclyde University behind him, the highlight had been the first gig he had ever promoted. Television were at the Glasgow Apollo, supported by Blondie, but at Strathclyde, Stuart had booked The Ramones supported by Talking Heads. 'When the Apollo show finished, the bands came up to see the university show, so we had those four bands in one room in 1977, the irony being that at that time Television were by far the biggest band.'

Dundee University became a testing ground for Stuart's ability to pick the right acts. It was on the college circuit but the first big success was in 1980. 'When The Pretenders played, they had just gone to number one with "Brass in Pocket" and UB40 supported them. I remember the medical students coming in to get tickets and it had sold out. They said: "But nothing sells out!"'

Not everything was a runaway success. 'We did lose money. I booked Def Leppard for £300 at 90p a ticket and the crowd was sparse to say the least – I lost almost £200 on that one. It was frustrating that people in the town didn't have the opportunity to buy tickets. I didn't like it and the bands didn't like it but we had no option – we were there to provide entertainment for the students. I remember The Ruts pulling fans in through the bathroom window.'

Good promoters generally have a bit of cheek and Stuart's real *pièce de résistance* came with a piece of classic front. 'I saw that Peter Gabriel was touring and had three days off between Newcastle and Aberdeen. It was the *Games Without Frontiers* tour, his first since leaving Genesis.'

He called Gabriel's manager and said: 'This is the social secretary from Dundee University. I see you have three days off. I know we're only 1000 capacity, but would you be interested?' When she called back, it was a yes but with a certain stipulation. 'She said, "Peter is very into castles at the moment. If you can find him a nice castle to stay in, that might swing it." '

Stuart did, but there was still the matter of the fee to consider. With a maximum budget of £400 for any band, he would need £2000 for Gabriel. He knew he could cover it by selling tickets at £8, but when he told the committee that he needed £2000 for a band, he was told where to go. 'I knew that the man in charge was the most *massive* Genesis fan. When I walked away, he said, "Who's it for anyway?" When I said, pretty casually, "Peter Gabriel," things changed quickly.' On 27 February 1980, Peter Gabriel's trucks rolled up to Airlie Place and the hall sold out at £8 a ticket.

That year Stuart also managed to circumvent the students-only rule by booking an act during a university break when the hall would normally have been closed. He convinced the committee to open it for Mike Oldfield on 13 April 1980. 'The Peter Gabriel gig was a real breakthrough,' says Stuart. 'It established Dundee as a great but kind of oddball little gig, where bands would do a warm-up. We built a reputation as having a great team to work with.'

COUNTRY BOY REJECTS THE CLUB

'Billy was the bridge between "that" London and Dundee,' says Tom Doyle, author of *The Glamour Chase: The Maverick Life of Billy Mackenzie*. 'You would see him on *Top of the Pops* on Thursday, then walking up Albert Street at the weekend. It just made the thing altogether more real and special. Before that, pop stars were aliens – it was Bowie as Ziggy – but this was somebody who was making an impression as a local dude.'

Following Steve Knight's departure, The Associates completed *The Affectionate Punch* for Fiction Records, quickly followed (in Billy terms) by *Fourth Drawer Down*, for the Beggars Banquet label Situation 2. As reputation-building albums go, they were successful and planted the idea of Billy in the musical psyche of the time as an operatic, uncompromising voice and worlds apart from those happy to step lightly on to the New Romantic bandwagon. The record-buying public was, therefore, more prepared for the whirlpool of aural delights that was *Sulk*.

The madness of its making has gone into legend, but according to Alan Rankine, it has been played down rather than exaggerated. Hotel bills soared, drug-dealers got richer, and Billy did roll around on a pile of cashmere sweaters – the advance was going fast, but at least the studio was block-booked.

Rankine, now a respected music lecturer at Stow College in Glasgow, recalled those times in a 2007 interview with the *Guardian*. 'We were all ridiculously profligate. But it wasn't entirely ridiculous to be doing things that way, because Bill would coax money out of record companies in a kind of mesmeric way. He thought that the more money we owed them, the more obligation on their part to make this work to get their investment back.

'If we hadn't spent the money, the album wouldn't have got made in the way it did. It was mental, but there was also a self-assured cockiness, because we knew we had these songs . . .'

That self-assured cockiness was a revelation to anyone watching The Associates on television at the time. Even in the more flamboyant context of 1982, it looked and sounded like a band of its time, maybe just not of this planet.

There can be few Dundonians of the *TOTP*-watching generation who didn't sit transfixed as 'that Dundee boy' gave performances of 'Party Fears Two' that gave a new definition to Rankine's 'self-assured cockiness', followed by 'Club Country' and then '18 Carat Love Affair'.

For an appearance for the latter in August of that year, Alan Rankine had chocolate guitars made, one of which he fed to the audience as the song progressed. They didn't know what was just around the corner.

That same month, on the day before the first of three gigs at the Music Room in Edinburgh, Billy pulled the rug out with typical flair. Steve Knight remembers the scene: 'They had had three hits. A huge tour was planned. They were in Edinburgh to do the first gig and Billy says, "I'm not doing it." Alan, of course, battered him. Who wouldn't?' A $600,000 offer for an American deal was also left on the table. The upshot was that Alan Rankine left the band.

When Steve met the singer at the art college bar not long after, Billy told him, 'It's there if I want it. I could have it all, but I'm not doing it.' Steve replied, 'Ah, go on, eh?'

'You have to remember, at that time U2 were being accused of copying The Associates. It's a great shame. Alan is such a great arranger. He could take all the madness of Billy and put it in perspective. He'd say, "I want a guitar sound like your underpants are too tight," but Alan could translate that.'

Steve was concerned when Billy got in tow with Steve Reid (formerly of Bread Poultice) as heroin had become an issue within that circle. 'I had fallen out with both of them but ended up in London, sharing a flat in Swiss Cottage with their ex-girlfriends Kath Smith and Christine Beveridge. I said to them, "A strict rule – no Steve Reid."'

However, Billy and Steve Reid had hooked up again for the first post-Alan Rankine Associates' album and were based in a Holiday Inn about fifty yards from the flat. It was the same Holiday Inn that had been used by the band (and a couple of whippets, who eventually had their own room) during the making of *Sulk*.

'They started coming to the flat rather than the hotel. Steve Reid had this huge ghetto-blaster and played what they had recorded that day at full volume – neighbours started going nuts. I was working at the time and it was doing my head in so I had to move out.'

TALES FROM THE SWAMP

In the early 1980s, London had its fair share of Dundonian musicians in residence. With few venues to play at home, it seemed like the only option for a gigging band to get a record deal. Chris Marra had already moved and found session work and a job playing bass with a band called the 45s.

Brian McDermott had also made the trip south. When a girl in Pete Lawton's office was leaving her flat, Brian took it over, something that he felt made it 'more serious'. 'I thought, "So I'm really doing this eh?"' The flat was tucked in behind Harrods in Knightsbridge, but once the drum kit had been brought down by the haulage company, there was barely room for a bed and chest of drawers.

When Gary first moved down, he was offered accommodation with friends of his manager but soon he, Ged and Derek Thomson were sharing a flat in Robertson Street, Battersea, affectionately remembered by all as 'The Swamp'. Maybe affection is a strong word, but with the distance of time it certainly seems to be less painful to remember.

'There was three inches of water in the kitchen, permanently,' says Ged. 'The first thing we would do every morning was check ourselves for slugs.' Little wonder that they would spend most of the time at Brian's flat. 'We would sunbathe on his roof,' says Gary. 'About five roofs across, the Bay City Rollers had a rooftop garden – we'd be outside in the sun with a ghetto-blaster, looking into the Rollers' garden and usually listening to Simple Minds' *New Gold Dream*. Ged was mad for that record.'

Back at The Swamp, conditions were cramped, damp and uncomfortable. Derek Thomson decided that London life wasn't for him and he headed back to Dundee, prompting some hasty rearrangements of the songs without keyboard parts.

Brian became the next to be consumed by The Swamp when he lost his place in the Knightsbridge flat. 'Gary would stay over some nights and we would be up all night playing music really loudly, but the final straw was I couldn't afford it anymore!' So it was over to Battersea, with the drum kit set up in Gary's bedroom.

'Actually, all the gear was set up in Gary's bedroom,' says Brian. 'I was curled up in the corner and he would only have room to sleep lying on the floor, with his head inside the bass drum.'

Ged was lucky enough to have a bed, but found himself sharing it before long. 'I had been meeting up with the guys for a pint in Clapham,' says Steve Knight, 'but I never went back to their flat, I always went back to crash at Chris's in Balham. When I had to move from Swiss Cottage quickly, they said I could move in.'

Steve has a deserved reputation for being dapper, so when he arrived, he was carrying armfuls of what he calls his 'posey clothes'. He realised that no one had been exaggerating about the conditions.

'I thought, "Holy f*ck, what is this?" It was two rancidly damp rooms, a toilet you wouldn't want to go near and *so* many slugs. I asked where I could put my stuff and they pointed to a cupboard, which was behind an ice-cream trolley! It seemed the landlord used it in the summer for selling ice lollies in Oxford Street. This thing was enormous. I tried to squeeze past it and tried to get my stuff in. I had to lie everything flat – how could I find anything? I had about forty suits!'

Brian recalls the shock of seeing Steve let himself go during that time. 'I might be wrong, but I'm sure he maybe even resorted to wearing a cardigan – once.'

Having no idea of which circle of shared accommodation hell he was entering, Steve had brought new bedding from Habitat. Ged had no opinion one way or another. He was too intent on alleviating what he called his case of 'Steve Knight hip', which began after waking up one morning and being a little too close for comfort. 'I decided that I was going to sleep as far away as possible, and on my side, so I developed this sciatic pain.'

The flat was a twenty-four-hour operation and a nightmare for Steve as the only one working. 'I had to work as I hated being completely skint,' he says. 'I would bring in food to the flat and take them to the local pub.' The Nag's Head was the unofficial living room – in bad times with no gigs and no money they would manage to stretch out a pint for practically the whole night, delaying the inevitable return home. 'We would write some really good poetry about the slugs though,' says Brian. 'And about the wee shop at the top of the road . . . the guy always thought we were going to nick stuff.'

Ged would use his catering skills to make meals that would last the whole week, cooking a large pot of mince, tatties and beans which could be consumed over several days, but as the mince went down, all they could do was add more tatties.

The spectre of having to work raised its head for Ged. 'I assumed I could sign on, but they fixed up an interview with Braithwaite and Taylor, a mail-order book firm. I went to the interview and tried to come across as totally incompetent – you should have seen the state of the writing. But at the end of the day they said mine was the best application so I ended up packaging up books. It could have been much worse. The Falklands War had started and we were more worried that they might reintroduce conscription.'

Knowing his story, Braithwaite and Taylor agreed to release him to go off on a tour supporting Chris de Burgh that he, Gary and Brian did as a trio. Getting to local gigs became something of a skill, as one of the guys would stand on the street with a small amp and hail a taxi. They would then take it around a corner where others would be waiting to pile the gear in.

Gary's manager at the time would turn up outside in his Rolls-Royce. 'He was the camel-coated, cigar-chompin' old-fashioned manager,' says Steve. 'He didn't even want to sit down, and absolutely refused a cup of tea – you should have seen his pus.'

Chris Marra managed to avoid The Swamp and didn't play live with the band in London, but when the 45s split, he became involved in the recordings, which were demos of songs like 'Mary's Prayer' and 'Davy'.

He had the opportunity to record an album with John Parr and stayed in London, while the rest disappeared back to Dundee. Brian and Steve had been back for a holiday and noticed a change in the city, particularly with the opening of a new nightclub called Fat Sams. It took more than a new club to convince Gary, however. 'I personally felt like going back to Dundee was giving up. But something started to happen. We would walk into the West End from The Swamp to get the NME and other music papers to find gigs. We started to see reviews by someone called Bob Flynn coming out of Dundee, from the Tayside Bar of all places. That would never have happened at the time we moved down. It seemed that we were in the wrong place to get a record deal at the time. The amount of interest in Scotland made it marginally acceptable for me to go back.'

Back in Dundee, Gary was surprised at the maturity of the work his younger brother was playing. Kit was five years younger than Gary and his twin Scott, but he had been influenced by growing up with a brother who had embraced music from such an early age. Their dad was a fan of jazz and the Clark household was always a place for people to perform at parties. 'There was never any differentiation between those who were musicians and who weren't – everyone did something and it seemed natural,' says Kit, who was always slightly confused that his dad would call himself a jazz drummer, not realising it was a local rhyming slang for 'plumber'.

Arriving at St Saviour's just as his brothers were leaving, it didn't take Kit long to put together his own band of school mates. 'I had asked for a saxophone for Christmas when I was about twelve,' he says. 'I had hated it when Gary was getting guitar lessons. I couldn't hear the TV for him sitting playing all the time, so I thought I needed to get an instrument to annoy him with . . . "What's louder? I know – a saxophone is louder." Also, I had always loved the contribution that the saxophone made to records that I loved, things like "Dr Wu" by Steely Dan. I realised pretty quickly that I couldn't really write things on it though.'

His enthusiasm to learn led to work experience at Allan McGlone's Inner City Sound studio. He would let Kit stay in the studio overnight and record his band, initially called Custard Hands and the Normal People, but eventually The Very Important Men. The line-up included Kit's best school pal Stewart Clark, who later fronted Citizen Kane and is regarded by some as one of the city's undiscovered talents, Mike Dailly, now the principal solicitor at the Govan Law Centre, and Mark Blyth, who at that point liked nothing more than to dress up in a binbag and flat cap, but is now professor of international political economy at Brown University in Rhode Island.

'We were allowed to rehearse in St Vincent's Church Hall,' says Kit, 'and the priest even managed to secure us a gig up at the Kyle of Lochalsh. Unfortunately he didn't tell us were expected to play for three hours – we had forty-five minutes of material at most.'

The worst part of the trip was getting back, however. Kit had borrowed Gary's guitar, a Stratocaster copy. 'I didn't take it up north, but it was packed away with all the other gear in the hall. When we got back, it was gone, along with parts of a drum kit and some other gear. There had been a jumble sale when we were away and the lovely wee wifies had sold all the gear. It took me about six months to tell him.'

Obviously distance had dimmed the memory, as Gary and Ged were keen for Kit to join the ranks of the band when they returned. He had already been accepted for RADA [Royal Academy of Dramatic Art] the idea being that The VIM would also move down and Kit could do both. 'Then I saw the costs of going to RADA. It was impossible – ballet shoes, which had to be from an expensive shop, books running to several hundred pounds . . . there were so many costs. I would have to get a job as well, so everything would have been half-assed.'

Kit recalls being in awe of figures like Chris Marra, Dougie Martin and Billy Mackenzie, but an afternoon gig at the St James Club showed how supportive local musicians could be. 'I had met Billy maybe once or twice – I knew his brothers and sisters quite well. On the day of this gig there was torrential rain. It was lunchtime on a Saturday and I saw him coming in, getting an orange juice, sitting down, and actually listening. My brother Scott had been playing football, spotted him, told him I was playing so he came along with the football team to support a young band. I thought, "He's just been on *Top of the Pops* and he's here to see me in a clubby." '

FINDING ALTERNATIVES

When Gary Clark left Dundee for London in 1981, the venues for live music, particularly new music, were practically non-existent. But in the time The Swamp was being overrun by Dundonians, the most unlikely destinations became the haunt of the city's musicians and trend-setters.

The Tayside Bar didn't cut any kind of aesthetic dash. It left that to the young crowd, who would walk through the shabby traditional pub at the front to see what was happening in the narrow, dark room with its tiny stage and seating booths, complete with historic microphone sockets for singalongs.

It had a reputation as the place to see alternative music, but in reality the fare was mixed, with more mainstream pop, and even the occasional heavy metal band also being given a platform. That platform was tiny and with the gents' toilets at the back, punters would briefly have to join the band on stage to reach them.

Nick Wright became a well-known figure at the time, particularly for the club nights he ran, initially at the Tayside Bar. He had moved to Dundee from Dingwall as a teenager and now he was involved in helping Stuart Clumpas's ents committee at Dundee University, exhibiting a flair for promotion and ideas, as well as designing striking posters and flyers. 'I was in bands like Waiter Waiter, which became Cattle,' says Nick, 'but I would hesitate to call myself a musician. The good thing about punk was that anyone could pick up instruments – it wasn't always great but sometimes there was a kernel that developed. The clubby scene was right across the road from the Tayside Bar at The Glass Bucket. We were pretty sneery, but there was some crossover. We weren't too chuffed one night when we came out and heard a clubby band doing a version of Orange Juice's "Rip It Up".'

The Soul Kiss Club was instigated by Nick, his brother Chris and Ian Duffy. 'It started with flyers and a fanzine, but it became a club night. There were rules: you couldn't play in your own band and if you did, you had to do cover versions.' When the Tayside Bar was knocked down to make way for a ring road, the club moved briefly to the Royal Oak.

There was an appetite for the alternative, which was satisfied from 1982 at the Tay Hotel in the shape of Club Feet, which played new wave music. If you believed every schoolgirl who managed to get access while underage, Billy Mackenzie was there every night.

There were bands who played at the Tayside Bar on a fairly regular basis, including The Scrotum Poles, Altres, Dundee's only reggae band The Grip, Aaga, The Junkies and a band with a drummer who had turned down the opportunity to rehearse with Billy Mackenzie a few years before.

Steve Aungle had gravitated towards St Andrews and had hooked up with Eddie Robertson, who had previously played with Lloyd Anderson and was friends with Brian McDermott.

'We ended up with a songwriter called Jeff Doran from Liverpool, and a bass player called Steve Duncan from Ardler, and started playing around 1982 as The Blush, particularly in the Tayside Bar. It was kind of new wave/psychedelic stuff and it fitted in with what was a really vibrant scene. There were a few bands who were quite serious about what they were doing, particularly us and The Grip, who were doing their UB40 thing. There was a bit of rivalry, putting posters over theirs, but nothing more serious – no aggro. Lloyd Anderson's band, No Fixed Abode, were also trying to do something. It wasn't my kind of stuff. We would call them "Nae Place Ti Bide" but no one could fail to be impressed by Lloyd's drumming and singing.'

The Blush fell apart around 1983 – a classic story of the contract argument. Fiction offered the band a publishing deal, but as Jeff was the songwriter the deal would be in his name only. 'I could understand that but Eddie and Steve had a problem with it, so we split up. There was one single, "Skipping", on our own label. That was before The Associates put anything out with the same name.'

Steve had taken over the studios in the Seagate, formerly run by Grant McDonald as SLR. 'I took it over about 1982 as a base for The Blush, but to pay the bills we did record other bands. I had it until about 1984 when Phil Ramsay took it over [as Watergate Studios] but that ended badly when he became involved with a pretty nasty crowd and the studio was used to stash drugs. There was a bust and he ended up in jail.'

Jock Ferguson was still one of the main figures at the Tayside Bar, even though he had stopped DJing and *Cranked Up* had closed in 1982. His next project was the result of the 'have a go' spirit promoted by the Soul Kiss Club. 'I was well into my twenties by then,' says Jock, 'and I was still writing for other fanzines on music and football, but things had moved on – it was much more art college than punk. I went to the football with two guys called Kev and Paul and found out they played guitar.'

Jock's plan was just a one-off, to have a laugh at the Soul Kiss with a *Rocky Horror Show*-style cabaret. The Beaver Sisters name was there from the beginning but over the next seven years, Jock was the only constant as a parade of musicians and backing singers (Beaver girls) went through its ranks. One Beaver girl, Donna Krachan, as feisty as she sometimes was, decided to try to reason with someone shouting abuse one night. 'Aw dinna heckle iz eh? Eh'm no good at that sort o' stuff . . .'

'For that first night we rehearsed "Sweet Transvestite", "Tomorrow Belongs to Me", and "Delilah",' Jock remembers. 'It was just me and two guitars. It was rough and ready but good fun. I could see some people were looking at me saying, "Did that guy not used to be the DJ?" and now I'm in suspenders.'

As rough and ready as it was, a big part of the Beaver Sisters' appeal was Jock himself, with the stage name Plenty O'Tool. A natural stand-up, he was as fearless on stage as he had been in print for *Cranked Up*.

'In the first year, people who came to see us – with some justification – could have said we were barely competent. That changed. We had better musicians like Anth Brown and Barry Gibson from Better Backwards.'

Gordon Walker says that in his bands following The Quick Spurts, 'Competency was never issue for us. It was never really about the music, it was just about having a carry on really.' From 1981 to 1984, the bands went under the names of Dirtbox, Doghouse, The Raunchy Guys, Slim Disney and the Tennessee Three, and finally Eric Poodle and Sunshine. 'We had to keep changing our name,' says Gordon. 'No one would book us twice.'

Dirtbox were booked to support The Junkies at a disco called Clouds in Edinburgh's Tollcross. 'This was in the days when we dressed up. My girlfriend at the time ran a stall selling vintage clothes in Dens Road Market so that night I was wearing a Lurex frock, and had my girlfriend's auntie's pants on – they were red with black fringes. I think this was a gay club, and it was weekday night in winter, so there were about fifteen people there. Jim Low, the singer, pulled my pants down, so I kicked them into the small crowd, which quickly parted to avoid them – they just lay there. I had to retrieve them after the gig.'

The band was asked to play a Christmas night gig at the Tayside Bar in 1981, much to Gordon's disappointment. 'Well *The Missouri Breaks* was on TV that night and I hadn't seen it. I just went along in a huff, wearing the brown zip-up baffies that I got for my Christmas.'

The Raunchy Guys were all bona fide members of the Dundee Country & Western Club, which met at the Ambassador and the Nine Maidens, but the favourite incarnation of Gordon's was Slim Disney. 'The agent Dougie Crumley had an office above the Hong Kong restaurant in the Seagate. He had booked us for the Invercarse Hotel but I wanted to see *Top of the Pops* that night so didn't go. He wasn't best pleased. Joe Jordan, known as The Bear, had given him a number for Jim Low's mum. She got a phone call saying, "A bear has just told me to phone here and ask for Slim Disney." She was confused, but you would be, really. He said he'd never book us again, so we just changed our name ...'

When competency arrived with The Beavers, the *Rocky Horror* theme was dropped in favour of a range of costumes, from a jester to the Haitian voodoo figure Baron Samedi, in top hat and full skull make-up. 'In the end, everyone dressed up. I would tip out a bag of costumes and the band would choose whatever they fancied. I always wanted to put on a good show.'

During the first few years of The Beavers, Jock left his job as a British Telecom engineer to join a theatre arts course. 'For me it was about learning better stagecraft, not really about becoming an actor, but subsequently, that's what I've become.'

After those seven years, playing all over Scotland, the Beaver Sisters were finally floored by an injury. 'I ruptured my Achilles pogoing,' says

Jock, laughing. 'That really wasn't an injury for a thirty-five-year-old man. When I was hospitalised, I realised that I had just lost interest, but it was OK. We knew it had worked.'

Barry Gibson's first band had been with Mike Brown and his brother Anth when they were teenagers. 'It was pretty noisy, thrashy rock really,' says Mike. 'Think New York Dolls, really, especially the hair.'

The Tayside Bar was the important place for Barry, who would go to see Mike Kane's bands Vex and Aaga, as well as the Soul Kiss nights. 'We had been playing together for a while, but it ultimately became Better Backwards about 1987 when Brian Lindsay joined.'

By that time Mike had taken over the studios in the Seagate with Stuart Firm and really made it a going concern. The only other studio was Inner City Sound run by engineer and sax player Allan McGlone (Donny Coutts also had an interest in the studio at one point). 'I had just finished my apprenticeship, the gear from Better Backwards kitted it out, and we took a PA on tick from Rainbow. I think at that point we moved into a band called Jih.'

Jih was essentially Grant McNally's vehicle with different backing musicians. They had started out as early as 1983 in London, and were championed by Billy Mackenzie, who arranged some studio time for them. Later Billy would produce a single for them, a cover of his own song 'Take Me to the Girl'.

The Tayside Bar and the studios in the Seagate would have a significant effect on Tom Doyle, Billy's biographer, one of Britain's top music writers, and a man with a few musical projects to his name. Like Mike Brown, his first gig had been Motorhead at the Caird Hall in 1980, a time when heavy metal seemed to be going through something of a resurgence in the city, even though local metal bands (as good as they were) never seemed to take off. Arrival, Lixx and Colossus, among others, would have their followings but apart from Foreigner's pub in Meadowside there was never a huge metal scene.

Add to that impressive list the mighty Spearhead, Tom's first band at the age of thirteen. He would be influenced by the characters he first encountered at the Tayside Bar. 'I was fourteen, and looked thirteen, but I managed to get through to the back to see bands if the owner Brian (Lindsay) knew I wasn't drinking. He didn't know someone would be handing me a joint as soon as I went through the door, though,' he laughs. 'When I was fourteen, I was drumming with anyone, anywhere, but the first recordings I did were at the studio when The Blush had it. It was Pavlov Orange, a synth band, but not too bad as synth bands go. I would go down to the studio and Steve would always give us the best possible gear. When The Blush played the Tayside Bar, they would pack that tiny stage with gear. They were amazing – a proper band. Inner City Sound was a great studio as well, and Allan McGlone a major studio talent.'

It was encountering the fanzine *Cranked Up* that lit a fire under his journalistic ambitions. 'It was bitchy and funny and I wanted to inveigle my way into that world. Someone had told me that if you worked for D.C. Thomson on magazines, you could go to London and interview bands.' During the legendary D.C. Thomson job interview, which lasted about two and a half days at that time, Tom stressed nothing apart from his knowledge of music. When he started in *Patches*, he was disappointed to be given the junior's duties of photocopying and making up horoscopes but the pop editor at that time (Bryan Burnett, now with Radio Scotland) was encouraging and allowed him do a few interviews.

'The first interview was The Blue Nile,' he recalls. 'That was mind-blowing. When I became pop editor, my mates would be at school and I'd be in London talking to The Cure and Talking Heads. We were told to turn nothing down, so I could be doing eight phone interviews a day. That's good training.'

An occasional visitor to the office would be Murray Chalmers, a music PR, who had left Dundee for London at the height of punk. 'Murray was always sound and knew his stuff,' says Tom. 'He would never steer you in the wrong direction. I do remember him having the bottle to wear a Gaultier dress in a pub in Dundee in 1984 though.' Murray was head of press at Parlophone for many years and is now running his own music PR firm, working with the likes of Coldplay, Kylie and Kate Bush.

The Tayside Bar is remembered fondly by everyone who walked through its doors. Jazz singer Alison Burns, who had her first gigs there, playing bass with bands like The Junkies, says, 'Most of it was enthusiasm and high spirits rather than musicianship, but it was great fun.' A few years later she played her first jazz gig there and she also performed there with a female vocal trio along under the pseudonym of The Canny Wee Fannies ... so the high spirits were still very much in evidence.

PERFECT TIMING

It was a short hop from being the pin-up of Dundee's punk scene to following her heart into jazz for Alison Burns. Her dad had played guitar in a semi-professional skiffle band and her mum played piano, and although she had grown up on a diet of classic musicals and the Great American Songbook, Alison left school as punk was happening and in the spirit of the time, picked up a bass and just did it. She was perhaps one of the most glamorous punks to grace a stage, even though she was also working at the Timex factory as an apprentice engineer.

Her tastes were also wider than the average punk. 'I went to see Michael Marra at the Angus Hotel and Clark's Commandos were supporting – it wouldn't have been long before they left for London. It was obvious there was something special there.'

Although she had been playing bass, singing was the goal. With jazz the ambition, she had heard of a great pianist who may be up for work. Steve Aungle had given up drumming and gone back to the piano. 'The pop scene in the 1980s was so bad I wanted nothing to do with it,' he says. 'My plan was to go back to the 1930s and forget I was in the 80s. I wore a red tuxedo, slicked back my hair, grew a pencil-line moustache and pretended I was Clark Gable.'

When Alison arrived at his Lochee Road flat, with an armful of sheet music and boundless enthusiasm to sing jazz, he was rather surprised. He had a baby grand piano in the flat and the two started putting their ideal set together. 'We rehearsed every night and all weekend to get that right,' Alison says. 'We wanted to get a huge repertoire together that would allow us to go out and get good work. We would also be doing what we wanted to do.'

The partnership worked as a duo and as part of a six-piece band called The Shoplifters, but it was the simple piano and vocal that was more portable and took them to residencies across Scotland.

They also had a residency in Dundee, in a retro bar in Union Street called Café Americain, where she would meet people who would change the course of her life, professionally and personally.

FACTORY FLOORS

It's an exaggeration to say that the opening of a nightclub changed the course of a city, but when Fat Sams opened in 1983, it provided a shell for events that helped the city to shake off its grim image.

It had already convinced Brian McDermott and Steve Knight to come back from London and now, not exactly for the same reason, Gary Clark and Ged Grimes followed – but they all liked what they saw.

Stuart Clumpas had headed for London following graduation to become a music business accountant. 'I absolutely hated it,' says Stuart, who only lasted nine months before heading back to Dundee to concentrate on his ambition to become a promoter. 'I would book the union on a semi-professional basis and brought bands like The Skids and The Smiths. I had also formed a good relationship with some of the new alternative comedy set. *Tiswas* had been at the union, as had Lenny Henry, and word of mouth was good.'

In October 1982, Stuart had taken another step and formed Dance

Factory Promotions, which booked nights at Teazers in the Royal Hotel, where the manager's name was Willie Rasche – honestly.

The first three acts booked for Dance Factory were Hey Elastica, Aztec Camera and The Monochrome Set. The posters and flyers that started to appear were stark black and yellow, with a sharp geometric feel. These were designed by Nick Wright, to Stuart's specifications. Nick would also hand-draw the tickets. 'My brother and I worked for Stuart on Sundays at Dance Factory,' says Nick. 'I worked on the door at Teazers, we would DJ and we made sure that band was OK and had their rider. I think it's called a promoter's agent but we didn't really know then.'

Still looking for venues for bands, Stuart booked the Coconut Grove to present the Eurythmics in February 1983. The Coconut Grove was the latest incarnation of the JM, which became the Barracuda and was subsequently sold to Mecca.

'We managed to get the Eurythmics for £300 and two weeks later "Sweet Dreams" was number five. The same thing happened with Big Country, who I recall had a mishap when the stage collapsed under the bass player. With the Eurythmics it was incredible, I had never seen so much money, but then I booked Kissing the Pink and lost it all again.'

Stuart was looking to expand his network and spoke to friends who owned Henry Afrika's in Glasgow about taking a Thursday night for live music. They weren't interested, but said they were thinking of opening a club in Dundee. 'They showed me the bare bones of Fat Sams and we went into the project together. They asked if I wanted to manage it too, but that really wasn't in my plan. I was a promoter, not a nightclub manager,' says Stuart.

That week, however, his car broke down and it was terminal. 'If I didn't have a car, I couldn't nip around with Chris Hudson, who was working with me then to get posters up, so I said, "If you buy me a car, let me carry on with the concert promotion, and pay me this much I'll do it." I managed to get Chris a job as my right-hand man, so that freed me up to do the promotion and run the club at the weekend. I was twenty-four, a middle-class kid in T-shirt and jeans, at a time when nightclub managers still wore suits and dickie bows. Guys would come up and say, "What do you mean, I'm not getting in?" I'd say, "I don't like your white socks and slip-on shoes." They would go mental, trying to get past the bouncers and shouting, "I want to see the manager!" They were even less chuffed when I told them that I was the manager.'

Fat Sams became a popular hangout for acts that had just played at the university, particularly stand-up comedians. 'Ben Elton loved it. As soon as he was off stage, he'd be saying, "Right, let's get to Fatso's."'

The club, or at least the cocktail-bar area, was also the hang-out for Dundee musicians, particularly on Sunday night when, for the first time since the Top Ten Club in the 1960s, music-lovers could see top bands every week.

Nick Wright remembers that Stuart's first promotion outside the university was Clark's Commandos and now they were back, working on getting a deal and hanging out in his cocktail bar.

'There was the guys who became Danny Wilson, and most of the other bands in Dundee, including Sweden Through the Ages, who everyone thought would make it,' says Stuart. 'They would be there week in, week out – they supported us so I tried to give them any support I could.' Billy Mackenzie would also hang out at Fat Sams, and on some Sunday nights, the party would carry on at the Mackenzie house on Bonnybank Road.

The bands were working in between propping up the cocktail bar and ordering newfangled foreign lagers, however.

'When we got back, Brian went off to join Steve Knight's band, which was a heartbreaker, but I completely understood,' says Gary Clark. 'Allan McGlone gave us some time in the studio to do demos and Kit was gradually finding his place with us.' There were places to play for the band, now going under the name of Spencer Tracy, but the trio found the most lucrative gigs were in the open air. 'As the Chili Peppers, we got a great reputation as buskers, and made some decent cash. We would take a guitar case full of coins into the Tayside Bar and Brian would change the coins into notes. Then he would change the notes into pints and pies,' he laughs. 'We would head over to St Andrews when The Open was on. We were doing the perfect material for the Americans, stuff like Sinatra and Bacharach. It fed us, watered us, and paid for more studio time.'

'The Chili Peppers was living the music and a nice wee sideline,' says Ged. 'It was just guitar, accordion and my tea-chest bass, which we just left at the back of Fat Sams. It was fine if it was out of the rain!'

Work was still going on at Inner City Sound on the Spencer Tracy demos and they were to find the ideal backing singer to complement Gary's vocals very close to home. 'I met the guys from the Chili Peppers during the Café Americain residency,' says Alison Burns. 'We would all go off to Fat Sams for a late bar when we finished, and that linked me into the group. Gary and I started going out, and I was invited to sing on some of the demos that they were doing at the time – "Monkey's Shiny Day" and "Broken China". I had been in the studio before with one of the punk bands, but they just tended to turn up p*ssed and nothing got done. This was different and felt serious. I feel really privileged to have sung on those.

'Those nights at the Dance Factory were fantastic. Everyone really made an effort and there was a very definite style to everyone who hung out in the cocktail bar. The diner was pretty good too,' she laughs.

One of the most memorable nights at the Dance Factory was a homecoming gig for Ricky Ross on one of the first Deacon Blue tours. Ricky had had some flirtations with the music scene during his time in Dundee, but came to it later than many, having been raised in the evangelical church. 'My life was pretty restricted in some ways, and the church was more defining to life than rock'n'roll,' he says. 'When someone came and played music for the church, and did material like Crosby, Stills and Nash, I liked that. It was strange as I didn't realise there was a life outside the church, really. I was listening to other things, but I remember my dad's reaction when I was listening to something like a Rolling Stones record, it was like "Woah . . ."' Ricky had been raised in Broughty Ferry and did play in bands, but he was off to Glasgow before Gary and Ged came back to Dundee.

In the *NME* of 13 December 1986, Bob Flynn reviewed Deacon Blue at Dundee Dance Factory. He wrote that Ricky 'has made something out of melody, fire and groove that resembles a Springsteen-fuelled Little Feat, with razor cuts and soul emotion'.

Now that Ricky has worked alongside Gary Clark as solo artists and shared the stage with Ged Grimes, he finds it strange to think they probably passed one another on the street. 'Circumstances had dictated that I had to move to Glasgow, but I also didn't think I would find the right people to play with in Dundee, even though subsequently I find out that Gary Clark was just living along the road from me. I've come full circle, playing with Ged Grimes and also Gregor Philp.'

Spencer Tracy didn't know it yet, but a Bob Flynn review would be something of a turning point for them. Until then it was comforting to have a high-profile writer in the corner of a venue, bringing attention to the city. Bob had also managed to organise some dates in Norway for them – but the next time they returned to Scandinavia, it would be to record a debut album.

THE UNDERDOG WAGS ITS TAIL

Without letting his dander get up, Michael Marra decided that if record companies weren't happy with the approach he wanted to take on the follow-up to *The Midas Touch*, then he would do things his own way.

'In Dundee, we had writers, musicians, arrangers, engineers, studios and producers. That was all I needed. The second album *Gaels Blue* was a complete departure from the first – the absolute opposite really. Lyrically, it is completely Scottish. They weren't too happy that I sang "wee" instead of "small", I also used an accordion on a track and was told, "I don't know about the Jimmy Shand vibe."

'I wanted to work in as many different styles as possible. It was time to relax and write about what surrounded me and also use how we speak.'

Michael says that the proof that Dundee had everything it needed came in the shape of Allan McGlone, a quiet, reticent figure who was respected as not only a superb musician but also a first-class engineer. He also points to the banks of talent he had to draw from – 'Gary Clark, Kevin Murray, Brian McDermott, Kit Clark, Christopher Marra, Derek Thomson, Ged Grimes, Frank Rossiter – the list goes on.'

He drew on this list to put together the Gaels Blue Orchestra for occasional performances, with a particularly memorable concert at the Bonar Hall in aid of The Samaritans which was compered by St Andrew, who is reported to have delivered the funniest raffle draw in history.

The *Gaels Blue* album, released in 1985, 'went about its business slowly' says Michael, and was well supported in folk circles. He was asked by Eclectic Records to make a follow-up, but didn't relish the thought. 'I don't like sequels of any kind. I saw the first James Bond film ... but that was it,' he laughs.

However, 'the guy was offering support,' adds Michael. 'He gave me the funds to make an album.' *On Stolen Stationery* was made in two weeks at Hospitalfield in Arbroath by Michael and Kevin Murray and despite the fact that he would rather the next album, *Candy Philosophy*, had been released first, *On Stolen Stationery* contains three of his best-loved songs, 'Hermless', also performed by St Andrew, 'Niel Gow's Apprentice', covered by Rab Noakes and Roddy Woomble, and 'Hamish', which was covered by Leo Sayer, despite the fact that it pays tribute to the Dundee United goalie Hamish McAlpine and covers the night Grace Kelly visited Tannadice to see AS Monaco play a UEFA cup tie.

The album also contains backing vocals by Alison Burns, who would also sing on *Candy Philosophy*. 'Her voice is just gorgeous,' he says. 'It's like it's 1948 and you're twenty-nine again.'

Michael Marra has a theory why Dundee has produced so many great musicians. 'I'm not a great salesman,' he says. 'An advertising company got in touch with me and asked what slogan I could come up with for Dundee. You know the kind of thing: "Fort William – Ultimately Disappointing".

I was the wrong guy to ask – when I really thought about it, what I'd like to see on a sign as people coming into Dundee is "Beneath the Underdog". That explains why there are so many great musicians here – they have to try harder.'

LET'S BE FRANK

As Spencer Tracy gigged around Scotland they hoped that the spotlight that had fallen on Scotland would eventually catch them in its sweep.

Talk to three different people who were at three different Spencer Tracy gigs, and they were all at the one where the band were signed. The truth is the interest came from Bob Flynn's *NME* review of a gig at the Sorbonne in Edinburgh.

'Everyone thought Sweden Through the Ages would get signed,' says Gary, talking about Steve Knight's band that had Brian McDermott on drums, Mike Knight on guitar, and Lloyd Anderson on vocals.

The night of the Sorbonne gig, Spencer Tracy had been left without a drummer, prompting a call to Donny Coutts, who promptly learned the set in twenty-four hours. 'He only had the soundcheck to rehearse,' recalls Kit. 'It was incredible – he added this amazing soulful touch to the songs.'

Chris Marra by this stage had been back and forward to London, mainly working with John Parr and living a life that was rather too rock'n'roll for his own good.

'When the guys had gone back to Dundee, someone had recommended me to John Parr, who was about to head to Miami to record an album. I thought, "Three weeks in Miami – fine." '

Chris then went on tour with Parr, a great excuse not to be in London. The next tour he did was a solid eight months, covering America on three separate tours with Bryan Adams, Heart and Tina Turner. 'Just before I left, we had just found out that my wife Irene was pregnant, and I only arrived back a week before Jean was born. That wasn't any life really.

'The drinking could be pretty over-the-top too and I would climb when I was drunk. I once edged around a tenth-floor ledge in Miami, with the waves crashing below me, just to get into someone else's room. It would never have occurred to me to use the corridors when I was in that state. The compulsion stopped one night at my flat in Maida Vale. I had forgotten my keys so climbed to the fifth floor to get in the bathroom window. When I got up there, I froze. It took at least half an hour to get back down, but I never did it again.'

Once Jean was born at the end of 1985, Chris decided it was time to spend more time at home, whatever he had to do.

'When it comes to good guitar, Chris Marra is the king as far as I'm concerned,' says Russ Paterson. 'I had a gig one night and went into Rainbow to ask Keith if anyone fancied playing it with me. He said Chris was just back from a tour with John Parr, but I didn't think he'd do it. But he did. He helped me out, and I helped him out by buying him a pint.'

As Chris was considering his next move, the deal that Spencer Tracy had been chasing had finally landed. 'Following the *NME* review, it was about four or five months of meetings with labels until we eventually signed,' says Gary. 'Bob Flynn wasn't exactly managing us (he had decided against it) but he was fielding a lot of calls. I remember the day the three of us were sitting in the pub and thinking "this is getting serious". So we agreed that day to shut up until it actually happened.'

He says that the work that Stuart Clumpas did at Fat Sams and Dance Factory can't be taken out of the equation. 'It was a seriously good venue that brought labels up to see bands. A&R men had expense accounts at that time and would be happy to come up for a weekend. The labels took the place seriously.'

With different labels offering their terms, it was time to stand back and consider what was important. 'When Ronnie Gurr from Virgin came to see us, we immediately had a fight,' says Kit. 'I liked that, actually. It showed he was being genuine. Other companies knew he had been to see us, so they started arriving. One offered a mansion each on Millionaire's Mile [at one point when the jute industry was at its height, Strathern Road in Broughty Ferry was said to be the richest street in the world] but I was just wondering how I would heat it. I was on the Broo, getting £18 a week!'

In the end, the band sacrificed noughts on the cheque for creative freedom. 'We had complete creative control at Virgin. For a breaking band to have that amount of freedom is unheard of now,' says Gary.

'There were these years of penury and not admitting how bad things really were,' says Ged. 'The vision we had – and the humour to get through that –was really important. There was a defined path about how you did it then. Get good, write material and develop a live act – then the record company come in and offer the contract, you sign the contract and then become like all these famous bands. Easy.'

Deemed to be the most responsible, Ged was put in charge of the advance cheque. 'I don't know why, I was as blootered as the rest of them sitting in the back of the taxi after the signing.'

SHORT AND SWEDE

Sweden Through the Ages, the band that had been expected to sign before Spencer Tracy, was still waiting on the break. 'I got the band together as soon as I got back to Dundee, really,' says Steve Knight. 'We had a chance to be managed by Stuart Clumpas, but I stupidly said no. Probably some daft thing about money at the time.'

Apart from being a drummer in demand, Lloyd had an increasing reputation as a singer. He had worked with Michael Marra, being introduced at one Angus Hotel gig as 'Dundee's answer to Barbara Dickson'. He had been playing in various bands including Spies with Gordon Douglas at The Bothy, managing to get a kit on a stage that he describes as 'no bigger than a piece of Ryvita, and it seemed every time you went back, someone had taken another bite out of it'.

Lloyd was actually playing in a few bands and not short of work, but agreed to sing backing vocals alongside Kim Pallas on Steve's new project. 'I did a couple of gigs but I was blowing out good payers to sing backing vocals, so I said I couldn't do it anymore. Steve said, "What songs do you think you can sing better?" And I had to say, "All of them."'

'Things really started to take off when Lloyd starting singing the lead vocal,' says Steve, 'particularly when we did a track called "I'm Only Here For The Summer". There was loads of record company interest after that.'

Chrysalis was the main contender and Steve was flown to London and offered £80,000 to sign for a full record deal. 'Go West were sitting in the next office. I loved the building – loved the set-up. We had a nice lunch and that was it. I told everybody we were going to sign with Chrysalis.'

A month later, Chrysalis had a new head of operations and the first thing he did was drop Del Amitri and their A&R man resigned in protest. Unfortunately their A&R man was also Sweden's and pen had not yet been put to paper. 'He went to A&M, taking Del Amitri with him, but didn't bother to tell us.'

Steve called the head of operations, who said he would need to see the band live, so it was back to showcasing again. He flew up to Dundee and Steve recalls that it was clear there was animosity between him and their former A&R man. Three months on, Steve had heard nothing so told him where to stick his deal; he would go to another company who had shown interest. 'Unfortunately in the record business, once something falls through with one company, the others take notice and lose interest. EMI signed my publishing and gave me a cheque for £10,000, but we really wanted the record deal. Meanwhile Spencer Tracy had signed to Virgin and wanted Brian and Chris back.

'I had the money, so we made our own EP, but I realised they had to go. Lloyd was heartbroken and I was twenty-eight, wondering what was next.'

There was another attempt at working with a singer, Paul Schofield, in London, but when that didn't work, Steve was thirty-one and admits the music business had burnt him out. Now a teacher, after getting a degree from St Andrews University, he is still writing and working with singers.

In 1985, his friend and former bandmate Billy Mackenzie finally released *Perhaps*, the follow-up to *Sulk*, still under The Associates name. The initial recordings by Billy and Steve Reid that Steve Knight had heard in the Swiss Cottage flat in 1982 never saw the light of day. The tapes were lost and the album was started from scratch. Four producers and £250,000 later, the album was released to typical critical plaudits, but only reached twenty-three in the chart, selling around 40,000 copies.

The next year saw the beginning of a musical partnership that would endure for the rest of Billy Mackenzie's life, with Steve Aungle, the student in a donkey jacket and specs who couldn't travel to Edinburgh to rehearse eight years previously.

'By 1986, I had given up the studio in the Seagate and had installed an eight-track recording set-up in my Baxter Park Terrace flat,' says Steve. 'I was friends with John Mackenzie – we had clicked right away when we met, not just as people but also musically. It was John who suggested to Billy that he should try doing some demos with me. Of course, I had heard all about The Associates and I saw it as a possible career move if things went well. I had got to know the family well, but hadn't met Billy. I was a rather tense, awkward individual at the time, but they seemed to accept me as I was without any hesitation.'

Billy visited Steve's sparse ground-floor flat across from one of the city's parks and once he recovered from the shock of the brightly coloured ABC wallpaper that adorned the walls of the home studio (Steve hadn't bothered to remove it since the previous occupant), they got down to work.

'I was reasonably pleased with our first recording session together. Billy was a bit demanding and full-on at times but there was a real natural charm and a sharp sense of humour.'

Billy suggested taking the demos to a studio in Edinburgh the following week, and as he didn't drive and his younger brother Jimmy had the Rolls-Royce that day, Steve was left driving an old, battered Ford Escort estate car, which he only learned halfway through the trip had no MOT. Billy didn't know what one was.

Steve found the results from the trip to Edinburgh disappointing. 'Sometimes the first version is the best,' he says. It would be four years before the two would work together again.

BEDLAM AND BREAKFAST

Not every band was looking for the record deal – many were happy enough to play for a living, for extra beer money, or simply for the fun of it.

Even with original material, Gordon Douglas had no intention of trying to sell his songs. 'With Spies it was back to The Bothy, and to be honest, it hadn't changed that much since the days when Jeff and I first played as a duo. It had been done up – painted, anyway – and they had put a carpet down, which obviously justified a hike in the price of the beer.

'The band always seemed to be moving on the stage. That wasn't us grooving: if you stayed too long in one position your feet stuck to the carpet. It didn't pay a lot, but the crowd were friendly.'

It all came to an end in the 1980s, though, when fire destroyed the building. 'It was a fire-trap, no doubt, but there wasn't enough oxygen for the flames to get a good hold until it was empty,' says Gordon. 'We all lost a gang hut and a home. Romances had happened there, children conceived (allegedly), love affairs begun and ended, and a great deal of beer went under the bridge. A lot of great memories, bands and songs were born there.'

While Spies were happy to stay at home, Alan Breitenbach decided to create Bedlam and take marauding Dundee musicians to the far north. 'At various points during the life of the band, Lou Lewis was in it, so was Chris Marra, Lloyd Anderson, Andy Robinson on drums and Ronnie Boyd. We had a gig in the far north of Lewis on a Friday night, meaning we would have to leave on Thursday to do a gig in Ullapool that night then, because it was too expensive to put the van on the ferry, all the gear had to go on the wee suitcase train. A guy would pick us up with a van on the other side and we'd drive to the island's most northerly point, to The Cross Inn at the Port of Ness.

'When we arrived, the bar would be full of guys dressed in overalls, speaking Gaelic, drinking heavy and rolling Golden Virginia. We'd have a wee kip to start at 10pm and they still were there. It was pub rock, the heavier blues stuff, which always went down well. We'd play all night and have a nightcap about 2am and they were still there in their overalls, drinking heavy, and rolling Golden Virginia. We would have to be up again to drive back to the ferry for 9am – no ferries on Sunday, of course. Then it was loading the gear on the wee train again and on the other side, a gig on Saturday night to break the journey back down.'

It was a far cry from the Parisian flea markets where he learned Reinhardt tunes but in 1986 he, along with John Whyte and Kevin Murray, decided to form a Django-style band and call it Havana Swing. 'The name came from a box of Cuban cigars in my house, but there's nothing Cuban about it. It's like Havin' a Swing.' Whatever the origin, Havana Swing has become one of the most popular gypsy jazz bands in the country, with invitations to play from specialist events right through to the Glastonbury festival.

OUT OF THE BLUE

Chambers in Castle Street and The Rendezvous in Union Street had long been popular live music venues. Dougie Martin and the latest incarnation of Mafia were known as the Chambers band but played both venues, while Donny, now playing with a different set of musicians, was in The Rendezvous.

'I was with Mafia until about 1982, but like many bands, tax affairs weren't always the best organised and as I was the one with the secure salary, I signed for everything. I paid for it in the end, having to pay a visit to the taxman.'

Donny did play with various other bands, including Quicksilver, but at that time he met a couple of up-and-coming young musicians. 'It's where I first met Gregor Philp and Simon Ciampi Deuchar,' he says. 'We were playing with Eddie Marra and Frances Carlin in Carlin Rose and her Mellow Fellows. What a name, eh?'

Gregor and Simon had met as children when Simon moved to Broughty Ferry with his family (his dad was jazz trumpeter Jimmy Deuchar). Gregor had already developed a taste for music, starting to play guitar at ten and spending pocket money that was meant for more practical things on a copy of *Sergeant Pepper* at twelve. 'I got up at 5am and played it very quietly with my ear pressed against the speaker. I'll never forget the feeling of that.'

Gregor and Simon had both joined the first year of the Perth College music course in 1986 but getting out and playing was the aim. For Simon that came when his bass teacher, Bob Quinn (a.k.a. The Man across the Pletty), gave him a 'them or me' scenario. He was not chuffed at the way one of his pupils was (as he saw it) being railroaded into slap bass. 'I left, because I valued his teaching ten times more,' says Simon.

'Another Sunday were my first band,' says Gregor. 'We played the university and supported Pete Shelley [Buzzcocks], but my musical education really began when I met Stewart Ivins. My mate Dave auditioned for a band he had at the time called The Headsquares, which did the girl-group stuff. When he got that job, I first saw Stewart with his black Strat and Fender twin reverb. I thought he was probably the coolest guy I'd ever seen.'

Ever the talent-spotter, Stewart introduced the young guitarist to Michael Marra. 'I played in a couple of bands with Stewart at that time, but my mind was on heading to London to become a session player. Thank goodness that nonsense didn't last long and I came back and started working in The Rendezvous with the Carlin Rose band.'

Gregor found plenty of inspiration in the way that Stewart, Donny, Dougie Martin and Gerry McGrath acquitted themselves musically. 'Between those four you cover off a lot of elements. It's really important that in the place that you're making music you have mentors, people that stand beside you. I've been more influenced by these people than records in the end.

'I was a real smartarse know-it-all when I was younger. Dougie would play something and I'd think, "That's the wrong chord." But it would invariably be better. He's more of an orchestrator than just a man who plays.'

At this time Donny was approached by a gangly young chap who was looking for a drummer. Keith Matheson had moved from Wick in 1985, two years after his older brother Alan, who had come down to join the magazine staff at D.C. Thomson, and two years before his younger brother Ross.

'I got a job working with Groucho's,' he says. 'I had been doing some shopfitting with Breeks and he offered me a job as manager. I knocked him back but changed my mind and went back the next week, but that job was gone so I joined as a staff member. I remember The Crypt was still open at that point, but I wasn't very trendy. I think the only thing I bought was a treble clef tie-pin.'

Keith had been playing in Wick since he was eighteen and on arrival in Dundee moved into a communal house in Windsor Street, where it seemed half the young staff of the *Beano* and *Dandy* lived at the time. There he met Kirriemuir guitarist Lindsay Duncan and they started working together on some of Keith's songs. 'The very first line-up of Big Blue 72 was me, Lindsay and Alan Murphy. We managed to harangue Donny Coutts to play with us, Steve Le Comber played bass on the first demo, but we also had Gary Fimister for live work.'

The cast of musicians who passed through the band is legendary, with one of the most settled line-ups including Alison Burns on additional vocals and Chris van der Kuyl on keyboards. 'We also had Ali Napier on keyboards at one point,' says Keith. 'Ali's one of these guys – I'm surprised he isn't a star. If someone had managed him as a solo artist he could have been huge. He's a genius player, a great singer and writes good songs.'

Chris van der Kuyl had been part of the musical group of friends at

St Saviour's, but his dad Tony's influence had already made a mark. 'Music was always a big thing in the house. Because my dad was on the folk scene, he had lots of musical friends.

'I was working in Rainbow and met Keith, who had already started Big Blue 72. Lindsay had already left to do something different and I think Keith was looking for a new sound. My mate Paddy Burns joined, as did a brass section and Gregor Philp. That line-up, with Alison, did the showcase in Bar Chevrolet which put the band on the final talent list for CBS.'

Keith is brutally frank about why he feels Big Blue 72 didn't get signed in the end. 'If I had written better songs, it might have happened. There was so much happening, and the opportunities were there. Gordon Charlton from CBS came up, Bob Flynn was kind of managing us, but the songs weren't good enough – I was always messing about with styles. I always surrounded myself with people who were much better players than me, who could play any idea I had.'

Donny Coutts believes that one of the most important things he brought to the band was a driving licence, so he could rent the van. 'There was a real "show must go on" moment at Fat Sams, where Chris had a terrible nosebleed. He carried on playing, while his dad was stuffing toilet paper up his nose.'

Shortly after closing the doors on Big Blue 72, Keith returned with Marshal Curtis, which brought Donny along but freshened up the personnel. 'To me it was kind of a way of renaming it, but I do think the songs were better. I was becoming a more focused writer.'

ON A WING AND A PRAYER

Once the signatures had dried on the contract, it was time for Spencer Tracy to start thinking about making an album. The crucial task was to find a producer who would be sympathetic to the sound. Howard Gray was the choice, a young producer who had engineered Simple Minds'

New Gold Dream. There was talk of using Abba's Polar Studios in Sweden, but they went to the next best thing, Puk studios in Denmark, which had been built as a carbon copy of Polar. 'There was accommodation at the studio and the closest town to Puk was Randers, about twenty miles away,' says Kit, 'so we were pretty isolated there.'

In hindsight Gary believes that level of isolation may not have been such a good thing. 'I think we went flying up our bums a wee bit. It was exciting, the first time in a new studio – you'll always want to dramatically rework things that really don't need it.'

One of the indulgences of the album that did work was a session with Lester Bowie's Brass Fantasy at his studio in Brooklyn. 'The main thing was how we were going to get to New York. From the advance, we were paying ourselves £80 a week and the rest was going into studio costs,' says Kit. Virgin had instigated a programme of live in-flight entertainment, and with a busking background they took the idea to Virgin that they would play on the plane in return for the flights. Even though they were Virgin artists, they had to audition for the airline, but passed.

For Ged, there was a major drawback. 'I couldn't take the tea chest on – it had to go in the hold. So I'm on the flight with my pole and bit of string and have an idea to use something else. The meals trolley made a fine makeshift tea chest and we played for twenty minutes, walking up and down the aisle. At the other end we went to collect the luggage and the first thing that comes off is the tea chest. We just left it going round and round on the carousel.'

Brooklyn in the mid-1980s wasn't quite the gentrified borough that stands today. 'We even found it difficult to get a taxi driver to take us out there,' says Kit. 'We were in Lester's studio and I thought, as you do, "I'll just nip out to the shops." It was the first time I had seen a normal grocery shop with full grilles and a hatch where they would hand your stuff through. When I came out, a gang of guys started to surround me but suddenly one of the studio engineers came round the corner and shouted, "Hey, he's with Lester . . . He's cool!"'

The song from the *Meet Danny Wilson* album that Virgin was pinning its hopes on was 'Mary's Prayer', which had been written in the damp, dank days of The Swamp. Before anything could be released there was the small matter of avoiding a good old Hollywood suing from the estate of Spencer Tracy, which wasn't best pleased that his name was being used.

And so the first single from the newly named Danny Wilson (a character in a Frank Sinatra film called *Meet Danny Wilson*) was 'Mary's Prayer', released in March 1987. It was released three times before it reached number three later that year. 'By the third time I was saying, "Please don't release it again,"' says Gary, 'but what convinced them was the rate it was rising in the American charts. We would get reports every couple of weeks and, sitting in Dundee, it was hard to believe that this was happening. It peaked at twenty-three on the main *Billboard* Hot 100, which is everything in the US, but everything is so segmented that they could see it was number one in the Adult Contemporary chart.'

The highest it had charted in the UK prior to that was forty-two, making it eligible for a Radio 1 poll to find out the listeners' favourite song that hadn't made the top 40. 'Mary's Prayer' won by more than four to one in what Gary described in an interview with *Scotland on Sunday* as the 'Top of the Flops' poll, saying rather drolly that people probably liked it 'as it took them back to their youth'.

With a genuine hit comes the onerous responsibility of talking to the teen mags. 'We were being pushed to do all sorts of press,' says Ged. 'The music wasn't out-and-out pop, but I think there was a desire to make us work across the board. I mean look at us – we're hardly pin-ups!'

It seemed that the fun of promotion lessened as the band became more established. In the early days, the three would sit together, having a laugh and providing great copy. Gary told *Smash Hits* that he was thinking of having an extra head put on, in order to wear more than one hat at a time; and Kit revealed that after the band had been on *Wogan*, they sneaked on to the set afterwards and saw that Terry's chair was covered in stains.

The band was the first to be signed to Virgin America. The marketing plan used posters of the individuals bearing the slogan 'Who's Danny?' – which didn't exactly help to stop the confusion that none of them was actually Danny Wilson. There was an opportunity to tour North America with Simply Red, however, and it was the excuse they needed to get the band back together for the road-trip of a lifetime. Bringing in Brian McDermott, Derek Thomson and Chris Marra, with the addition of Frank Rossiter and Gary Thompson as the horn section, they set out for three months across Canada and the US.

'On the first day with the tour bus, I was so excited,' says Ged. 'To get the chance of spending three and a half months touring this amazing country. I bought a massive map and pinned it up on the bus so we could chart our progress. I came back on the bus and someone had written, "Let's get the f*ck out of here" on the first cross.'

Gary felt no homesickness during what he coined 'Dundee Goes to Hollywood'. Living in London for so many years meant that being away from Dundee was natural. 'In fact we loved the travel part of it. You would go to a new city and generally someone would be there to show you the best stuff in the time you had. I think the American tour was an amazing thing to share together. Early on, I suffered quite badly from stage-fright – I was fine after a few songs, but I felt like throwing up before I went on.'

The same sense of humour that had seen them through the darkest days of the London experience shielded them from the fawning nonsense of that world. 'These daft American lassies would come up to us and say, "Hey, we gotta keep in touch,"' says Ged, 'and we'd say, "OK, here's my address. It's 123 Fish Supper Crescent . . ."'

Gary's vision of Dundee Goes to Hollywood was never truer than during the band's stay in LA. 'They put us up at the Hollywood Roosevelt. Now it's hyper-trendy but at the time we got a cheap deal on cabanas at the pool – you could dive straight into that David Hockney painting.

'Kit, Ged and I had to get dressed up in the suits and the hats and head off to do promotion, but we walked past the guys who were all relaxing around the pool. What a sight – these wee, white, skinny Dundee bodies! Derek Thomson was floating about on a lilo and Chris was on a lounger with a giant strawberry daiquiri in his hand and his head tilted back to the sun. He didn't even open his eyes, but just as we went past we heard, "Ahhh. I wonder what the poor people are doing now . . ."

'It's absolutely true that Chris was the bravest of us all,' adds Gary. 'He went out there a number of times, going off on tour to make a go of it for his whole family. It's a huge commitment and sacrifice and it doesn't always pay off.'

Chris felt that sacrifice all too keenly again. 'I had done the American tour thing, but I hadn't done it with my best pals, so I had to say yes. But during that tour my father died. I had to fly back for the funeral and then turn right round and fly back out to join the tour. I was thinking, "Is this what your life's going to be? Is everything important going to happen when you're away?" '

The work continued and one thing a tour of that size did was improve the band's stagecraft. 'We started to work out some stage moves,' says Kit. 'There was one that Gary and I worked out for "Aberdeen", where I would sing the second verse. I was playing tambourine on the first and then on the second, he would whistle. I'd spin it and throw it to him. We perfected it one night at The Venue in Edinburgh, which was so wee that Ged practically needed to crouch so he didn't hit his head on the lights. The next night we played Wembley Arena, and did the same thing on "Aberdeen". I looked across and Gary was so far away that I saw the tambourine flying through the air and it barely made it halfway . . .'

The isolation of making the first album was turned fully on its head when Danny Wilson started work on the second release at Allan McGlone's studio the following summer. Gary had received three nominations in the Ivor Novello awards for 'Mary's Prayer' and the critics were generally pretty approving of the ambition of the songwriting and the complexity of what the band were trying to do in a three-minute pop song.

'We decanted back to Dundee,' says Ged. 'And it was fantastic. That feeling that we didn't have to go to London. The hunt for producers started again, leading to the bizarre sight of Don Was (of Was Not Was) in the Campbeltown Bar. He was keen to work with them but felt that the demos were already ninety per cent there. 'The rain sound on "Shirley Maclaine" was recorded as rain fell on plastic bags outside the studio,' says Gary. It was back to the DIY sounds and memories of Kit playing house bells instead of proper tubular bells (for the proper Menzieshill sound).

Virgin rejected album titles such as *Disney Punks* (too litigious) and *Huckleberry F*ck* (naturally) so were probably happy to go with the obscure *Bebop Moptop*. The first single, 'The Second Summer of Love' cracked the top 30 again.

'There was a really young audience on the tour for that album,' recalls Chris. 'The support included a specky boy from Glasgow [it was The Indian Givers] and I was watching them from the balcony one night. He had all these teenagers watching him and he says something like, "Somewhere above us all Aldous Huxley is laughing like a madman." What?!

'We actually had the same specs and for one song he would take them off and put them on the amp. I swapped them one night while he was singing. He came back to get his specs, put them on, and couldn't understand why he couldn't see anything.'

It was a time when pressure was beginning to show – Brian was no longer with the band and had joined Del Amitri. 'I would rather have been playing the Danny Wilson stuff but they decided to use someone else. I had six or seven years with Del Amitri, and to be honest, they treated me brilliantly and we had an amazing time.'

Danny Wilson were still on the promotion treadmill, with Virgin determined that they would be a pop act. Meanwhile, the band's priority was crafting songs well, and increasingly all three wanted a hand in the writing.

A *Smash Hits* interview at the time signed off: 'Three cheers for the Wilson – the happiest men in pop.' They were putting on a good front.

SWEET SUCCESS

While Gary and Ged were away from Dundee, their girlfriends were creating a project of their own. Alison Burns, along with Ged's girlfriend Tricia Boyle and Jane Grimes – a former Grimes Folk Four member – brought honeyed harmony and 1940s glamour to Dundee in the mid-1980s, with the Penny Dainties.

'I had always had an ambition to do something like this,' says Alison. 'I had started something similar with two school friends, but they weren't as keen at the time so I went off and joined bands instead. I had met Jane and Tricia through Ged and knew that they sang, so I mentioned the idea to them on New Year's Day 1986 at a party.'

A week later, the girls had learned three classic swing songs in full three-part harmony and took it to the streets. 'We did quite well,' says Alison. 'We were rumbled when people kept going past and we were singing the same songs again, but we made £15 and took it straight to the Pizza Gallery.'

Alison was working on another project simultaneously, with Danny Wilson keyboard player Derek Thomson, who wanted to create a band for his songs. He had previously worked with a female singer called Kim Pallas in The Quiet's Over, and now he teamed up with Alison for The Rainmates. 'We had record company interest pretty quickly,' she says, 'but we turned them all down. The offers were based on short-termism. It was the case of releasing singles and seeing where things sat, but we wanted an albums deal.'

She had also been part of Cat's Oot The Bag theatre company, which culminated in the large-scale community project, *Witch's Blood*. 'Alan Lyddiard at Dundee Rep offered me a professional role there. He had given away the allocation of Equity cards for that year, but he said, "If you can get an Equity card off your own back, you've got a job." I managed to get all my contracts for singing and other work I'd done and I qualified easily.'

Alison was still working at British Telecom at the time, but resigned to take the Rep job. 'My workmates asked me what they could buy with my leaving collection and I asked for a map of the world and a ghetto-blaster – that's been the template ever since.'

While The Rainmates were gaining interest, she auditioned for Dave Anderson at the Wildcat Theatre Company. 'I went along in my usual bizarre garb at the time and also took my bass. I sang with Dave playing piano, I played bass, and I did some acting. I was offered the chance to join.' However, Alison decided to continue with The Rainmates. 'That was the crossroads. Things like that happen quite often, but it's the only one I look back on and say, "What if?"'

When The Rainmates split, Alison had to get working. 'I got a whole box of backing tapes, a crap PA and loaded them into my car, which was about to die on me. I went out and did solo gigs with tapes, just to pay the bills. It was lonely and I had never been so miserable.'

The bright spots during that time came with the attention that the Penny Dainties were receiving. 'We did the pilot for a Channel 4 show called *Halfway to Paradise* with Stuart Cosgrove, among other television spots. It was an easy thing to take out and gig – three mics and a PA were all we needed. Those were happy times.'

Helen Forbes had moved on from gig-crawls and conning policemen into getting a lift home, to playing in bands as a traditional whistle player. 'I played the piano, but the whistle came about because I moved into a flat and couldn't get my piano upstairs. I didn't have much money, but I loved playing that music and lots of sessions were springing up.'

When Mike Ward from the Tannahill Weavers moved to Dundee, he and Helen's father approached the Occidental Hotel in Broughty Ferry to set up a session. It moved to The Ship but finally found its home at the Fisherman's Tavern. 'Jake Donnelly ran a folk club in The Bothy and brought people like Dick Gaughan to Dundee. My dad and I would do floor spots, with dad playing uillean pipes, which he bought from Dublin.' It was in Ireland that Helen learned from Mary Bergen, arguably one of the best whistle players in the world. 'I idolised her and would get lessons anywhere and anytime. I'd play for eight hours a day and forget to eat.'

The practice paid off and Helen joined The Foundry Band along with her dad, touring and making albums. Her next project would be something of a mission, however, as the idea of an all-female folk band in the mid-1980s was still rather unusual.

'To say the least,' says Helen. Through Lou Lewis (now her partner), Helen met Shirley Potts. They were joined by Karen Valentine and Jae Austin, and from 1987 Blon a Gael took on the folk scene. 'We really fought for it and it was hard to get the gigs at first,' says Helen. 'It meant travelling everywhere to get £40 but we knew we had to travel out of Dundee and get to the west coast – the Scotia Bar in Glasgow on Wednesday nights was great for us. We supported Boys of the Lough and Eric Bogle and sold out our Edinburgh Fringe show five years in a row.

'We liked to have fun, I would almost call it vaudeville folk. It was a great band to be in. When that came to a conclusion in 1994, I carried on playing whistle with bands and solo and I do quite a bit of teaching.'

Around 1987, there were some Dundee girls in tartan, but they were playing far from traditional music. The band known at that point as It's a Crime had started as Visions two years earlier, with Maggi Fenwick (keyboards), Carol Air (guitar) and Ailsa McInroy (bass). They would eventually settle with Mary McInroy (Ailsa's sister) as the lead singer, with Wayne Hutton drumming.

In 1987, when Varie Mathie replaced Wayne, they were gigging extensively and had a friendly local rivalry with a band called Six Appeal. 'We had to race them one night along Berriedale Braes to our gig,' says Ailsa. 'They passed us on a bend at god knows what speed, all the time mooning out of the open windows! When we got to the gig they pretended we were double-booked with them!'

That year they were approached to back Jessie Rae, the Claymore-wielding Scot in full regalia, who had a minor hit with 'Over the Sea', and had also written 'Inside Out' for Odyssey. Varie was out by that time, so drummer John Russell was recruited from Six Appeal and they became known as The Thistle Warriors, clad in tartan with kilts that barely covered their bahookies. 'We were accompanied for many of the gigs by a Cairn terrier called Mhairi,' says Ailsa, 'who Jessie insisted be on stage with us to sing "It's Just the Dog & Me". He would introduce it by howling like a dog with Mhairi. A lot of time the dog could be found sleeping inside John's bass drum throughout the gig. She was a tough wee thing!'

When the girls left Jesse Rae in 1988, they recruited a young drummer from the Highlands called Shona McLeod, and became Adam 812. They recorded for the Precious Organisation and over the next two years went on to do television and videos, but according to Ailsa the proudest moment was headlining the 1991 Octocentenary Celebrations in the City Square.

The band decided to take a break in 1993, but a reunion became out of the question in December of that year when Shona, just twenty-one at the time, sustained serious head injuries in a car accident. 'She was in a coma for nine months, before waking to a life requiring twenty-four-hour care,' says Carol. 'This put an end to what was potentially a great career as a drummer.'

MEETING THE PUBLIC

During a Rainmates' rehearsal in Fat Sams, one of the lighting engineers spoke to bass player Colin Davidson during a break. He asked if he thought Derek Thomson would mind if he had a 'wee shot' on his keyboards. Colin gave him the go-ahead, and after a few minutes said, 'You're actually pretty good, eh?'

Ali Napier had been picking out tunes on the piano since he was three years old and after a few weeks of lessons, the teacher gave up, saying he had learned too many bad habits already.

'So they sent me to violin lessons. The teacher was Andy Lothian, the bandleader, who had retired but was teaching peripatetically around schools. He had played with my dad in the past, so there was a link. Also, he was teaching us music that I identified with, Scottish country dance music.'

There were instruments all around the house and after a broken leg at the age of fifteen he picked up a guitar and used the enforced eight-week lay-off to add another string (well six strings) to his bow. Genesis changed everything, however. When they came to Dundee in 1980, it was Ali's eureka moment about becoming a keyboard player. He also loved the feeling of being in a band.

'A bunch of mates getting together and making music and being loud was fantastic. I came from quite a conservative and church-oriented family, and the music was all very tame, so I was the mental child to them . . . My older brother loved it, however. He had, to his sorrow, no musical ability at all, so loved the fact that I was doing it.'

The only person that Ali came across at that time was Gregor Philp. There was a link between the two in John Berridge. 'I remember being at Berridge's house at Strawberry Bank and this guy was a mind-blowingly good guitar player – that was Gregor. There was obvious envy straight away,' he laughs.

Following a few years at university in Aberystwyth, Ali arrived back in Dundee in 1988. 'I had missed out on everything that was happening in town with Danny Wilson and I wasn't hooked into the musician scene at all.' Colin Davidson was also playing with Stewart Clark in Citizen Kane and knew they needed another keyboard player. 'That was the start,' he says. 'From there I also joined Big Blue 72, but the band I did most with was Joe Public. So from doing nothing I was playing with everyone, being a bit of a tart. It's not like there was any money in it though.'

Joe Public were a high-energy band (think a mix of pop and rockabilly – popabilly) fronted by the vocally dextrous Caragh McKay. They were a popular touring band and had some high-profile support slots including with The Big Dish. 'We managed to get a big hit of publicity during what turned out to be the last big adventure, touring the UK with The Bhundu

Boys.' On the second night, Shakespeare (Shakie) Kangwena received the tragic news that his wife had died. It looked like the tour was over, but when they asked if Ali could stand in, he said he would 'give it a blast' and managed to learn the set in fewer than forty-eight hours.

'We met up to rehearse and it worked. By the time we reached the Town and Country Club gig, it was a fairly big story in *Melody Maker* and *Sounds*.'

A PASSAGE TO INDIE

From the mid-1980s, the pages of the music papers were undergoing something of a revolution. Although John Peel had paid a visit to Dance Factory in 1984 and the Tayside Bar had been the home to a thriving indie scene, Dundee still had a reputation for what was called 'blue-eyed soul'.

Not so for Alan Cormack, who listened to Peel's show and found little to his taste in Dundee. 'I had gone to see Simple Minds with my friend Craig McNeil in about 1982 and thought that Derek Forbes looked really cool, so bass was my instrument of choice.'

Alan and Craig agreed to sell their precious CB radios to raise funds for instruments. 'I sold mine for £25, went to Forbes and bought a K bass. The next years were spent listening to Joy Division and learning to play.'

Alan's family moved from the Kirkton housing scheme to the leafier surroundings of Broughty Ferry in 1984, which didn't please him at first, as he liked the 'mental stuff' that would sometimes happen in the more notorious areas of the scheme.

A year after he moved to the Ferry, he came into contact with people who would be influential later, but at the time, like all good indie kids, they stared at their shoes and said nothing. 'I'd be sixteen and getting on a bus to go into town. My friend Paul Munro said, "I think you should speak to my pal." I thought the guy sounded interesting but I probably just shrugged.

'The place to hang around was Foreigner's, even though we weren't into heavy metal. It was the place to be if you had a leather jacket and dyed black hair. The first time I understood there was a scene of any type was about 1986 when Craig and I went to Dance Factory.'

Craig had bought an Ibanez semi-acoustic guitar with his CB loot but was going to guitar lessons and intent on playing more than three chords, despite Alan's protestations that they just needed to get the band going. 'The Housemartins were on that Sunday and he said, "If the guy is decent and playing three chords, we'll do it." He was happy enough so we did.'

They put out ads for another guitarist, a singer and a drummer, saying they had to be into The Doors, Velvet Underground and Echo and the Bunnymen. The first person to call was Paul 'Lefty' Wright. (Lefty now has a collective of musicians across the generations called Lefty and Friends and has recently learned sitar in India.) 'He was a real heavy metal guy at the time and I said to Craig, "I canna be in a band with him – he smells of patchouli oil." I think The Doors were that crossover band between metal and indie.'

That was the beginnings of The Sandflowers, initially called The Pretty Little Eskimos. The first gig was at Dundee Rep in February 1988, with a band called The Wildhouse, with a singer called Kenny Gall who worked at D.C. Thomson and Roy Anderson on drums. 'Kenny was going into Groucho's a lot,' says Alan, 'probably because of Moog Rogers who worked there, but not long after that Breeks wanted to put a flexi-disc on a magazine called *East Coast Rumble*. It was to be us and The Wildhouse – it came out on the Dark Side of the Haggis label.'

The Sandflowers were a musical world apart from bands who had enjoyed recent success. 'There was a thought that bands like Big Blue 72 and Danny Wilson looked down on us, thinking we couldn't play our instruments. We'd be sitting in the pub and one of the guys from Danny Wilson would walk in and we'd be like, "Yeah, they're crap, we're much better than them, we should be on *Top of the Pops* not them . . ." We had a huge chip on our shoulders.'

Craig McNeil asked Alan to come and check out a band called The

Hate Foundation at Café Club, just in case they were competition. When Graeme Ogston walked up to the mic, Alan had no idea that this was the same guy that Paul Munro had recommended he speak to years earlier.

'Graeme introduced the band and then there was five minutes of tuning up – we felt quite smug. Even though The Sandflowers weren't technically gifted to the outside world, we made a point of being tight. It was going to be competent, even if people thought we were crap.'

The Sandflowers came to an end when Craig went off to work in London. 'He went to college about 1989/90 and through his own cheek, really, managed to get a placement with the *NME*,' explains Alan. 'When he was there I was asking, "Have you given them any demo tapes?" He always swerved the subject but when he came back, things had changed and he was obviously looking to move on. He managed to get a job in the press office in Polydor and now he's a director at Beggars Banquet records. So indie did no' bad for him!'

JOHN, PAUL, GEORGE AND BINGO

Like garlic to a vampire, the working men's clubs were anathema to the shambling indie kids. However, the clubs (or 'clubbies' in local parlance) have long been a source of entertainment for those looking for cheap booze, bingo and a band – usually in that order, with some putting bingo in the top spot. They have also been the source of much-needed income for musicians. The Thursday night entertainment pages of the *Evening Telegraph* would be littered with ads, advertising which bands were playing over the weekend.

'There has always been a real work ethic to music in Dundee,' says Stuart McHardy. 'Few people had pretensions. If there was work, they would do it and get paid. Fantastic.' When he came back to Dundee from London in 1974, Stuart hooked up with Colin Speed, who he had known through the folk scene. 'He asked if I fancied doing the odd gig, it was mainly country stuff in pubs and clubs. The work just poured in. I believe that was where I learned to be a musician – I may have known a lot technically but I wasn't the finished article.'

At a gig in the Happyhillock area, Colin hadn't broken the news that their second set would involve audience participation. 'Singers. I had never come across this before. The first one came up and wanted to sing "St Therese of the Roses" in G. Go. When I got into it, I realised I could do it.'

Stewart Ivins and Gus Foy were well versed in the art of backing singers. 'My favourite was the guy who said, " 'Danny Boy'. C. Nae laughin'!"' says Stewart.

'And of course,' adds Gus, 'they would have more keys than a locksmith. They keep changing key and looking at you as if you're daft.'

During their gigs at the Civil Service Club, Gus remembers a woman who would sit quietly, dressed from head to toe in black. 'In the break she asked if we did any Elvis numbers. We didn't so she was NOT happy. She says, "How no'? I'll get you barred. I'm still mourning for Elvis and I will only dance to Elvis." So we had a blether and we all knew bits and pieces – enough to throw a wee Elvis thing together. When we started she was up like a shot, pushing everyone out the road, giving it laldy . . . We stopped and she sat back down and didn't move again all night.'

Agents have been notoriously 'creative' when getting their bands work and Skeets Boliver often found themselves at a gig which would turn out to be a wedding. 'We struggled with that,' says Stewart. 'People would be expecting "The Grand Old Duke of York" . . .'

They would also expect the 'Hokey Cokey'. Gus remembers one instance in particular. 'It was a wedding at the Inchture Hotel and someone says, do you know the "Hokey Cokey"? Everybody's on the floor and we all spot that there's a guy with one arm – we're all looking at Stu, thinking, "What's he gonna say here then eh?" '

Skeets were also booked to play a club in Kirkcaldy and proceeded to hump the gear, PA, and a desk up two flights of stairs. They had set up when the owner came over and said, 'You guys play all the top twenty, eh?' When he was informed that was far from the case, the gear was packed up and straight back in the van. 'People would come up and say, "You ken any Queen?"' says Gus. 'We'd say no and then they'd start singing it at you anyway, as if that would help!'

There were some lucky breaks, however. 'Our favourite had to be the bingo in Arthurstone Terrace,' says Stewart. 'We had to play for fifteen minutes as they came in. They got their books and started, so we went to the pub. We went back to play for ten minutes in the break, then back to the pub again. Then it was back to play for fifteen minutes at the end. It was good money too.'

The strict rules applied to everyone. The dress codes, always carrying drinks on a tray, and never carrying that tray across the dancefloor. The social convenor ran the club and whatever he said went, whenever they wanted to say it.

'At a place in Forfar we were always expected to do The Eagles tune "Lyin' Eyes",' says Gus. 'I could never remember the words, probably because I hated it, but it was a good clubby song. One night I really thought I was going to get through it, no problem, and right over the top the social convener starts shouting, "After this number, it's the bingo, right ..." I totally lost it.'

Andy Pelc remembers a particularly vocal convenor taking over at a St Andrew gig at Douglas Amateurs Football Club around Christmas. 'I'm singing away, giving it a' that and the convenor starts waving his arms and shouting, "Stop, stop!" So the band stop mid-number and he starts, "Just to let you know there are some remote-control trucks here for the kiddies." Then a remote-control truck starts trundling across the dancefloor. "Bra' for the kiddies. Get your trucks for the bairn's Christmas. They should be twenty quid but we can sell you them here for a tenner." So I'm looking around at the band in total disbelief and Gus Foy and Eddie Marra are getting the wallets out to get some!'

Audiences didn't always show respect for the performers either, but seasoned performers have coping strategies, finely honed over the years.

'There was always the statutory wedgie as they walked behind me on stage,' says Alison Burns. 'I had joined up with Chris Marra and Calum Mckenzie [Havana Swing] who were already going out as a duo called The Culprits, but I convinced them that they needed a singer. The Black Watch Club in Arthurstone Terrace is a place where I remember we were really ignored,' she laughs.

When the going got really rough, there was only one solution to the boredom. 'Out the corner of my eye I would see Chris nodding to Calum and then they would carry on with what they called "Knobs Oot". With instruments shielding their 'organs' they would play away quite happily in the knowledge that that the crowd were ignorant of what was happening on stage. I'd be howling with laughter through the singing, but desperately keeping my eyes to the front!'

Keith McIntosh saw Calum in another coping-strategy mode. 'I stood in for Chris one night at a miners' club in Fife and no-one was slightest bit interested. Alison was saying, "Not one person is paying any attention to us," but Calum was of the "Don't worry, we're getting paid" attitude. He then said, "Watch this," and took his microphone, stuck it down the back of his trousers and let rip. You could hear it all around the hall and no one, not one person took a blind bit of notice.'

In his clubby years, Steve Aungle also learned to keep his eyes to the front. 'I was playing keyboards by then, but being a drummer I could always work out what was going on behind me. One night, I thought the drummer was a bit off, so I turned and saw him playing with one hand and smoking a fag with the other. He put the fag down, I thought to pick up another stick, but he lifted a pint instead.'

Another night, the band started with some background music but then shifted into a set for dancing. 'I spotted a man at a table close to the stage. He was taking off a false arm . . . Then he reached into a holdall and put on another arm that was bent at the elbow. Obviously his dancing arm.'

Ricky Ross never played the clubs, but what went on there held a fascination. 'When I had an after-school job in Wm Low's supermarket in the Overgate, one of the guys played in a club band. He would hang his "clubby" suit up in the staffroom and there was a bit of me that was fascinated by it and thinking, "That's a really interesting world, something that I know nothing about." The only time I went was to see a girl who I was at college with. We did our teaching practice together at Glebelands and she invited me to come and see her band. They did a lot of Abba and chart hits. It was a new world for me. My parents had never gone to clubs like that.'

When Mafia had a residency at the Ambassador, part of the job was to back the acts that were passing through, playing clubs all over Scotland. 'One woman was having a massive diva fit,' says Dougie Martin, 'shouting, "I can't go on, I can't go on!" She was obviously looking to get a wee ego massage, but Jim McAra was having none of it and said, "That's a good idea. If your rehearsal was anything to go by, maybe better no . . ."'

When a magician in yellow hipsters tried to take his sawing-the-woman-in-half act to new heights, his calculations were ever so slightly off. 'It was an electric saw and the lead wasn't long enough, so he had to dismantle the box and move it closer to the plug.'

Norrie Maiden was a legend among agents, but he also went out playing the pubs and clubs as Dean Eastwood. Dean and Dawn were the best-known of his acts, having recorded a tribute to Dundee. 'It was called "Proud of Our City",' says Gus Foy. 'The worst record you've ever heard. As an agent, he kept the best gigs for himself, but it backfired on him sometimes. They billed themselves as International Recording Artists, but someone had misheard him. He turned up at a gig in Auchterarder or somewhere, with Dawn, a guitar, and her tambourine. The place was full of people in kilts looking forward to seeing Dean and Dawn – international accordion artists.'

'Peter Benedetti used to go out under the name of Pepe Supersax,' says Gregor Philp. 'During the 1960s, he would swing on stage wearing a Tarzan outfit, while playing his sax. One night he was playing in Teazers

[Royal Hotel] and the breakfast stuff was all set up behind the curtain for the next morning. Having a Teddy boy suit, there were huge pockets so he started stuffing them with condiments. He also had lighty-up shoes, which were battery operated. Part of this act was that he would cart-wheel on stage before picking up the sax and started playing.' Unfortunately he had forgotten about the booty in his pockets and it was 'like a Catherine wheel with vinegar, salt and sauce flying everywhere . . .'

Dundee clubland had some leading lights and none more so than keyboard player Stuart Duncan, known better as Kez. Steve Gaughan played with him and bass player Fraser Adam in a band called Go East. 'That was a direct response to Go West, so we started playing about with other eighties band names. Kez said it couldn't be anything serious and was keen on either Chip Shop Lassies or Curiosity Killed the Doag!'

Go East were playing at The Logie Club and were really impressed by the facilities. 'In the break we found a room with loads of wigs and costumes,' says Steve. 'So we put the wigs on, but Kez is still fully dressed up when we get back on stage. Halfway through a song he disappears and as we look round, we can see him doing a handstand, with full stockings and suspenders.'

At a gig in Arbroath, however, Kez was one of the better behaved members. 'It was a Saturday,' recalls Keith McIntosh, 'and Fraser got a bit p*shed. Steve and Kez had to find him, get him to the gig and prop him up on a chair, where he managed to get through it. At the end though, the convener said, "Big hand for the band, folks – and a special round of applause for the handicapped laddie on the bass."'

THE NINETIES

The Nineties

WHERE EVERYBODY KNOWS YOU'RE HAME

There's a bar I know that's supposed to close at midnight
But when I come home, they lock me in 'til five
I've been on the road all day
And I'm half a mile away
And I'm hopin' they'll be open when I arrive
          – Gary Clark pays tribute to the Westport Bar in
                   'Hopin' (They'll Be Open)'

When Gus Robb opened the Westport Bar in 1988, the gleaming chrome and lasers of Da Vinci's had gone in favour of a team who set about creating a bar that would offer live music and good food. Talk to any of the people who made it their second home during the 1990s and they will say that the 'Westie' was much more than a pub. It was cheerier than *Cheers* and something of a community centre for musicians.

'I knew Kit Clark from way back,' says Gus, 'and I met him with his brother Scott in Tally's just after they came off tour in 1988. I think Allan McGlone was the first to jump ship and drink at the Westie and it just snowballed from there.'

Gus had his own playing background. 'I had a great education in music,' he says. 'I lived in Cleghorn Street and used to hear the sound of a bass or guitar from Bob Quinn's window. When I left school at fourteen, I would stay up all night with Bob, drinking endless cups of tea, but he would introduce me to so much music. We listened to Stanley Clarke and Bootsy Collins, but he always insisted that we listen to classical as well. I loved being in his company.'

Gus played in a few clubby bands, but early on decided to get involved in music through business. Shortly after taking over at the Westport, Gus approached Nick Wright to join him there. A few years before, Nick had moved the Soul Kiss Club to the Blue Mountains, which became one of the 'feeder' pubs for Dance Factory nights. He also took over the cooking and as a self-taught chef introduced the Dundee public to tasty green stuff – pesto, mostly. Now the Soul Kiss Club had become the Krush Club at the Royal Oak.

'I was hoping to make music a big part of the Westie, and Nick seemed like a natural – one of these cool characters who knew his music – so we moved the Krush Club to upstairs in the Westie.'

Nick initially came in as a chef and music adviser but eventually became a partner in the bar. 'Gus downplays his role in the music side of things,' says Nick. 'He had the connections with people like Michael Marra, who used to rehearse upstairs.'

The idea was to have a mix of bands, local and out-of-town. The Beaver Sisters, Better Backwards and the Penny Dainties all played in the early days and from out of town were the Balham Alligators (with Robin McKidd from Dundee, who had previously worked with Rab Noakes), the Milton Balgonies and the Scooby Doo Orchestra. Sometimes they just struck lucky.

'I was walking down the Hawkhill one Saturday night towards the bar and saw a queue snaking up towards me,' says Gus. 'As I got closer, I saw that it was for us. We had Teenage Fanclub that night but I had had no idea of their underground status when we booked them.'

They also benefited from the loyalty of local musicians too, with Gary

Clark playing there with Boo Hewerdine on his first solo tour after Danny Wilson. Gary appeared on the Sunday morning with his girlfriend in an open-top car and told Gus that he had written a song about the pub. Sure enough, 'Hopin' (They'll Be Open)' appeared on the King L album *Great Day For Gravity*.

Fairly early in the Westie story, Timex came out on strike and the workers were duly sacked. Gus spoke to Michael Marra, who agreed to play a benefit concert, backed by the Penny Dainties. 'He thought we could maybe get Pat Kane and Ricky Ross was a possibility, but I really wanted to get Billy Mackenzie,' says Gus. 'I was advised that the way to approach it was not to give him any reasons NOT to do it. I primed Ali Napier to learn his material, so that Billy couldn't come back and say that he didn't have a piano player.'

Hearing that Billy was at a studio in Auchterhouse, Gus decided the best plan would be to go up and ask face to face. When he arrived, he was shocked to see that Alan Rankine was with him, as there had been no talk about them ever working together again. 'As I watched them in the studio, Rankine didn't seem overly enamoured with the place.' Gus couldn't convince Billy, who didn't say no, but didn't say yes, much to Gus's disappointment.

('Billy told me he was going to try to reform The Associates with Alan Rankine,' says Steve Aungle. 'It was at the instigation of Chris Parry from Fiction. He also said they were going to demo some songs and asked if I minded them doing a version of a song we had been working on. He invited me to come up to the studio where they would be working, near Auchterhouse, so I dropped in. I had always admired Alan and was looking forward to meeting him, but I don't think the feeling was mutual. Obviously the attempted reunion of The Associates fell through. I think Alan wanted Billy's full, exclusive commitment and he wasn't prepared to give it.')

The *Beat the Drum* concert did go ahead in November 1993, with Ricky Ross and Pat Kane joining Michael. There were also his own gigs. He was using the upstairs room to rehearse with the first proper touring band he had put together. 'They left from here to go to Glasgow to record the *Pax Vobiscum* live album,' says Gus. 'A wee while later my friend from Inverness, who was a massive fan of Michael's, phoned me to say, "How did you get a mention in the sleeve notes?!" I was really chuffed by that.'

One of the tracks on *Pax Vobiscum* was 'Julius', written for Dougie Martin's dog. According to Michael (in *The Rock n Soul of Dundee* DVD), Dougie told the dog fibs when he was about to head off to Skye for gigs. 'I felt sorry for the dog, so I felt I had to write him a wee song.'

Dougie and his Mafia were still attracting audiences and played upstairs at the Westie. Mafia offered more than just their normal show and would often bring in some guests, as Gus recalls. 'I was behind the bar on a Saturday afternoon when Alan Gorrie walked in and said, "Is this where Mafia are playing nowadays? I'm just going to see my mum in Perth, but would you let Dougie know that I'll be back later?" Of course, I was straight out to the blackboard, writing, "Mafia tonight with special guest Alan Gorrie from the Average White Band". About half past four a few American servicemen came in and asked if it was true. They asked what time upstairs opened, and at 7pm on the dot, a bus arrived from RAF Leuchars, packed with servicemen.'

Another regular act upstairs was Howard McLeod, back in Dundee after having lived in Yorkshire and the Channel Islands during the 1980s. He had signed a deal, lost the deal and realised that he should come home to Dundee. Ali Napier played with him there in the band McLeod. 'When I was working in Sound Control one day, in walks this bizarre black guy, with his ego preceding him. He said, "My name is McLeod and I'm looking for the best keyboard player in the town." I felt I had to say, "That'll be me then . . . What can I do for you?" So we started writing, recording and gigging.'

Nick's creativity with a club night came through, and the most memorable events for locals weren't the big-name bands. 'We had our themed nights, where everyone would choose a song to cover from a chosen artist – Abba, Blondie, The Human League's *Dare* . . . and our *Top of the Pops* night was particularly popular, with Pan's People including Stewart Clark, Keith Matheson and his brother Alan.'

Alan Matheson is described by everyone who knew him as a 'powerhouse of ideas'. He organised his own club night called Theme Park at the Westie, but was constantly on the lookout for ideas to promote both his brothers' musical endeavours and those of the wider music community.

He was also the first MC for what became another institution, the Groucho's music quiz. Always one for a sense of occasion, Breeks had bid in a charity auction for the jacket that Bamber Gascoigne wore as quizmaster on *University Challenge*. It didn't fit him, but Alan was smaller so was happy to take charge of proceedings. (Alan died in 2002 at the age of forty-two as a result of an accident, but is still remembered for the passion that he brought to everything he tackled.)

'When we gave up the Westie, Nick concentrated more on his considerable culinary talents and I also stepped away for seven years while I concentrated on running nightclubs, but then opened the new Fat Sams Live venue in 2006,' says Gus. 'Fat Sams had been open for fifteen years before I got here, and it was time to resurrect its place on the touring circuit. It has gone from a 500-capacity nightclub, and now over four rooms it's 3500.

'Nothing is ever the same as in the days when things were pretty harum-scarum – we even bounced back from a time when we lost the alcohol licence for a few months. In terms of atmosphere there's been nothing to beat it and it has to be said some of my favourite nights had to be our Mardi Gras with Boogalusa.'

SQUEEZE THE DAY

Dave Oudney painted the sign above the Westport Bar. It's just as well he did a decent job – he would be seeing it on a regular basis for years to come.

He had first picked up an accordion as a child, and like most Scots with a box saw little potential in what it could offer, unless he joined the Jimmy Shand circuit.

'I didn't play at all for ten years, and then at the age of twenty-four, I picked it up again. That break was important as I was looking for a style to play at that point.' Having tried Argentinean tangos and Irish music, Dave heard a Zydeco track on Alexis Korner's radio show in 1979 and immediately bought the album it was from. 'It became a bit of an adventure, as I started visiting Louisiana nearly every year to hear the music, and to buy Cajun accordions.'

From the Bayou to The Bush (the Seagate, not Australia) and in 1989, his band Baton Rouge was in the process of disbanding, leaving Dave in serious need of some new hombres. At one point, he had also had a band with Stewart Ivins, Gus Foy and Tam Parks called Tall in the Saddle, which turned out to have an unfortunate acronym.

There have been many tales of great musical discoveries, but when Dave visited his favourite watering hole, the Tay Bridge Bar, barman Alan Wilson picked up a triangle and added some rhythm to the session going on at the time. Dave noticed and asked if he fancied playing washboard in the new band. 'At first I said, "No, that's too complicated," but six months on I'd been watching the first guy try it and I realised I could do it,' says Alan.

Dave was welcomed back to play at The Bush with Boogalusa, a line-up that also included drummer Rab McGlone, fiddler Stuart Morrison, guitarist Bill Higgins and bass player Ian Sweetman.

With six members crammed into a tiny corner, Alan (or Washie as he has become known) was forced to stand on a shelf designed for a speaker. And they were loud. A few weeks into the residency, there were complaints from people in the flat above and after the council stepped in, they had to leave.

'In a way, it was the best thing that could have happened,' says Alan. 'We had to look around for a new venue and identified the Westie. We agreed a fee with Gus of a fiver each and free drink, but he soon realised that it was going to be cheaper to offer £15 each and four pints – and that's when it was a pound a pint!'

During the first few months, the crowds were worryingly sparse but Gus urged them to hang on in; it was summer and things would get better. He was absolutely right. 'Once the students came back, things really took off and it was packed every night we played. Tuesday nights were queued around the block,' says Dave. 'We recorded a gig in November of 1990, which became the first album *Slave to the Zydeco*. We sold about 500 cassettes, so there was obviously an appetite for what we were doing.'

It was time to get some gigs outside Dundee and after taking cassettes to venues that were on the wish list, there were gigs at the Renfrew Ferry in Glasgow and The Venue in Edinburgh.

'Things started to take off pretty quickly,' says Alan. 'The BBC came to record us for radio and then a TV show called *The Insiders* (co-presented by Gordon Kennedy and Alison Burns) filmed us at the Westie. The first single, "Little Women", was about to come out and Gaelic TV came to film us there too.'

A businessman who had seen a couple of Edinburgh shows funded the recording of an album, no strings attached. 'He wouldn't even take more than a couple of CDs when we offered him a dozen.' The record company, Club, wasn't quite sure what to make of them, says Dave. 'We weren't Celtic and we weren't traditional – that was what they understood – but we were making inroads, so they thought they'd better hold on to us.'

Television invitations kept coming. They became the resident band on *The Funny Farm* on STV and in 1994 received a call to head off to Birmingham to do *Pebble Mill at One*. 'The company said, "How did YOU get that?"' Alan laughs. 'It must have seemed like a dream for an artist of theirs to get exposure like that. I'm pretty sure it came through Andy Kershaw, who had been up to record us – I think his producer worked with someone at Pebble Mill. They phoned me direct and said they would like us to be on.'

They did it and Alan got a £200 fine for having a trailer in the fast lane of a motorway – he did get it back with the next gig money, however.

'I think the strangest TV we did was *The Big Breakfast*,' says Dave. 'They would show up at someone's house at 8am and launch into something. Paul Ross was doing it that day, which was seemingly National Turkey Day. So they went to this family's home near Douglas and knocked at the door. When someone answered, they were given a live turkey each and had to race them in the garden. We were deemed to be ideal background music for this.'

The global nature of the music and the fact that it didn't sit comfortably in any of the conventional traditional genres meant that the band was in demand at festivals. 'We started to go to Shetland early on but we did others in Europe, Ireland and Orkney. Kevin Findlay was now the fiddle player and he and I were the only ones with full-time jobs,' says Alan, who works as a journalist with the *Courier*.

'My shifts at the paper were flexible. I worked all my free time with the band but I did consider taking the leap to becoming a full-time musician. At that time Salsa Celtica, Shooglenifty and the Peatbog Faeries were doing the same circuit as us. There was a thought that we would all make the commitment to do it, but there was a double blow. With four kids under the age of eight it was becoming too difficult for Kevin to go on (he rejoined at a later date, however), then Bill Higgins left to do his own stuff. This was just after the new album was recorded and we couldn't promote it properly.'

Dave says they took a long time to recover after that, especially when it came to replacing Kevin. 'Finding someone who was half as good and was committed to being in the band for any length of time was proving impossible. And, although we found Ralph Teviotdale pretty quickly, it took him a while to find his feet, as he was a rock guitarist. We ended up touring the album but we weren't really firing on all cylinders for that.'

There were personal appearances in record stores to promote the album but with only half a band it never really made an impact. With the worst timing possible, they had a launch at King Tut's in Glasgow on the same night that Phil Collins was in town to launch his new album. 'So you know where the press went. It cost us hundreds and we had three men, no dog, and five people from the record company,' says Alan.

Dave's trips to Louisiana became less frequent but with such specialist equipment it was occasionally required. 'I remember him going off to buy a very particular type of reed,' says Russ Paterson, who is also father of the current bass player Steve Paterson. 'He was living above Forbes music shop in the Nethergate, and subsequently found out that he could have just gone downstairs to get it.'

A washboard isn't something that can be found easily and Alan's are sourced from an importer in North London. When the band played the Ceilidh Tent at T in the Park, Alan could compare washboards with his opposite number in the Scooby Doo Orchestra, a young musician by the name of KT Tunstall, long before her breakthrough.

'The biggest gig we ever played was Hogmanay 1998 in Edinburgh,' says Alan. 'We were on the Waverley Stage, looking down Princes Street and across Waverley Bridge. There were tens of thousands of people there and when we looked to the left, we saw we were on a huge screen. There were people standing on bus shelters, people up lampposts. Unfortunately everyone was so packed in together, there was no room to dance. As we played over the bells, snowflakes were starting to fall – it was spine-tingling stuff.'

Back on home turf, the Tuesday night residency at the Westie was becoming a spectacular, especially with the annual Mardi Gras. In the kitchen, Nick would be cooking up gumbo and the room was decorated with theatrical props, instruments and giant cactuses. There were other bands on the bill on these nights and tickets would sell out so quickly that they had to move them to larger venues in subsequent years. 'It really felt like the ceiling was going to collapse in that room. It legally held about eighty – but there were about 200 jammed in there.'

The tales from the road of pure cheek are many, with one from Bath summing up the fun they had on tour. 'We were playing a pub,' says Alan, 'but they had decided to accommodate us in another pub they owned across the road. We would be sleeping IN the bar. They had obviously never met us before. So, with the gear stored in the pub we were playing, it's party time for the boys in the sleeping quarters. There was a loud knock on the door, which caught Rab in the middle of pouring a nip and he mumbled something like, "Just getting some peanuts, mate." The guy said, "Couldn't care less, mate, I'm the cleaner. I'll come back later . . ."

'Then, when we go back to the pub, all our gear had been shifted to the cellar! I start to see the guys carrying Rab's drums out without the cases. They come later clinking very slightly on their way back to the van.'

Alan believes the band has survived twenty-one years by being true to what they have always done. They are the first choice for organisers looking for a good party but as Dave says, 'We do love it when people dance. It's not just party music but it's definitely dance music.'

MOVING ON FROM THE RAN DAN

The statement was very simple: 'The band feels that, artistically, their material is best served by undertaking separate projects.' And that, in 1989, was the end of the band called Danny Wilson.

'I honestly can't remember the pressures that broke the band up,' says Gary. 'The major issue for me was that I wanted it to be a vehicle for the music I was making – and as the band got bigger, Ged and Kit wanted to contribute songs. It's not that I didn't like what they were writing, it was the fact that there were going to be fewer songs on the records. We had so much going for us that, maybe in hindsight, it would have been better to just take a break and go back to it, but when you're inside you don't see it like that.'

Ged sensed the unrest that was happening. 'There was so much creativity going on, and with only one record every two years and twelve tracks between three, that wasn't going to satisfy anyone. There was also the reaction to the second record. Virgin America didn't want to release it.'

Kit found himself in a difficult position. 'Gary and Ged were being told that I was planning a solo career – and that wasn't true. There was a real divide-and-conquer thing going on and I'm amazed we came out the other side as well as we did.'

By 1989, Kit was still only twenty-two, a fact that wasn't lost on Ged. 'There was no apprenticeship for Kit, he was whisked off his feet and straight into a record deal at seventeen. Gary and I had a run-up to things with the time in London and it was strange enough for us with limos picking us up when we couldn't even afford taxi fares, so it must have been doubly so for him.

'For me, I was also in the middle of brothers. I know from having brothers of my own that they speak to each other in a completely different way. It could be difficult to be in the middle of that at times, but I love them both to this day. Once the decision was made, there was a huge sense of relief: I don't have to be in Danny Wilson anymore.'

Kit remembers a difficult few days before they were due to go out on tour in 1989. 'The budgets were tighter so we had to strip the band down. Everyone had to be multi-instrumentalists, really. One reviewer thought they were criticising us when they said, "They even had the audacity to drag out a tuba." Chris Marra was doing all that AND played a tuba – how brilliant is that?!

'We were supposed to have a five-day break and then head off to Australia, Japan and Europe, but the roadies were acting rather strangely.'

The bombshell was dropped the day before. There was to be no tour, just TV shows in Germany and Belgium.

Shortly after that, Kit did what he needed to do, and got away from the situation. 'I went AWOL. At least I tried to but I got nabbed,' he laughs. 'I decided that I really wanted to see my mum and dad, and as I was walking up their path, my brother Scott spotted me. He had been doing some tour managing for us and the manager had phoned him about something else. He hadn't actually realised I had gone.'

While Ged made the trip to Dundee to propose to his girlfriend Tricia, Kit told Gary that he felt he couldn't carry on with the band. 'Ged came down and we got his brilliant news about them getting married and then we had to speak to him about what we had discussed,' says Kit.

Although the press officer was happy to put out a statement to say they were splitting because of height and weight differences, it was stopped at a higher level.

Gary was picked up as a solo artist on another Virgin label and went about making his solo debut, *Ten Short Songs About Love.* 'From a song point of view, it was the Danny Wilson record that I wanted to make. Ged and Kit both played on it – there was never any animosity.'

Although Gary put his 'heart and soul' into the album, it didn't sell nearly as well as the Danny Wilson records. 'At the time I had started to write what would have been the second solo album, but I was also asked to go to LA to write for an album project, which in the end didn't happen.' It did introduce him to Eric Pressly, however. 'We were born two days apart on opposite sides of the world, but in terms of the music we had grown up loving, it was a parallel existence.'

What was to be the second Gary Clark album became a band project. Eric brought in a drummer and Gary asked Neil McColl of The Bible to become involved. 'I had a realisation that people seemed to invest in bands and when I broached it with the record company, they thought it was a great idea.'

They were called Napoleon Starfish 'for about a week and a half', says Gary. 'I think some gigs came up and we had to think of something really quickly, but the name didn't stick.' It became King L, and the *Great Day For Gravity* album, released in 1995, was well received but didn't sell well. 'I think people who liked Danny Wilson found the slightly harder edge to some of the stuff – and the rock guitar – a bit hard to take. It was an amazing band live. I wish we had more live recordings.'

King L were dropped, but Gary was asked by Eric to work on some tracks for his girlfriend Keely Hawkes (sister of Chesney). The demos found their way into the hands of a DJ at a show called *Morning Becomes Eclectic* on KCRW from Santa Monica. 'It turned out that because the show plays anything and everything they like, including demos, A&R men listen to it.'

After dropping Gary from the label, Virgin were back on the phone to ask about this new project they had heard about. 'Eric was keen for the project to become a band with the three of us. I wasn't sure but I went ahead with it, so Transister was signed by Interscope in the US and Virgin for the rest of the world. I think everyone thought "Look Who's Perfect Now" was going to be a huge smash, but it wasn't,' he laughs.

They started work on a second album in LA, but for Gary it was like 'pulling teeth – everyone was going in different directions'. There was also the promotion aspect, which finally hit home when the band were heading to a festival in the far north of Sweden. 'It took two days to get there on a bus. I was so tense, thinking, "I just want to get off this bus and DO something!"'

Gary went back to London for a break and gaining some clarity through distance, decided to leave the band and concentrate on full-time writing and production. The studio had always been a wee bit of a playground, however.

'We played everything on the Danny Wilson records,' says Ged, 'maybe not always proficiently, but we were picking up instruments and finding out how to make a sound. However, those songs still sound perfectly whole with just an acoustic guitar.' That messing about with sounds put Ged in good stead for his next incarnation as a composer of music for computer games. 'I did some live stuff with Eddi Reader but it was a bit strange really, in that it was the first time I had done anything on that scale that wasn't Danny Wilson. They were all great people but I felt what a lot of musicians must feel – going to the four corners of the globe with a bunch of people you have no shared experiences with. There wasn't that feeling of a band really pulling for one another. It was a job.'

Setting up his own studio in Dundee, he concentrated on games music for a while, a band being the furthest thing from his mind. 'And when my first son Jack came along (the studio is called Jack's Hoose), I decided I was going to be at home. It was ten years before I went out and played live again.'

For Kit, the contrast of being inside the bubble of the record contract to outside was the most marked. 'It was a total change of life. Where Gary stayed within the music industry, I went to do what I wanted to do while being on the Broo. The woman there told me that music isn't a real job and offered something else in entertainment – maybe a bouncer? She said, "You could still talk to people around music if you did that." '

Sharing a flat with his brother Scott on Broughty Ferry Road, he made his first EP, *Lovedung*. With some interest, he was back in the studio with Howard Gray, taking Chris Marra and Stewart Clark with him. By that time Howard had Metropolis studios and was working with Apollo 440. 'I went back to Dundee, listened to what we had done there and decided to put out the original myself.'

Shortly after doing some work on *Ten Short Songs*, Kit moved to Budapest briefly. 'My girlfriend at that time had a chance to work with the British Council there. My pal used his air miles to get me a return flight to Budapest. It was ridiculously cheap to live there at the time, so if Gary sent me £5 a week from the session fee then I could stay there for two years! I also did some illustration work for local magazines. Getting some distance from the whole situation was probably a good thing at the time.'

Unlike other bands of the time, there is no consideration of wheeling out Danny Wilson for the quick retro buck. 'We may do something together again in the future,' says Ged, 'but it will be something new.'

TENNIS THE MENACE

If *Raintown* had established Ricky Ross and his band Deacon Blue, then the album *When the World Knows Your Name* had something of a prophetic

St Andrew napalms the
White Heather Club.

Clark's Commandos record at Inner City
Sound before heading to London. From
left: Gary Clark, Derek Thomson, Brian
McDermott and Ged Grimes.

Mafia at the time of the 'Rescue Me' single.
Back from left: Allan McGlone, Gordon
Dougall, Gerry McGrath, Donny Coutts.
Front: Peter McGlone and Dougie Martin.

Groucho's poster (signed by Billy)
for the gig that was cancelled,
heralding the end of the
Mackenzie/Rankine partnership.

Nick Wright's flyer for the first event by Dance Factory Promotions.

The souvenir Unlucky Bag on sale at the 'last' Woollen Mill gig in 1983.

St Andrew and the Woollen Mill, backstage with John Cooper Clarke at Dundee University (front). From left: Gus Foy, Chris Marra, Jonathan Ogilvie (Jog), Michael Marra, Stewart Ivins, Andy Pelc.

Danny Wilson's 'Mary's Prayer' which cracked the US.

Almost there: Sweden Through the Ages in the Fat Sams foyer. From left: Brian McDermott, Mike Knight, Steve Knight and Lloyd Anderson.

Taking on the menfolk. Blon a Gael from left: Jae Austin, Shirley Potts, Helen Forbes and Karen Valentine.

Deacon Blue, after selling out the reopening of the Caird Hall in 1988. From left: Jim Prime, Lorraine McIntosh, Ricky Ross, Graeme Kelling, Dougie Vipond and Ewen Vernel with council representatives.

Indie kids The Sandflowers at an open-air concert in Dudhope Park. From left: Craig McNeil, Roy Anderson, Kenny Gall and Alan Cormack.

The Penny Dainties backstage at Channel 4. From left: Derek Thomson, Gregor Philp, Caragh McKay (deputising for Tricia Grimes), Jane Grimes, Alison Burns, Brian McDermott and Colin Davidson.

© JOE ROZSKOWSKI

Boogalusa live at Dundee Blues
Bonanza 2011. From left: Rab McGlone,
Alan Wilson, Steve Paterson, Dave
Oudney and Kevin Findlay.

© COLIN DAVIDSON

Sunday night in the Westport Bar and
Kit Clark and Colin Davidson (both Swiss
Family Orbison at the time) entertain the
Westport Bar crowd as The Mudskippers.

© RAB ALEXANDER

Ali Napier rehearses with Mafia.

© GED GRIMES

Modern-day glamour and nostalgic sounds
with the Penny Dainties.

Musician, composer and Billy Mackenzie's trusted collaborator Steve Aungle.

Spare Snare going places. From left: Barry Gibson, Graeme Ogston, Alan Cormack, Jan Burnett and Ross Matheson.

Jimmy Deuchar guests with Havana Swing at McGonagall's, from left: Alan Breitenbach, Jimmy Deuchar and Kevin Murray.

Stuart Clumpas at Balado for T in the Park 1999.

© DONNY COUTTS

The latest stage as Donny Coutts, Drew Larg and Dougie Martin play together in The Bond.

© DONNY COUTTS

Alan Gorrie, still touring with the Average White Band.

© P3 MUSIC

Alison Burns realises her dream as a jazz singer.

© ROBERT ADAM

Voice of his generation, Dave Webster.

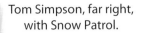
Tom Simpson, far right,
with Snow Patrol.

The Hazey Janes, from left:
Liam Brennan, Alice Marra,
Andrew Mitchell and
Matthew Marra.

The singular voice of Michael
Marra still rings true.

Guitar man Stevie
Anderson.

Early days for The View.
From left: Kieren Webster,
Pete Reilly, Kyle Falconer
and Steven Morrison (Mo)
at The Windmill Bar.

© TWO THUMBS

Keeping it local: The
View's Record Store Day
2011 anthem, 'I Need That
Record' with Groucho's on
the cover.

© 1965 RECORDS

Crowd pleasers The View
on the main stage at T in
the Park .

© LOUISE WILSON

title. With a major European tour, Ricky wanted to support someone who had been an inspiration to him back in Dundee. 'I had met Ricky much earlier,' says Michael Marra. 'He was kind enough to write to me after a Gaels Blue Orchestra event and I wrote back to encourage him.'

Ricky invited Michael to support them, and he agreed. 'I also thought it would be good for me to try to write on tour. I always wrote in my studio, nowhere else. In a way it was an attempt to get past all the neurotic conditions I need when I write. Coffee, fags, pencils and paper – a pencil to be used for the first two drafts and pen for the third.'

Outside of that comfort zone, there was certainly inspiration from the surroundings. 'The Berlin Wall had just come down. There was a quiet mayhem with people treating those who had come from the East horribly. One night in Frankfurt, someone was thrown from the top of the building – this is someone who got through the wall when freedom had finally come and was then thrown to their death. That became a song called "Lieblings in the Absence of Love".'

Inspiration also came closer to home, as Michael wrote 'The One and Only Anne Marie', about a girl who had seen every Deacon Blue gig. 'That might sound like a small subject but I found it tough going – they have big emotions, these songs.'

A pre-gig stroll in Milan brought some welcome light relief, however. Michael had arrived by train from Paris early in the morning and was walking across a piazza when he saw two women walking towards him. 'I thought, "I know that woman – she comes from Blairgowrie," so I'm already giving her the nod. She acknowledged this so I stopped to speak. I say that I'm surprised to see her here, all the time trying to think of what context I know the woman in. Had I met her at the berries or something?'

Eventually Michael blurted out something in Italian, then French, and suddenly realised he was chatting with tennis champion Martina Navratilova. 'I must have looked so flustered that Judy Nelson started laughing and consequently Martina melted slightly. "Please forgive me, I didn't recognise you, are you in Milan for a tournament?" She said she was and I told her I was there to perform. "I'm a musician. Would you like to come to the show?" She looked dubious but Judy seemed quite positive and asked where I was playing. I said, "Club Rolling Stone – so, will I put you on the guest list?" And Martina said yes. So I went back and told the guys that Martina was on the guest list. She had beautiful posture. I don't meet many people like that. I found her to be beautiful and once she melted she was very nice to me.'

The songs for *Pax Vobiscum*, which included 'Lieblings' and 'Anne Marie', were written during that tour. Recorded at a gig in the Tron in Glasgow, the band of Chris Marra, Gregor Philp, Calum Mackenzie, Kit Clark and Lloyd Anderson had one take at every number.

As the 1990s progressed, Michael set about making another studio album with Allan McGlone and Chris Marra producing. 'Posted Sober was a complicated record and took a long time.' Michael left the choice of songs to Alan and Chris and wonders how they 'got so clever'.

'Actually, I don't know how I got so clever to just leave it to them. They got it absolutely right. It's a proper collection that travels through as one piece of music.'

Chris is always the test for Michael's material. 'I never know if anything is good or not. I'll play something to him and he'll say, "Dinna play that in public … It would be a bit unfair to sing that to people. Why don't you use that one? That's not too bad." That's about as good as it's going to get with Christopher. He's trustworthy and he's always right. He can think of what kind of record it can be, from the roughest demo. He's interested in that sort of thing. I am up to a point; I'm just more interested in writing.'

NOWT AS DEAR AS FOLK

Michael Marra once said that when Hen's Teeth split up, Dougie McLean went off around the world – and he stayed in one room. McLean was taking musicians with him, however, and showing them that some parts of the music business were actually quite respectful of musicians and treated them well. Ali Napier was one of those.

'Working in Sound Control was a dream job. Getting cheap gear, trying all the new gear, and a chance to meet everyone. There was an element of shop loyalty with Sound Control or Rainbow, but there was always some crossover. It was my first proper job but I was never really cut out to be a salesman. I was one of the two or three go-to guys for keyboards – not many people do keyboards because they're expensive, and not really very portable!'

One regular customer was Dougie McLean. Ali first met him when 'Caledonia' had taken off, but when he was looking for a new keyboard player, Mike Ward had recommended the Sound Control guy.

'My first gig with him was the Glasgow Royal Concert Hall, during Celtic Connections. I had had two nights' rehearsal for the biggest gig I'd ever done. No wonder I got a nosebleed ten minutes before going on.'

Ali toured with Dougie pretty solidly for five years in Europe and the US. 'It was such a different world. The folk scene can be quite lucrative, as fans will pay money to see good traditional music and buy merchandise, particularly at Dougie's level. There were proper dressing rooms, lights, PAs, hotels and great guys to work with.'

Ali had now tapped into the traditional circuit and also worked with Freda Morrison (BBC Scotland) and through her met Paul Anderson, a traditional fiddle player.

Heading back to university in 1996, Ali was officially 'a made guy' in Dundee music, when he was invited to join Mafia. 'What a singer Dougie was – back in the day you couldn't watch him without your chin hitting the floor. I had three years playing with them and it was just hilarious. Dougie once counted how many people had gone through that band and I was member number fifty-eight . . .'

A WALK IN THE PARK

For the majority of bands who blossomed in the 1980s, the dance culture of the 1990s was a time to retreat and ride out the guitar-free zone. That wasn't an option for Dance Factory Promotions, but the shift in culture meant it would have to look at its public image.

'When Dance Factory started, the DJs did play dance music, but it was indie dance – things like The Cure and New Order,' says Stuart Clumpas. 'Then Lil' Louis came along and everything changed – rave became dance. I remember The Almighty asked us how they could be promoted by something called Dance Factory. To them dance was Ecstasy and beep noises and the absolute antithesis of rock, so it was a good time to change the name to DF Concerts.

'Things had been changing as the eighties came to a close. My girl-friend Judith [now his wife] was promoting bands like Texas and Deacon Blue in England and I was managing Love and Money, while still a director of Fat Sams. Things had stalled in Dundee too – I thought it was going to build on the vibe that had happened, but it didn't.'

So, when Glasgow became City of Culture in 1990, Stuart and Judith opened King Tut's Wah Wah Hut and although Judith was managing it, Stuart was spending so much time in the city that it seemed the right time to go.

Stuart had been sure that Scotland could support a music festival, even with the weather. 'We thought we could have our own Glastonbury. The great outdoors in Scotland is greater than most countries and there was that fierce pride in Scotland.

'Tennent's had already been involved in music, sponsoring Tennent's Live, but they decided they wanted to start promoting huge acts. I told them that a festival would be a much better thing for them, creating something rather than just presenting.' They weren't convinced at first, but when the respected Irish promoter Denis Desmond said that would be the best way to go, they realised Stuart's instincts had been right.

'The first thought was that Loch Lomond was the place and we shopped around for a bill. We went back to them after three days with acts like INXS and Morrissey and they were impressed enough to give us the go-ahead. By that time we had lost Loch Lomond, so we decided to look at the next year. I had my eye on Strathclyde Park.'

They could afford to lose a certain amount of money before going bankrupt, and they lost that amount. Stuart remembers driving along towards Strathclyde Park, thinking, 'You've spent the past three months digging your grave and next week you're going to jump in it ... You d*ckhead.'

However, on Saturday 30 July and Sunday 31 July, 1994, the first T in the Park took place, with Cypress Hill headlining on Saturday and Primal Scream on Sunday. Other acts included Björk, Del Amitri, Teenage Fanclub, Rage Against the Machine and The Saw Doctors. Day tickets were £23.50 with a weekend deal for £39.

'There was a great amount of support,' says Stuart. 'The next year we got it right and sold out. By year three we were financially back on track. I genuinely thought that bringing the festival close to a city was the best option – I really didn't think Scotland would want a camping festival. I got that bit wrong,' he laughs. 'The next year we moved to Balado.'

Seven years after the first T in the Park, Stuart was out. He moved to New Zealand. 'For me the buzz had gone out of it. I never started doing it just for the money. Also my health wasn't great. I had developed Crohn's Disease and had half my gut taken away in 1997 – stress isn't great for that condition. My children were four and two and New Zealand seemed like a good place to raise them.' He says he knew certain elements of the press would point to another reason for leaving: a burglary in the days after T in the Park 2000, when thousands of pounds in charity cash raised by the festival was stolen from his home, but one aspect of Stuart's success has been not listening to those who find a negative spin on events.

'I love that T is getting better and better,' he says. 'It's a great pleasure to go back and see what you started. While I'm a Glaswegian I have a much stronger affinity to Dundee. I spent much more of my adult life there and it's great to see how things are moving on.'

DIFFERENT DRUM

Although dance had taken a hold, bands in Dundee were drawing on a range of musical styles to create something of their own. The Sandflowers had scoffed at The Hate Foundation, who seemed to trump them for lack of technical ability, but the band were playing long after Craig McNeil had departed for London.

They had started playing in 1989 with Graeme Ogston, Ross Turriff, Paul Munro and Graeme Watt, who now runs Seagate Studios. 'The gear we had wasn't great – it would detune if the temperature shifted by one per cent,' says Graeme Ogston. 'In June 1990, we were asked to support Teenage Fanclub, who weren't a big band at the time, but told us they were off to the States. When they came back, they signed to Creation.

'There was obviously an interest in what was going on at the time here. Out of the blue, I got a call from Geffen Records asking for demos, as they'd seen a review in *Music Week*. By 1995, though, we felt we had taken it as far as we could. I was working in Groucho's and started a project called September 70 which was mainly instrumental – I was probably DJing more at the time.'

Alan Cormack was still intent on making loud noises and scoffing at what was seen as the acceptable face of the Dundee music scene at the Westie. 'I really think there was a split with the indie kids at Bar Chevrolet, where I also worked. That came down to even having five-a-side football teams that played each other. It crossed over once or twice – when Teenage Fanclub played and the night Alan Matheson walked into Chevy's. It was unusual to cross over into each other's territory.'

Alan met Barry Gibson, who had played with Better Backwards and the Beaver Sisters and said that he wanted to start something grungy and noisy. That became Muppet Mule.

Jan Burnett was one of the DJs in Bar Chevrolet. 'He said to me, "I'm putting out a single – I'll give you a copy." I didn't hold out much hope for liking it. Jan was a guy who I always thought was a bit strange. He came across as a boy who should still be wearing shorts and his mum taking him to school – and I still have that opinion in some ways. Not the coolest of guys, put it that way . . .'

Jan had been part of the Tayside Bar scene, playing with Brian Hayes in Let's Evolve. 'I was making recordings all the time, usually with Mike Kane in his kitchen. He was quite an inspiration for *not* learning guitar. He's a great guitarist, but his deal was that he could almost make his own chords out of it.'

'I was DJing in various places for about nine years and sometimes worked as a DJ duo with Graham Anderson. We were the first DJs at King Tut's, because of the Dance Factory connection.'

Still messing about with recordings, Jan put together a track under the name the White Leather Club. 'It was called "Shandy on the Rocks" and was me doing a rather crap rap over a Jimmy Shand backing track. It was a one-sided seven-inch single, with a hand-painted postcard. Graham and I toured Scotland on a wee camping trip, going to radio stations to hand out copies of the single along with cans of shandy.'

The 500 singles were handed out rather than sold. One was sent to a label in Minneapolis, who contacted Jan to say how much they liked it. By that time he had also completed the first Spare Snare single. (The name came from a night when The Darling Buds played at the Dance Factory. They had soundchecked but hadn't moved all of the drum kit. It stayed there when another band's gear was moved on, prompting Nick Wright to comment, 'Look at that – they've got a spare snare.') The US label liked the Spare Snare stuff too, asking for 100 copies to distribute; unaware that Jan had only printed 110. They were keen to have the band over to play live.

'Of course, there was no band,' says Jan. 'That forced me to do something very out-of-character – talk to people that I only vaguely knew to put a band together. I went loads of gigs and spoke to Alan, who came as a duo with Barry. Paul Esposito joined us on guitar and that was it.'

When Alan eventually got the first Spare Snare single he was surprised. 'I really thought it would be like the Pet Shop Boys, who he was really into, but I thought it was brilliant. He was making plans for a US tour and asked if I wanted to join the band. Well, yes!'

There was one warm-up gig at the art college coffee bar, but the first time that Spare Snare played for any length of time as a band was on an American tour.

'The first gig was in Minneapolis and I was amazed,' says Alan. 'Sixty people there and none of them could possibly be friends or family. The only reason for being there is liking the record. We worked our way back across to the east coast and at the final gig in Cambridge, Massachusetts, there were about 250 people. Back in Dundee it was thirty people and we kind of knew them all.'

The band were given enough in a publishing deal to make the first album, still recording at home (releases went out on Jan's Chute Records), hire a proper van and do a UK tour. There was a second US tour, playing New York and Boston, and around that time they also supported Placebo. Alan says, 'Brian Molko came up to us and said, "Hey, you guys are from Dundee – so am I!" And I thought, "Aye right . . ." He said, "I am – my mum's from the Hilltoon," and then I thought, "Yeah, I believe it now."'

When they reached the third album, Paul had left and the band was down to a trio. 'If someone had wanted to sign us at this point, it would have cost them a lot of money,' says Jan. 'We were all grown-up with jobs and mortgages, so we decided to do it for fun and split all the writing credits – and that's how it's been from then.'

Even those Dundee exports who didn't fit the blue-eyed soul genre that he shunned needed to do a lot of impress Alan. 'We thought we were the first Dundee band to get a John Peel session but The Associates did one. We argued that they weren't living in Dundee when they got it and they're not all from Dundee – anything to justify it!' he says. 'I was never a big fan of The Associates at the time – it was only later I realised how good they were. When I was working in Bar Chevrolet, Billy would come in quite regularly and order a cappuccino. I'd be bursting to tell somebody I'm serving Billy Mackenzie.'

YELLOW CAR IN GERMANY

Billy was supporting young bands whenever he could, and at the beginning of the 1990s helped out a young musician who would go on to pay it forward fifteen years later. Grant Dickson, now manager of The View, was in a band called Yellow Car, who played at an event called Five Live at Fat Sams. 'I think Marshal Curtis played and maybe The Sandflowers,' he says. 'We had just done a demo at Seagate and were sending them off with cheeky wee letters. There was some great feedback but nothing was happening. Billy Mackenzie was down at the gig, and came up to say he really liked what we were doing. He was working in Germany at the time but asked us to get a copy of the demo to him.'

Grant went off to university in Aberdeen with his friend Blair, also one of his band mates. A poster went up in the union one day which said: 'Do you know any of these people? Phone this number to your advantage.'

'It was everybody in the band,' says Grant. 'We called the number and it was a record label in Germany who had heard the tape through Billy and wanted to sign us. So we chucked the maths and engineering and headed off to Germany, touring around Europe with Green Day, Nirvana and Supergrass.'

After one album on the German label, Geffen Records came in and offered a deal. 'The guitarist said he wouldn't sign unless he got £70,000 in his hand from any advance. There was some financial pressure at home and he had been offered the chance to join the police force. It was all handled so badly because we didn't have a manager. That's one thing I tell The View now – I became a manager because I know every way to f*ck it up. I know how mistakes are made.'

Grant came back to the UK around 1995 and started to learn the business. 'I thought I needed to wise up and find out what was happening in the minds of record labels. The label I was working for looked after a band called The Porcupine Tree, bringing them up from nothing to a band with a huge underground following.'

CHATTANOOGA CHEW CHEW

'It's true to say that no one has played better since Jimmy Deuchar,' says Martin Taylor. 'But it was more than that. He was a great writer and orchestrator too.' The jazz world lost Jimmy Deuchar in 1993 at the age of sixty-three. As well as working with local bands such as Havana Swing, he was in demand as a player and arranger until his health deteriorated.

He had also been, in a strange way, encouraging of his sons' musical ambitions. Simon Ciampi Deuchar recalls that, out of the blue, his dad would say: 'Tomorrow night, Angus Hotel. Put a nice shirt and tie on and come along and play with me at my gig.'

'He never had a bad word to say about anyone,' says Simon. 'He realised that people had failings and sometimes he had to make concessions, particularly with the kind of people who are attracted to the music business. He was actually a man of few words.'

His most important piece of advice to his sons was, 'Timing. That's the most important thing. Don't spend all your time getting your act together then miss the train.'

Dundee's swing trio the Penny Dainties had been together for ten years in 1996 and it was time to record an album. A few bottles of wine later, the trio were in the bathroom of Ged and Tricia Grimes' home, recording vocals.

'Always a good acoustic,' laughs Alison. 'We were so lucky to have such incredible players to help us. I think it was the last session that the fantastic accordionist John Huband did.'

When the album was launched, the gig was in the Westport Bar. 'We decided to have a wee bit of fun with it. The guys – Chris Marra, Calum Mckenzie and Mark Hunter – dressed up in our frocks and turbans, with plenty of lippy, and we dressed as them and picked up the instruments, then we all mimed to a couple of tracks.'

Mark Hunter left in 1997 to work on the QE2, so they were on the hunt for a good jazz drummer. 'I had been to see Martin Taylor play his *Spirit of Django* set and liked what the drummer was doing, not knowing at that time it was Martin's son.'

The Penny Dainties approached James Taylor, who was drumming with a range of bands at the time. 'He said yes, but then he cancelled on us as he had been offered a cruise, and set us up with another drummer. But then his cruise fell through and he called us back. I told him it was too late, but he told me it was OK, he had called and cancelled the other guy!'

James joined the band, and too not long after, he and Alison were a couple, marrying in 2004. Martin Taylor took a greater interest in the band, which led to some anxiety for a guitarist. Steve Gaughan had been working with Lorna Bannon since she left Shakatak and had a few dance hits under the name of Lorna B, but he was looking forward to playing some jazz. 'It was a set of around twenty songs and there were a few solos which guitar wasn't right for, so when Jack Emblow came in to play accordion it was just amazing.

'I had a couple of solos and, being the thief that I am, I had pinched some bits from Martin Taylor and patched them together with some of my own stuff. We walked on stage, and who was sitting in the front row – Martin Taylor. My solo wasn't for about half an hour, and all that time I was sweating, thinking, what am I going to play, what am I going to play? Eventually I realised I would just have to play it as planned. I played it OK in that I didn't make any mistakes. When we were backstage after-wards, Martin approached me and told me that he had enjoyed my playing. I said, "You should have – half of it was yours." And all he said was, "Where do you think I get my stuff from? Everybody does it." What a gentleman.'

GREAT CRACK ON THE PAVEY

The 'farewell' gig in 1983 came complete with souvenir St Andrew and the Woollen Mill Unlucky Bags (containing clothes pegs and money-off vouchers, mainly). Since then, Andy Pelc had made occasional appear-ances as St Andrew, but it was *The Word on the Pavey* album in 1995 that finally brought the American Dundonian to the attention of a wider Scottish audience.

Written by Andy with Michael Marra, the sessions went on late into the night, as Michael's daughter Alice remembers. 'My brother Matthew and I would hear him arriving in the middle of the night – he'd prob-ably been away fishing – and they would start writing. The laughter that came from my dad's studio was incredible. We would just think, "I canna wait to hear this when it's finished."'

Andy describes the album as a monumental job and was surprised by the following that it received. 'People obviously got a laugh from it but it was more than that – there was great playing on it. There was a lot more going on than just a wee daft comedy record.'

Peter McGlone was involved in the marketing of the record, which they decided to only sell (at first) through the famous peh shop Wallace's Land O'Cakes and Dundee's chipper of note, the Deep Sea. There were television appearances and the support of the press, including Tom Shields through his Diary in the *Herald*.

Michael Marra calls the album, 'an awful lot of mischief – healthy mischief and great fun. The best part of the experience was writing the glossary. Some of these words hadn't been written down previously so the fun was in getting a spelling. We decided on *pussait* for an annoyance, a hassle. It may not have been right but we fancied starting an argument about how it should be spelled.'

Janice Forsyth on Radio Scotland had been a supporter of St Andrew for many years. 'I was out fishing in the River Tay one day and my mobile phone rings,' Andy recalls. 'It's Janice's producer saying, "Are you listening to the radio just now Andy?" I told him I was kinda in the middle of a river, but he still carried on. "Would you like to do a wee live link as St Andrew with our guest, who's a fan?" I said I couldn't but asked who the guest was. "Rolf Harris," he said. Now I'm a huge fan of Rolf, but I was fishing and St Andrew doesn't fish.'

Stuart McHardy, well versed in the importance of the Scots language and former director of the Scots Language Resource Centre, says, 'I don't know Andy well, but I do know he's a genius. The night *Word on the Pavey* was released there was a wee gig at the Printmakers' Workshop in the Seagate. I was involved and did the first half. The second half was going to be Mick and Andy Pelc. I had the first album, which I thought was OK, so I didn't know what to expect. Mick did a short set and then he introduces Andy – now he's not a wee guy, but that night he's wearing platforms, so he's a giant.

'He looked enormous on stage, but it was more to do with the transformation that happened rather than the height. I had never laughed as much in my life and I haven't since. My ribs were sore. I've never come across anyone who can affect an audience like Andy Pelc.

'The thing about *Pavey* is it's not just Dundonian, it's Scottish. I think it's one of the great Scottish works of the twentieth century.'

The album came at a particularly busy time for Michael, with work on *Posted Sober* and a Rep production called *The Mill Lavvies* going on simultaneously. 'They all got finished, but none of us were speaking to each other at the end – well Christopher and I never fell out. It was just too much at once and absence for a wee while in those circumstances can be a helpful thing.'

Liz Lochhead, who has worked closely with Michael over the years, is similarly convinced of its worth as a Scots-language work, saying it made 'an interesting read' as well as something to listen to, and Celtic Connections invited him to perform in 2009, with his Rare Wee Helps (Michael Marra and Kevin Murray).

Sue Wilson, reviewing a December 2008 show in Edinburgh, applauded the song 'The World is Phuhl o' a Number o' Things' as a '. . . hilariously extended non sequitur comprising seemingly random lists of foodstuffs, buildings, modes of transport etc, sewn together with a gift for rhyme which elsewhere, cherishably, paired "jannie" with "Modigliani".'

'When the CD was on sale in Groucho's there was one of those promotional stands on the counter,' says Andy. 'A lassie called Ted Rogers was working there at the time and glanced across at a guy who was looking at the cover. She said, "Sum pus, eh?" To me that says everything you need to know about it.'

AT THE EDGE OF THE WORLD

Jim Mackenzie found the lifeless body of his son Billy in the garden shed behind his home on 22 January 1997. Jim had been trying to get help for his son in the weeks leading up to this. There had already been a suspected overdose on New Year's Eve, although Billy insisted he had taken too many sleeping pills mistakenly.

With no idea of what had been happening in Dundee, Steve Aungle had last seen him a week before, when a publishing deal with Sony was signed. 'Billy looked terrible,' recalls Steve. 'He looked pale and weary. I asked him what was wrong but he said he just had a dose of the flu.' Once the papers were signed, there was no celebration, Billy saying that he didn't feel up to it. 'He walked away and after about 100 yards or so, he stopped and turned. He gave me a wave and I waved back. I never saw him again.'

It had been an eventful time for the new musical partnership. By 1990, Billy was living in Hampstead, signed to Circa Records, while Steve Aungle was in a shabby council flat in Stockwell. Although the Edinburgh recordings in 1986 hadn't been satisfactory to Steve, the experience of working with Billy was something he was happy to repeat. 'I soon had my equipment installed in the Hampstead flat and before too long Billy appeared, having just returned from a walk on Hampstead Heath with his whippets. Some of the material we worked on ended up on the *Outernational* album, which initially suffered the same fate as his previous album *The Glamour Chase*, and was shelved by Circa when the label was in trouble.'

The relationship with Circa over, Billy went home, now to Auchterhouse, just outside Dundee. 'I went to visit him there,' says Steve, 'and the fact that he wasn't signed to a label didn't appear to be having any effect on his enthusiasm for making music. I was only up in Dundee for a few days, on a visit from London where I was still living, but I left with rough demos of two new tracks, an instrumental called "A Mood for All Seasons" and a song called "At the Edge of the World". I told Billy I would work on them and return in a few months.'

When Billy moved to Edinburgh in 1994, Steve decamped and they shared a two-bedroom flat on Great King Street. It was Billy, Steve and the whippets, Drummond and Sophie. 'She was a human in a dog's body,' says Steve of Sophie. 'She didn't accept me at first and expressed this by defecating in my bedroom repeatedly. It was no use closing the door – she could open anything. But early one morning she entered my room and got into my bed. She nuzzled up against me and I knew she had relented. The defecation stopped immediately.'

Steve had a piano at his sister's Edinburgh home which made the move into the flat. 'We worked very hard – sometimes doing fourteen-hour days – and it wasn't uncommon for Billy to wake me up during the night to start working on an idea that had just come to him.'

Later that year, armed with new material, it was back to London to get on the trail of a record deal, with Steve in Chiswick and Billy staying with a friend in a small flat in Notting Hill. 'They had frequent blazing rows in that confined space and Billy would turn up on my doorstep with a huge suitcase, saying, "Can I come and stay here for a while, Steve?" But he would always go back.'

They continued to write songs, and in November of that year set themselves up in a flat in West Kensington and found a manager who was confident of securing a deal. He duly did, bringing Nude Records on board in September 1996.

Steve detected a flatness in Billy's response to the deal, putting it down to the fact that he had gone through this process on several occasions in the past and knowing it didn't mean everything would necessarily work out well. The following month, they started recording in Red Bus, Martyn Ware's studio in London. It was their last recording session together.

A few days after signing the publishing deal with Sony in January 1997, Steve called Billy in Auchterhouse. At first they spoke about music and the fact that Apollo 440 had agreed to produce them. 'There was a pause and I asked, "What's really going on with you Billy?" He then told me he had been hallucinating and said, "What am I going to do when I come back down to London, Steve?" I said, "Get yourself a nice flat with your dogs, Billy. You can afford it now." The conversation ended quickly, which was unusual. It was normally a case of trying to get Billy off the phone.

'Not long after that I received a phone call from John Mackenzie [Billy's brother]. There was no preamble. He just said, "Billy's dead." He was going to hang up but, of course, I demanded an explanation. "He killed himself – took a load of prescription drugs." I was stunned and couldn't reply. John hung up.'

Steve travelled to Dundee for the funeral on Monday 27 January. It wasn't until this point that he was able to react. 'When I saw people gathered outside St Andrew's Cathedral crying, I went to pieces myself. At the wake, there couldn't be the usual celebration of a person's life – there was too much grief and hysteria around. People soon dispersed and I retreated to a pub with some friends where I drank myself into a stupor.'

ROY TOYS

When Kit Clark arrived back in Dundee from Budapest, the enforced lay-off would, he hoped, provide some perspective. Gary and Ged had moved on to their respective projects and it was time for him to take his next step.

The Swiss Family Orbison name had raised its head years before as a potential replacement for Spencer Tracy, but this Swiss was to take a different approach, still based on the craft of songwriting but consuming the influences that had passed through his life since Danny Wilson split.

The original line-up of Swiss included Howard McLeod on drums, along with Ali Napier and Stewart Clark on keyboards, Gregor Philp, Colin Davidson and Keith Matheson.

Kit had already been impressed by some of the work that Keith had been doing with Big Blue 72. 'We corresponded when I was in Budapest and when I came back I produced a song for him during his lunch hour from Groucho's.' Keith was someone Kit was keen to work with. 'The rest of the guys were asked one night in the Westie, and at Howard's insistence, they agreed,' laughs Kit.

The band gained some interest fairly quickly and soon Kit was back discussing his future with A&R men. 'I was in London for the signing, but we decided to put it off for a week, as I wanted to iron out the situation on retainers for the guys in the band, and couldn't get a meeting with the lawyers right away. I was staying in Gary's flat while I was there and couldn't reach the label. Then there was a weird message on the answering machine to meet up. The company had been bought over.

'At that point, we had to scale everything down and ended up as a much smaller outfit.'

It dealt a blow to the keyboard players. 'It was a great band, but then it seemed we were out,' says Ali Napier. 'We knew it was a vehicle for Kit's songs, really, but it wasn't great when it got pulled from under our feet.'

The original drummer Howard McLeod had already gone, 'It wasn't my thing as a drummer, so when Kit started looking around for a deal I had to say that I was out if it happened.' Next in the seat was Dougie Vipond, who had been missing live work since Deacon Blue had stopped touring.

'The first gig that Dougie played with us was Hooks in Kirriemuir,' says Gregor. 'It wasn't a great place but we were well treated. I watched him as he set up his stool and looked around as folk were getting physically ejected from the pub. I said, "I'm sorry, Doug. This must be . . ." but he stopped me and said that he was absolutely loving it. It was around Christmas, so we had snowball fights in the town square across the road.'

The band spent some time in London sharing a flat with others, including *Trainspotting* actress Kelly McDonald. 'She was pretty famous by this time, and of course took a shine to the ugliest member of the band, Colin, who looks like Spud,' says Gregor. 'She would say, "Colin you're dead cute, just like my pal Spud."'

The first album was released in November 1997, on Boo Hewerdine's Haven Records. It received good reviews, with some constructing a pedestal that would be hard to stay on. Tom Morton, reviewing a live Radio Scotland session recorded at The Lemon Tree in Aberdeen in the same month, wrote in *The Scotsman*, 'There is a real magic in hearing unfamiliar music on the radio that reaches out and shakes you with its brilliance . . . Hugely impressed, I determined to buy the album when it came out. And then the following day the album itself – not due until January – arrived out of the blue. It was as if some divine plot was under way by which I was to be convinced of the band's brilliance. Enough, already, I am.'

Kit and Keith started working very closely together. 'I think when I was working alongside Kit, we produced the best material either of us had ever written,' says Keith. That partnership was put to the test when they were asked to support the Saw Doctors on a tour in 1999. 'We were due to play the Royal Albert Hall as a trio, but Gregor decided to leave the band the day before. They were happy for Keith and me to do it, so we stayed up overnight to rewrite the set to suit the two of us in Keith's flat in the Hilltown, then got straight on the train. I can vividly remember the three-minute call, then the two-minute call – I thought this must be what it feels like when the priest leaves on Death Row.'

With two people on stage, microphones are usually placed pretty closely together, but they had been set at opposite ends. They lifted them and took them both to the centre. 'That got a round of applause anyway,' recalls Kit. 'They obviously had a "good on you for giving this a go" attitude. We opened with one of Keith's songs that we had just finished the night before but after that it's a bit of a blur. The thirty-five minutes were an amazing experience. From the Hilltown multis straight to the Albert Hall and you walk out the door with no money to buy a pint. To be honest, after doing something like that, anything else was almost impossible – things just drifted.'

Keith believes that the band may have had a better chance if the partying culture hadn't been embraced so warmly. Not by every band member, however. Dundee didn't exactly embrace the dance culture of the 1990s but some were happy to wear the accessories. 'It all fell apart through over-indulgence really,' Keith says. 'There are so many "ifs and buts" when it comes to Swiss. I think if we had had decent management, the Saw Doctors dates could have been the game-changer. After that I started playing with The Pearlfishers. My brother Alan had been in touch with Davie Scott, so that's how we met. What a change that was – tea and cakes backstage. I loved it – I really enjoyed not getting hammered before playing.'

Prior to The Pearlfishers gig, Keith was working with Gregor on an idea called Bikini Machine. 'The idea was that they only existed in the ether – and this was a year before Gorillaz appeared. We wanted to do something that wouldn't restrict what we could write. They would appear at times through history, so we could write stuff like Slade, The Beatles, Led Zeppelin. It was a chance to be much wider.

'As far as Swiss goes, I think that, without going major, we were as successful as we could have been.'

STAYING COOL

The art school had been producing musicians since the early 1960s and, with changing tastes, it was now producing DJs. Tom Simpson from Monifieth was at Duncan of Jordanstone studying drawing and painting, but his ambitions lay with a set of decks.

'I had initially been into hip hop, but as I grew up I became more interested in where the samples on the records had come from. That's when I started buying old soul records.'

Tom and a friend, Nick DeCosemo, who became editor of *Mixmag* magazine, ran clubs, including one called *Spaceship* in the art school. 'Apart from the Westie, there really wasn't anywhere to go to see bands. The occasional thing would come through the Caird Hall and the university, but dance was big with students.'

At one of their clubs, they would see the same 'strange-looking skinny guy' every week. Gary Lightbody had just started university in Dundee and liked the music they were playing. 'He had ill-fitting clothes and Mr Clumsy shoes, and he was dancing mentally to the music we were playing. He would come up to say he enjoyed it and ask, "What are you doing now?" We would invite him to whatever party we were going to and he would always insist on carrying the record box. I had this massive steel flight case, so I'd refuse and say we'd get a taxi, but he always wanted to. That went on for a few weeks and then he said one night, "My band's playing at the university tonight. Do you fancy coming to see it?" At that time it was called Polar Bear.'

Tom did go along and was asked by Gary what he thought. 'I said I loved it and thought there was a lot of great stuff in there. He looked pretty relieved and asked me if I wanted to do some recording with them, which turned into tracks for the first album *Music for Polarbears*.'

The switch to Snow Patrol came, as many band names do, through the threat of legal action. Eric Avery was using the name Polar Bear for his side project to Jane's Addiction and as Tom says, 'It was the big lawyers versus the wee lawyers.' The new name came from a friend of the band who always got the band name wrong – he had always called them Snow Patrol. 'Of course, as soon as we changed the name, the next time we saw him he called us Polar Bear,' Tom laughs.

The band asked Tom if he fancied going out on the road with them and, becoming disillusioned with the dance scene, he left his voluntary work for the arts charity Generator and headed out on the road.

Tom's involvement with the band was growing and soon he was standing in front of a keyboard with black tape on the keys to work out where his fingers had to be. 'I was terrible when we started. I had to learn to play, so Kit Clark would come down to my house in Monifieth three times a week to give me lessons. He advised me to get proper lessons, so now I can play to a fairly good standard. I still have a cottage in Monifieth – it's the place where I anchor myself.'

The band decanted to Glasgow, where they signed to Jeepster Records, the home of acts such as Belle and Sebastian (who have a Dundonian trumpeter, Mick Cooke). 'The first two albums were actually pretty well received, but that wasn't reflected in record sales and we were dropped. I saw the label owner not long ago, and I said, "No hard feelings. We don't owe you any money do we?"

'There was a lot of touring and getting drunk and sleeping on floors. Sometimes the only way to make the floor comfortable was a half bottle of whisky. We would have been better off signing on, we were so broke, but through belligerence and the fact that we were unemployable by that point, we stuck in.'

The band were signed by Fiction in 2003 and the work paid off with a breakthrough album, *Final Straw*.

'At that point I was about thirty and my dad was saying, "What are you doing son? Is this going anywhere?" I told him that I would give it one more year, and if it hadn't happened, I would do teacher training and be an art teacher. They're proud of it now. That's why there's a dedication on the albums saying, "Mums and Dads of the world, be patient with your children."'

THE NOUGHTIES

The Noughties

YOUNG GENERATION

Buzzing from a new recording contract, Snow Patrol returned to their spiritual home to play in the Westport Bar. That night they were supported by a young band called The Hazey Janes.

Andrew Mitchell, Matthew Marra and Alice Marra were joined by their new drummer, Liam Brennan, for the first time that night. Liam, who had been heard to shout, 'I want to be in your band!' (often and loudly) at gigs was the replacement for Michael Benbow. 'When Michael decided to leave, we looked at each other and thought, "We'd better phone Liam,"' says Alice.

All four members of the band came with a substantial musical pedigree. Alice and Matthew are the children of Michael Marra, Liam the nephew of Gerry McGrath and Andrew the grandson of Alexander Mitchell, who sang with The Mitchell Brothers.

'There's a recording of me at about eighteen months, singing something that's definitely an original melody,' says Alice. 'The words are kind of "anee anoo", but I'm definitely trying to get something over. My dad's playing the piano and I'm singing along. Then there's a recording of me at the age of about seven singing "Mary's Prayer" and really trying to copy Gary Clark. I just always loved to sing.'

Alice was about sixteen before she picked up a guitar, and liked what she heard through her dad. 'People like Eddi Reader and Rab Noakes. I remember him giving me a hard time when I was REALLY young about liking Kylie – I couldn't have even been ten yet – and then he said, "Don't worry. One day you'll discover Joni Mitchell records and everything will be all right." '

Meanwhile Matthew wanted to be a drummer and played 'a wee bit of keyboard and dad's guitar'. He started to look at the guitar more seriously at about the age of sixteen, but started playing drums with Andrew. 'Another friend of ours was a better drummer, so I started to play bass – the luck of having a former bass-playing dad, there was one in the house. It combines playing drums and guitar for me.'

Andrew would sing with his mum, and like the others picked up the guitar at sixteen and found that, 'nothing else made me feel like playing music did. I managed to get some cohorts at school. I always loved the physical aspect of singing, but things moved forward when I saw that The Beatles played guitars. My mum was in Liverpool in the 1960s and had a Cavern membership so there was always Beatles stuff in the house.'

Liam's family were involved in the Dundee music scene, but he was also lucky enough to find Billy Mackenzie's mum living next door. 'Billy would come to the house and give me his new singles when he got back from London, even the stuff he did with Finitribe. My grandad played bass drum in the Black Watch pipe band, but I'm the first drummer since him. All my influences were singers. I went to see Gary Clark on his *Ten Short Songs* tour and his voice was just too big for the theatre. My mum would also sneak me just inside the door of Chambers to see Mafia and that really stuck with me.'

Andrew and Matthew had already started playing together when Alice, who had already been in a band with Liam, joined them in rehearsal.

The band were bright-eyed and bushy-tailed and the bane of someone's life with it. 'We would want to rehearse from 10am on a Saturday morning,' says Andrew, 'and Ecky [the rehearsal studio manager] would come along, bleary-eyed and hungover, cursing us for making him get up so early.'

When Liam joined the band, it became more focused. 'They were telt!' he says. There was definitely a greater sense of purpose to the gigging and writing, which culminated with the first release in 2004, an eponymous mini-album, recorded with Mark Freegard, who had worked with Del Amitri and the Manic Street Preachers.

'We needed to get our stuff out there,' says Matthew, 'and the idea of a mini-album rather than an EP was that it would be stocked with albums rather than singles, so have a longer shelf life.'

The interest generated by that first album continued with the momentum of *Hotel Radio*. It was recorded in 2005 in the Paco Loco studios near Cadiz, and there were sound reasons for choosing to 'head to the sun' for a few weeks. 'It was actually cheaper to go out there at the time,' says Liam. The studios were residential and that also provided opportunities to come into contact with figures who would be influential.

'We couldn't believe it when Gary Louris from The Jayhawks came through the studio. We were also really excited that John Agnello (The Hold Steady/Sonic Youth/Patti Smith/Dinosaur Jnr) was there and engineered the album.' Agnello was impressed and told the band: 'Not bad for a bunch of punk kids from Dundee. You guys want to cut a record in the US, you give me a call.'

The reception that *Hotel Radio* received was almost unanimously positive, with Andrew Harrison from *Word* magazine saying, 'Dundee's Hazey Janes do it well because they keep the energy levels up, punking out on every fourth track and remembering that this stuff is nothing if it doesn't brighten your day . . . instantly wins you over.'

The most repeated quote came from a 4/5 *Mojo* review by Johnny Black, which although positive, was tinged with a slightly questionable reference to their nationality: 'Life-affirming debut from sparky quartet . . . The Hazey Janes may just be the best haggis-powered country rockers yet.'

'Those were all very well,' says Liam, 'but my favourite was the Ceefax review that hated it, calling us The Samey Shames. Brilliant.'

What followed was a period of making the most of *Hotel Radio*'s reputation, travelling the length and breadth of the country and playing as often as humanly possible. 'Even if that meant coming off stage in London, getting in the van, driving to Portree on Skye and setting up the minute we got there,' says Alice. 'We did our own tour and then went out again with the Electric Soft Parade, then Brakes and then the Cosmic Rough Riders.'

There was also a trip to the industry's biggest talent showcase South by South West (SXSW) in 2006, when they became the first Dundee-based band to play there. In the US they found a natural home for their sound.

'We had a chance to play in New York, supporting Susannah Hoffs,' says Liam, 'but then we found out that her backing band was Velvet Crush. That was a moment and a half . . . We played in the corner of a building that had glass walls so I was stuck right in the corner, with no clue what was going on behind me,' he says.

'I remember turning round and there was a guy holding up a sign saying "CAIRD HALL – DUNDEE",' laughs Alice. 'You just canna escape it!'

The punk kids remembered John Agnello's offer and in March 2007 headed to his studio in Hoboken, New Jersey, to record another album. It was March and it was brutally cold. The experience was everything they expected it to be, having enough distance from New York City to concentrate on recording, but close enough to be able to experience and soak up the thrills of Manhattan when they needed an escape. Pounding the streets of the city was business as well as pleasure, with one photo session lasting ten hours during a day in blinding sunshine. 'It was worth it when we ended up walking across the Brooklyn Bridge during the most spectacular sunset. Absolutely unforgettable,' says Andrew.

With another trip to SXSW breaking the recording, it was back to Hoboken in July. Instead of hugging the heaters, in the sweltering summer heat they were fighting to be closest to the air-conditioning. The album

Hands Around the City was completed, with the single 'New York' released in May 2008, inspired by their experiences there. A fourth album, *The Winter That Was* was recorded closer, just outside Dundee, and releaseed in October 2011.

After a break with the management, it was time to regroup and think about what was next for the band. Advice may have been close to home, but there was no paternal push into music in the Marra household. 'I wouldn't actively persuade them into an insecure way of life,' says Michael. 'I would never say to them that it's a grand laugh at the songwriter gig. It's something that they would choose to do or not to do – and both have. However, I haven't discouraged them.

'The good thing is, they both enjoy it more than me. My example I suppose is I've always been working – that's the big trick. I also work hard to get it right every time. Every single time.' He then adds, laughing, 'Also, if you keep gigging you live longer. If you have a gig there's less chance of you dying.'

An opportunity to relax in New Jersey came when they were invited to board a yacht and sail around the bay and across to Ellis Island to view the Statue of Liberty from the water, complete with champagne in hand. 'These opportunities only come about because we are playing music. It's a wonderful thing to share with your friends,' says Andrew.

That sentiment is shared by Tom Simpson of Snow Patrol. The Hazey Janes' first gig had been supporting them, and their biggest was also with Snow Patrol at Meadowbank Stadium.

'It is the greatest job in the world,' says Tom, 'and getting to travel the world with your best pals just makes it all the better.'

VINTAGE CARS

The rise to stadium gigs for Snow Patrol came with *Final Straw* in 2003. Gary Lightbody had said, 'We spent ten years making records that 6000 people bought,' but in the year following the third album's release there was a sudden change, best illustrated by their headlining of the King Tut's Tent at T in the Park 2004.

'That's when we knew things were changing,' says Tom. 'Before *Final Straw*, we were playing to crowds of about 200.' Now, at T in the Park, it seemed everyone was moving towards the tent, which held about 8000 people. 'They had to lift the sides up as there was another 8000 or so outside the tent. When I walked out, every hair on my body stood on end. The first song was a nightmare – we forgot everything and were just completely overwhelmed by what was happening.'

If *Final Straw* was the momentum, then *Eyes Open* was the explosion, with one song in particular. 'I remember Gary playing me a song he had been messing about with in demo mode,' recalls Tom. 'It was obvious that it was a huge hit straight away. Three chords and the truth, as they say.'

The song was 'Chasing Cars', which went on to become the most played song of the decade, according to Phonographic Performance Limited (PPL) the official UK music licensing body. Aside from that, it was nominated in the Best Rock Song category in the 2007 Grammy awards and reached huge US audiences through *One Tree Hill* and *Grey's Anatomy*. It had more than 100,000 radio plays in the UK, two million downloads in the US, and it also closed the final edition of *Top of the Pops* in July 2006. The effect on the *Eyes Open* album was phenomenal, leading to a final sales tally of 4.7 million copies worldwide.

'With that song the stars just aligned,' says Tom. 'Sometimes it needs a song like that for people to take notice. There's a certain element of luck, but we did work our backsides off with three tours of America. It was just a constant circuit, and as we toured the audiences got bigger and bigger.'

Snow Patrol's reputation as a stadium and festival band grew, something that Tom believes came from that old-fashioned paying of dues. 'We had to cut our teeth on the toilet touring circuit and we didn't get too much too soon. There was also a period of learning how to tour with each other and because we took the blows in the early days, we're a bit more resilient when the blows come now.'

There have been a few testing times. There were cancelled US gigs as *Eyes Open* was building in the US, when Gary had vocal polyps; and there was a potential cancellation of a T in the Park main-stage headline slot in 2007, when Tom was arrested straight after appearing at Wembley Stadium for Live Earth. He missed a festival in Dublin but was released without charge from Uxbridge Police Station in Middlesex in time to make it on stage at Balado.

There was relative disappointment in late 2008 with the next release, *A Hundred Million Suns*, which didn't quite get to number one, being held at bay at number two by Pink. A great result for most bands, but following the sales of *Eyes Open*, it had to be a disappointment.

'Take in a financial crisis across the world and particularly in the US, and sales of albums and live tickets are going to suffer,' says Tom. 'We were still able to fill the O2 for multiple nights and I still think that reputation is down to the live show.'

With that behind them, the latter part of 2010 saw the band resident in a house in Malibu to record a new album. 'That was the way to do it this time. Not in a residential studio but by bringing the studio to the house. The views across the Pacific were incredible. There were whales breaching,' says Tom. 'There were also schools of dolphins, just like the River Tay. Maybe that's why I felt so at home.'

MULLING THINGS OVER

Michael Marra also had the chance to work by the sea, invited by the An Tobar arts centre in Tobermory to live on Mull for a month and write about whatever he encountered.

'Unfortunately the first thing I encountered was racism – an anti-English feeling that was apparent in the pub. I went away thinking, "I better not mention that . . . I better not." But then I realised the way to tackle it was by poking fun at it, which I did in a song called "Gossip". There was a lot of talk about locals not being able to buy houses as folk from the south of England were moving in, but I don't blame anybody for wanting to live there.'

Michael encountered a songwriter on Mull who was surprised when he mentioned a song from her past. 'I asked her if she was the same Lesley Duncan who wrote "When My Baby Cries",' he says. 'I told her I was a fan of the song and had heard the Poor Souls' recording of it. I said that Dougie Martin had spoken very highly of her, and she seemed very pleased with the news.'

The success of the Mull EP, *Silence*, was followed by the later *Quintet*, with five songs about musicians (including 'Peter' for Peter McGlone) but since *Posted Sober* there have been no full-length studio albums.

'I don't have a manager, being completely unmanageable, but I have an agent who is very understanding of my theatre work.' In this respect Michael has been busier than ever since the turn of the decade, working with Liz Lochhead on *In Flagrant Delicht*, writing an operetta and a play and having the dual role of songwriter and actor in a production of *The Demon Barber*. A full-length album was released in 2010, but this time it was a live recording of a series of concerts with Mr McFall's Chamber. 'This is chamber music with a difference,' says Michael. 'They will tackle everything from Frank Zappa to Joe Zavano.'

There was also a return to the madness of St Andrew with a mini-album of six songs called *Hubris*.

'My preferred title was *Ratify my Hubris*,' says Andy Pelc. 'There was no point in doing another *Word on the Pavey*. And it certainly isn't that. St Andrew can work whenever the time is right for him. Maybe we can do more when my bairn's grown up a bit.'

Michael has his own take on it. '*Hubris* is an unusual record. "Mental" would be the word I would use,' he laughs.

Those who were with Michael in the earliest days are still with him now and believe he has more to offer than ever. 'Michael Marra, in my opinion, is truly original and one of the most important cultural figures in Scotland,' says Barbara Dickson. 'He is able to be the voice of his generation, his class, his neighbourhood and his country. I find his songs timeless and he has a quirky, subversive quality which intrigues me. Michael writes with the world in mind. He typifies what Bashevis Singer said about if you write in truth about your surroundings, the work speaks to the world. That's Michael.'

PENNIES IN HEAVEN

Alison Burns, the singer who inspired Michael Marra to feel like he was twenty-nine again, was creating her own opportunities to fulfil long-held ambitions. In 2000, the Penny Dainties had the opportunity to take their harmonies to the Manhattan School of Music to work with the New York Voices. 'Apart from the excitement of doing that, there was also the idea that we may be able to meet the women who inspired what we did – The Dinning Sisters.' Accordionist Jack Emblow had been working with the trio and just as The Dinning Sisters inspired the Penny Dainties, so Art Van Damme, who played with the Dinnings, had inspired Jack.

'He contacted Art and asked for Ginger Dinning's number. I had to steel myself and just phone her. I asked if we could send her the album and told her we were coming to New York and would love to meet her.'

So when Ginger Dinning walked into their Manhattan hotel, Alison, Tricia and Jane were ready to welcome her. They also agreed to come over to New Jersey to hear a women's vocal group she sang with. 'The woman running the group took us aside and told us how much it had meant for her to hear from young women who were continuing their legacy,' says Alison. The Dinning Sisters had been stars in the 1930s, with their own radio shows while still in their teens. 'We missed the last bus back to Manhattan and Ginger insisted that we stay with her. While we were there, she called her sisters Lou and Jean to let them talk to the girls who sang their parts.'

Alison was getting used to taking opportunities. She had got to know Martin Taylor through James, and he would encourage her to join him on stage, but she was reluctant, holding off for several years. 'To be quite honest, I just didn't feel worthy.'

We all have now-or-never moments and Alison's came at the Chet Atkins Convention in Nashville in 1999. 'Chet Atkins was still alive at the time and there were guests like Duane Eddy and Tommy Emmanuel. I thought if I didn't take the invitation at that point, I wouldn't deserve another one. It actually gave me my first American review, but they did call me Welsh!'

Alison wasn't so shy after that, doing more jazz gigs, while still working as a lawyer, earning her the nickname of 'the singer suing machine'. The turning point came in December 2005 when James's twenty-one-year-old brother, Stewart, committed suicide. Alison says, 'That was another *carpe diem* moment. One of the reasons I had made the decision to leave my job was my brother had died in the Falklands and I didn't want to let life pass me by. In 2005, we felt that we had been working so hard on other people's music careers, we were neglecting our own.'

James was the driving force. He booked a studio and told Alison to get a set together to record an album. 'I was so nervous the first day of recording, as I had the very best musicians. I knew I had to raise my game. I was a very lucky dolly and couldn't mess this up . . .'

Despite the familial relationship, Martin Taylor would not work with a singer unless he felt that there was a musical connection and they offered an extra element. 'The thing about Alison is she fully understands the language of the music she sings. It's important that the singer isn't just there to sing the melody and lyrics – they are there to interpret. Her acting background has helped her with that. All the best singers understand the lyrics and Alison does that. She's also blessed with a deep, warm voice.'

The album *Kissing Bug*, released in March 2007, became the first album by a Scottish jazz singer to reach the jazz top 10 and was followed by an album with Martin called *1AM*. Concerts in Australia, Sri Lanka, Thailand, Europe and the US have followed. Finally, that map of the world she received from her colleagues is being put to good use.

Only six months after Alison left her job, she bumped into a former workmate who asked how she was doing. 'I told her things were OK. I was getting a few things but it would take a while to build up. She said, "Uch well hen, yi tried yir best!" Fantastic!'

FOLLOWING HIS HEART

Gordon Douglas, with his theatrical pedigree, was approached to write what he believes is his most satisfying project to date. 'Through a friend called Gary Mitchell, I began working with children and young folk who were in need of some help. I would work on songwriting with them. You would be amazed what the achievement of writing a song can do. These aren't *X-Factor* children, these are young folk who are really achieving something by being able to perform at the end of it.'

In 2006, that led to a bigger project run through The Prince's Trust. 'We were working with young people who were children of asylum-seekers. They were from all over – Cameroon, Kosovo, Nigeria . . . We had residential weekends at Pitlochry where we sat and worked with them and listened to their stories. Then we went away and wrote a show for them to perform. It was called *Heart of Gold*, with the book, lyrics and music written by myself and Gary. It is probably my greatest musical experience, because of what they gave you back.'

The band was his own Prisoners of Fender – Gordon, Billy Fisher on drums, John Fitzgerald on bass and Lindsay Duncan on lead guitar. *Heart of Gold* ran for three nights at the Edinburgh Festival Fringe at Stockbridge Parish Church. 'I just laugh now when some people say, "Did you used to be Gordon Douglas?"'

FEELING THE BYRNE

Gregor Philp had secured a loan from his father to finance a second Swiss Family Orbison album. That project was never to happen, but being the supportive father that any creative son would appreciate, he asked how Gregor could use the money to help to making a living in music.

'It allowed me to get finance to set up a studio and start putting together demos for TV music. The wide range of music that I had been playing meant I could recreate different styles, which is essential for soundtrack work.'

Demos impressed and Gregor was on his way to creating music for some of Scotland's best-loved TV programmes. Invited by director Brian Kelly to visit the set of a new children's history programme called *Chuck Wallace's Middle Age Spread*, he was more stunned than surprised to see George Wendt (Norm from *Cheers*) standing on a bridge in Stirling spouting forth about Scottish medieval history. 'It seems that George is something of a Scottish and Irish history buff and agreed to do the show in return for a paid holiday. When we got to talking about music, his taste was Nirvana and the Seattle grunge stuff – again, totally unexpected.'

When the cast and crew retired to a hotel in Bridge of Allan that night, George walked into the bar and it was all they could do to stop themselves shouting, 'Norm!' Gregor asked what he would like to drink. 'I couldn't believe that I was buying Norm from *Cheers* a beer,' he says.

More work for Channel 4 followed, including working with Toyah Wilcox on *Barmy Aunt Boomerang*, and then across to BBC Scotland for the shining light of children's TV, *Balamory*.

It was music for *Taggart* that led to collaboration with a musical hero, however. 'I got a phone call from a DJ called Gill Mills, who asked if I knew anything about the David Byrne project, and then went on to say that he wanted me to help him out with some music for a film. I thought this must obviously be a David Byrne with an accordion orchestra in Kirkintilloch and not *the* David Byrne from Talking Heads.'

Gregor had forgotten that months earlier he had been asked to submit a piece of music for a sampler. He had chosen a piece that he had been happy with, but it had been rejected by *Taggart*. 'She went on to say, "You're a percussion player right?" and – wanting to work with David Byrne – I didn't argue with her. She said he would call or e-mail.'

He did call and much to Gregor's relief said he knew he wasn't a percussion player, he recognised that the work had been done with samples. The next step was for Gregor to take his gear down to Ca Va studios in Glasgow where David was working with the cream of young Scottish talent, including members of Belle and Sebastian and Mogwai.

'He was the polar opposite of a control freak. When I asked what he wanted, he would look over his specs and ask what I wanted to do. Whatever I said, he was cool with. The great thing was he loves the slightly dark, leftfield Scottish sense of humour. Even though he left Dumbarton at an early age, that has never left him.'

The results can be heard on *Lead Us Not Into Temptation* – songs from the film *Young Adam*. Not the most successful movie in Ewan McGregor's canon, but a great musical experience for several Scottish musicians.

The spirit of collaboration was alive and well in Dundee, and through Kit Clark, who was writing and teaching, Gregor met Andrew Mitchell of The Hazey Janes. He was keen to work with Gregor and the pair wrote an album which was released under the name Heavy Little Elephants. Bringing Ged Grimes in on bass and Dougie Vipond in on drums, he was introduced into the Deacon Blue stable and started playing guitar with them on live dates.

Gary Clark's decade started with a high-profile songwriting project. Since the break-up of Transister in the late 1990s, he had been working to establish himself as a songwriter and producer. Anne Barrett, Natalie Imbruglia's manager at the time, contacted Gary to ask if he would be interested in doing some co-writing and producing a second album, which became *White Lilies Island* (on which Ged Grimes played bass).

In 2003 he was given the Performing Rights Society songwriting award at the annual Tartan Clef awards in recognition of his work with a diverse range of artists. To date that list in writing, production or both includes Melanie C, Skin (Skunk Anansie), kd lang, Liz Phair, Skye (Morcheeba), Emma Bunton, Mark Owen (Take That), Guy Sebastian, Ashley Parker Angel, Nick Carter (Backstreet Boys), Lloyd Cole, Ferras, McFly, Demi Lovato, The Veronicas and Delta Goodrem.

'I always liked the idea of moving into songwriting for other people when I got older and I thought, naively, that writing songs for other people would be easy, but it's much more difficult than writing for yourself,' he says.

'I may be a lot less successful than other professional songwriters in the way that I operate, but I make an effort to be couture rather than production line. I work in exactly the same way as I would for a band – it's just for them rather than my band.'

Ged Grimes has begun to experience the band mentality again on a bigger scale than ever. He joined Simple Minds in 2010 – coming full circle from the young musician in London listening to *New Gold Dream* on Brian McDermott's Knightsbridge rooftop.

'The first gig I did at three days' notice with no rehearsals,' he says. 'We were in the back of a car in Paris going up to the venue and Jim [Kerr] casually drops in that the gig will be broadcast live on French radio.' It also turned out to be the Fête de Humanité, an 80,000 crowd and the biggest gig the band had done since Live Aid. 'I saw the flood-lights at the top of the hill and it seemed like no time at all until I was on stage and Mel Gaynor was counting me in for a ninety-minute set. The Chili Peppers busking came in really handy there.'

Gary doesn't get back to Dundee as often as he would like, but the feeling when he does is the same. 'I remember in the early days, when we would be driving back from London, we would round that corner and see the skyline over the bridge. It was a great feeling. Later, when it was a plane, it descended towards the landing strip – you would see the two bridges and get that amazing feeling of home.'

ROOTS MON

Traditions have a habit of adapting to suit their time, and this is true with roots or folk music. At the start of the decade, Stuart Fleming and Kerry Fowler had decided to make their home in Dundee, as Stuart was the regional representative for the Performing Rights Society. Coming into contact with musicians of all types opened their eyes to the range of styles that could conceivably come under that roots banner.

'I was speaking with musician Dave Arcari about this in, I think, 2004,' says Stuart, 'and we agreed that there was amazing roots music out there that didn't come under straightforward folk, blues, bluegrass or Americana. At that time I thought it would be an interesting idea to represent seven or eight acts to try to place that music in film or TV.'

Both Stuart and Dave were busy and the idea lay on the shelf for a couple of years, before Stuart and Kerry came across an eighteen-year-old singer-songwriter called Amber Wilson. 'We saw something in her that was exceptional. We realised that she would probably need management as that was where she was lacking direction. So that's how Jagged Roots as a management company began.'

Jagged Roots has also become a label, with Amber recording her first EP at Willie Hastie's studio with the help of Gavin McGinty. Jagged Roots had funded it, so by default became the label, but realising that sales of physical CDs were dropping, they felt that working online was the way forward. 'We really only pressed CDs to fund Amber's tour,' says Stuart, 'to sell as merchandise for extra income, as well as for promotion to press, promoters and festivals.'

Early in the life of Jagged Roots, a French distribution company contacted them to say they would like to work with them for worldwide distribution. Eventually Stuart and Kerry agreed and when they did, they started picking up sales in every corner. 'In mainstream companies, artists would be dropped without hundreds of thousands of sales, but here the costs are minimal, so we can develop artists. Kerry had been working on material and that has been distributed through Jagged Roots,' says Stuart. 'Most of her sales are in the Middle East. We would never have had that reach, working in a more conventional way.'

Any new artist would be considered, as long as they fitted in with the original ethos of Jagged Roots. The next artist to come on board was called Panda Su, and was working between Dundee and Tayport.

Still in her early twenties, Su (real name Suzanne Shaw) has her own label, Peter Panda Records, but has benefited from Stuart and Kerry's experience when it comes to touring and getting her music out to a wider audience. A song, 'Eric is Dead', was used in E4's *Skins*, taking the original idea behind Jagged Roots full circle.

At the same time, Kerry was putting together a nine-piece Slavic gypsy folk band from Dundee, writing and singing Macedonian and Bulgarian folk songs, fronted by a burlesque show and a character called Smug the Elder who wears a rather fetching goat's head. The Lost Todorovs emulate the wandering troupes of musicians who would entertain throughout eastern European villages and towns, but with a collection of Dundee's best roots players.

In what could maybe be regarded as more mainstream roots, the Woodlands Folk Club also had resurgence in 2006, as the Out of the Woods Acoustic Music Club, this time run by local singer-songwriter Pauline Meikleham. As well as the stalwarts of the former folk clubs such as Michael Marra and Rab Noakes, the new Woodlands featured contemporary acts who could sit comfortably in that area, such as Aberfeldy, The Hazey Janes, Martin Stephenson and Karine Polwart.

Russ Paterson was invited along as a guest performer at the opening in 2006. 'When I played the Woodlands again, I was terrified. When Pauline announced me, I was blethering away to Gus Foy so I didn't hear. Suddenly Rab Noakes is tugging my sleeve and saying, "You're on." The second time I did it was with my two sons (Don Paterson, the well-known poet and author and Steve Paterson, renowned portrait sculptor and Boogalusa bass player) so that wasn't quite as nerve-racking.

'I still head across the bridge to the Newport Hotel for a session once a week – and I still do a lot of stuff I was doing at the folk club. It's good to see new people coming through – of all ages. There has always been an element of do it yourself in folk and I don't think that will ever change.'

PEEL APPEAL

Spare Snare had already decided that doing it themselves was the only way to proceed and by 2000 Ross Matheson, brother of Keith and Alan, had joined. 'Jan came in to Groucho's, where I was working at the time,' says Graeme Ogston. 'They had nearly finished *Charm* but he needed to get another guitar player. I liked them so said I would do it. As soon as it was agreed he said we had a gig in three weeks – a showcase gig at Manchester: In the City. I had three weeks to learn the songs they were going to do.'

There was a T in the Park appearance in 2001, but when Ross left in 2002 that was the line-up until the *Garden Leave* album in 2006, when keyboards were required. Adam Lockhart was in a band called Condition Blue who had released on Chute Records, and has been in the band ever since.

The live appearances have been infrequent, with each treated as something of an event now. 'That's not why we avoid the live stuff,' says Jan. 'I enjoy it but it's also a real financial drain. It's about making the records for me. I like the fact that we did three John Peel sessions – a gig we did at Reading also went out as a session.

(Spare Snare are in the bizarre position of being the only band to have recorded sessions for John Peel and Aled Jones. In 2008, they recorded a version of 'Amazing Grace' for Jones's Radio 2 show.)

'The Peel sessions were all done on Sundays, so he wasn't there at the time but I did meet him later. He was so accessible. I sent him the first single and he responded with a postcard, and by playing it. Then he phoned and asked if we wanted to do a session.'

The biggest thrill was a track called 'Taking on the Sides' featuring on a compilation called *Kats Karavan – the History of John Peel on the Radio*. 'That meant everything,' says Jan.

Alan Cormack is happy to let Jan take the lead on whatever happens with Spare Snare. 'If Jan decides it's over, then it's over. There will never be an Alan Cormack's Sound of Spare Snare.'

NEW VOICES

It's unfair to make comparisons of any kind, particularly where the spirit of Billy Mackenzie is involved, but Dave Webster is widely regarded as the most exciting vocalist produced by Dundee since.

The singer and songwriter received some recognition in a band called Luva Anna, who were paying their dues like any other young band, through support slots and working through the festival stages.

His influences as a child came from sources as diverse as Donovan, The Jacobites, Robert Burns and Alex Harvey. 'My mum had loads of old punk records but I never heard them – they were locked in a cupboard because she had written sweary words all over them. We did share some things though. Every Christmas we'd all have an envelope and we opened them at the same time – it was always a ticket to that year's Michael Marra concert. A brilliant annual event for our family.'

Dave was singled out for his vocal ability at school and believes that the only reason Morgan Academy kept him into sixth year (to do one Higher) was to put him into competition to sing for the school.

There had been bands at school, but when he started the Dundee College music course he met Drew 'Boy' Gray, who would become his closest musical collaborator (he would also meet Kieren Webster who was mucking about with a few friends in a band that would become The View).

'Drew and I bonded over The Smiths – always a band that brings people together. We started rehearsing and worked on each other's tunes, but we never intended to play live.' That only happened when a friend who was in a band called Page 6 invited them to play on a bill at Drouthy Neighbours. Two other band members were drafted in from a school band and they played the gig. 'Kieren was there with Kyle Falconer and they asked us to play with them at a pub called Stuzzi's (now The Bond). We kind of became a band by accident.'

Guitarist Stevie Anderson joined his first serious band through the classic route of answering an ad in a local rehearsal studio. 'It's a total cliché but I would pretend to play guitar with a tennis racket when I was about six years old. My mum and dad asked if I wanted lessons, but at that point I was quite happy with a tennis racket,' he laughs.

'Not long after, I got a wee half-size nylon string acoustic from Forbes and started going to a guy called Tom Cleary for lessons. He gave me great basics – accompaniment, singing, the first tunes you learn on guitar; also a bit of notation.' When Stevie was about twelve, he switched to a tutor at Stage 2000 to learn more about lead playing. 'It was scales and stuff like that – everything I can't remember now.'

His first band was at the age of twelve, all the time still soaking up influences. 'The big shock was one day my mum started playing Chopin on the piano. I was fifteen and had never known my mum played the piano.'

When Stevie answered the ad, Stuart Purvey, Simon Donald and Martin Donald had been together as a band for several years, but when the new guitarist joined in 2004 there was a change in direction and name, to The Law.

'We had a few line-up changes with Luva Anna,' says Dave, 'with people heading off to university or jobs. We were lucky to get Robs Ward in on bass and Billy Fisher on drums. I had known Billy for years. We went to Russia with the Boy Scouts together. I was also jealous because I had won the Leng Medal at School, but he had a Gold Leng Medal,' he laughs.

The Leng Medal, run by the Sir John Leng Trust, is an annual competition for solo singing of Scots songs, held in schools in Dundee and surrounding towns. Each school would have a Silver Medal winner each year, who would then go on to compete for the Gold.

Luva Anna's combination of what could be called folk rock with some manic episodes singled them out of a raft of bands trying to emulate the likes of Oasis and Franz Ferdinand. 'We played T in the Park in 2008 and I have to say I was pretty worried when we went out for a sound-check during the fifteen-minute changeover. Everyone had left the tent when the previous band finished. There were maybe ten people there and I thought how embarrassing it was going to be.' Dave went out to the backstage area, had a drink and tried to not worry about it. 'Then we just heard this noise, the crowd was unbelievable. We filmed the gig and can't hear the band for the crowd singing.'

The following had been built through constant gigging. The Doghouse was a second home to Luva Anna, The Law and The View, with the followers of one supporting the others.

'I was also working for Capability Scotland at the time and my boss said she was coming along to a gig in Glasgow. Sharing a bottle of sambuca before going on was definitely a bad idea, as I ended up completely naked on stage. My boss said it was "interesting" and a journalist gave us the only bad review we got: "2/5 – average at best". I don't know if that was me or the band.'

The band also played the last night of the Westport Bar. During the japery of the favourite set closer, 'Angry Fat Bouncer', Dave jumped off stage and started swinging on the lights, which came away from the ceiling. The police were called and – showing that they were as rock'n'roll as anyone else in the room – asked Dave, 'Who do you think you are? Jim Morrison from The Who?' Dave says they held the laughter in until later.

'It took us a couple of years to get going as The Law,' says Stevie, 'but the guys encouraged me to write songs and we really had a chance to rehearse properly. Having the rehearsal space upstairs in The Doghouse saved us a fortune and Grant Dickson helped us by putting us into Tpot Studios to record with Robin Evans.'

The Law released two singles in 2007, 'Milk and Honey' and 'Still Got Friday to Go', which gained them attention from the music press and led to the XFM Rising Star Award at that year's Tartan Clef Awards. Grant was helping the band, with Paul Grieve handling the day-to-day management and taking the guys out to South by South West. Dougie Souness of No Half Measures took over the band's management and funded them to go into Sawmill Studios in Cornwall. With a deal on the table from EMI (Relentless) the well-publicised buy-out of 2007 put an end to that. In the end, the album *A Measure of Wealth* was released on their own independent label in 2009.

In addition to airplay in the UK and US, earned by the graft of endless gigs, the band had tracks featured in a network American television show *GREEK*, which used 'Still Got Friday to Go' and 'Man in the Moon'. The album's first single 'Don't Stop, Believe' was also used in the international trailer for *The Men Who Stare at Goats* with George Clooney and Ewan McGregor.

With The Law and Luva Anna playing on the same bill, with and without The View, Stevie and Dave realised they had a shared love for country rock and the blues. 'I passed up the opportunity to play with Stevie in a studio, thinking he was just Joe Guitar,' says Dave Webster, 'then I saw him play a few months later and thought, "What have I done?" I think we've both learned so much since then though and have a better idea where we're going.'

They are now working together with Billy Fisher, Gavin McGinty and Robs Ward on material that moves them into that direction.

'There's no point in restricting yourself musically,' says Stevie. He met 'wild man' Peter McGlone, who only returned to the sax a few years ago, and the two have been working together. 'Stevie is very open and all these young guys are very welcoming and inclusive of us old fellas,' Peter laughs.

Dave Webster has also found a mentor in the shape of Steve Knight.

'I've always been writing and I have some great songs just waiting to be recorded,' says Steve. History repeated itself in some ways, when Steve heard Dave sing at a party, in the same way he had first heard Billy Mackenzie. 'He was just incredible and sang "Hallelujah" brilliantly. I thought, "I could write for you . . ."'

Dave's interest in singers verges on the obsessive. 'If I hear something I like, I'll try to do it and if I can't get it, it will bother me – I've been close to falling over a few times, just singing one note.'

Stevie says, 'It's been a great few years in Dundee and the next few years are looking just as good, but really, it was The View that threw the recent spotlight on Dundee.'

VIEW FROM THE BRIDGE

When Grant Dickson arrived back in Dundee, he was trying to make sense of what had happened since seeing that sign on the notice board at Aberdeen University and starting his own musical journey.

That journey had brought him home, and although there was no intention of getting another band together himself, he was determined to show that success could be achieved directly from the city.

He started working with local promoter John (Lemuria) More and after meeting record producer Robin Wynn Evans in the Twa Tams in Perth, he found out about the Tpot Studio that Evans was running in rural Perthshire, having moved from London with his wife, the singer Sam Brown, and their young children.

John and Grant were running club nights, primarily in The Doghouse, a venue that had been identified as a place that could be the centre of something they were planning to create. The idea was to record bands under the name the Lemuria Recording Company and Tpot was the ideal location. 'We had sessions at Tpot with the Dubhead Orchestra,' says Grant, 'which showed a whole new way of how music could be presented. It would be like a gig, with people watching the recording. It was all very utopian really. We filmed quite a few sessions, but the guy who was filming was also lecturing at Dundee College and handed me a demo from a student called Kieren Webster.

'After starting a label, I was always getting CDs, but I put this one on and liked it straight away. I didn't know how old they were or what they looked like. I just knew they had recorded these six tracks at Willie Hastie's studio and they were good.'

Apart from Dubhead, Lemuria had made an album with Michael Rattray in Perth. The album launch was in The Doghouse, with Sam Brown performing at it. 'Sam was upstairs in the backstage room with a curly-haired kid who was singing songs at her – he was being kind of annoying, but in a good way.

'When I was in The Doghouse two weeks later I heard music from the stage and thought, "That's that CD" – and when I looked at the stage, I saw it was the kid. Within three songs, I knew that I had found my band.'

When they came off stage, Grant told them not to leave until they had all got together and spoken to him. He said if they were interested they could sit down and look at making a plan, maybe recording an album.

'I said, "Don't leave your jobs just now," so of course they came in next day and said, "Right we've packed our jobs in. When do we start? We'll start now, will we?"'

They had got together a few years earlier, first as friends and then, at about the age of fifteen, picking guitars up. Kyle Falconer, Pete Reilly and Steven Morrison (Mo) had gone to the same primary school, but knew Kieren as his grandfather taught there. When it came to secondary, three went off to St John's, with Mo heading to Harris Academy. They all picked up guitars at the same time but Kieren says, 'I realised Pete and Kyle were good so I learned to play the bass.'

There were two important bands – Oasis and The Beatles. Pete remembers that everyone who played guitar learned 'Wonderwall' as a first tune.

They played the school talent show – 'the toughest crowd we've ever played,' says Kieren. 'In between songs, someone would shout, "Scum!"' Pete thinks they were lucky being in the cool group, 'The Irish dancers got a really hard time.'

So Kyle and the Casuals, as they were hastily named, played three songs – 'Get Back', 'Day Tripper' and 'Live Forever'. All except the barre chords, that is. 'We hadn't been playing that long,' says Pete, 'and I couldn't do them yet, so I was kinda dipping in and out . . .' The repertoire was also limited so, as the winning band, they did 'Get Back' again for their encore.

'It did give us confidence to go out and play, though. We were only fifteen but we managed to get wee gigs in pubs,' says Pete. 'We played in the Smugglers with Dougie Martin, because Kyle's sister knew him. When Kyle went to sing the mic collapsed. I'm sure Dougie did that to wind us up.'

'We hit all the high spots,' says Kieren. 'Next on the list was the Red Lion Caravan Park in Arbroath. We look on that as our Hamburg.'

With rehearsal space prohibitively expensive, any empty rooms were welcome. 'We rehearsed in Murray Royal [a psychiatric hospital in Perth] and also out at my dad's cottage in Errol,' says Pete, 'but it was getting The Bayview that really kicked things off.'

Before finding that base, there had been a gap of about six months between the end of the covers band and beginning to write their own material.

'We were still pals and seeing each other all the time,' says Kieren, 'and we knew we should be doing something, but when the chance to use The Bayview came up it felt right.'

The first songs they worked on were 'Street Lights' and 'Time', and at that stage Mo came in to replace Ryan Brown. The Bayview was owned by Kyle's cousin Kenny, who was understanding, but only up to a point. 'We had the run of the place, apart from the weekends,' says Kieren. 'I'd get a phone call on Sunday morning: "Get this drum kit oota here –

there's a christening on!" I was the only one who had a car, so it was always me that got phoned to shift the gear. It got to the point that if Kenny phoned on a Sunday you wouldn't answer it.'

The Bayview became a second home. If they weren't rehearsing, they were playing. If they weren't playing they were 'trying to rob the puggy ...'

Kyle would also play acoustic sets at The Bayview, choosing from the hundreds of songs he has stashed away under that mop, for a couple of pints.

Once the band, now named The View as a tribute to their second home, had eight or nine songs, it was time to get out and play. From their second home, they found another, when they were asked by The Killer Angels to support them at The Doghouse.

The demo that Grant Dickson had been impressed by had been recorded on Pete's eighteenth birthday and had the benefit of Willie Hastie's experience, talent, Rickenbacker and bacon rolls.

'I think Grant saw our second gig at The Doghouse,' says Pete. 'He instantly gave us a bit of direction. He said he thought we should do an EP, and that we could rehearse in the upstairs room at The Doghouse. I was an apprentice joiner, and when I told my dad I was going to give it up for the band he just shook his head and said, "F*ckin' idiot."'

Kieren had left a job for the Dundee College music course but 'then I dropped out of college'.

Grant was so sure that he had found the band, he remortgaged his house and went back to live with his parents. 'I knew I had to give it my all. The band would spend eight to ten hours a day working on songs in The Doghouse. They had no money to buy drink so they just put their heads down.'

In the aftermath of the Michael Rattray launch, John and Grant went their separate ways, Grant feeling that he was doing most of the work while John enjoyed being the party host. 'I had just met The View and there were things that I didn't want them to get involved in. I think John was concerned that I would use the name Lemuria, so Robin and I became Two Thumbs.'

At their first Tpot session, The View met The Law for the first time. The ticket for a Tpot session included drinks, so the band started to work their way through a bin full of lager.

'We still have these conversations today. Start drinking at 2pm and by 6pm you can't play. You'll hate yourself tomorrow. By 6pm, they were totally bombed and made an arse of that one. The Law were playing well and were really tight so that made it worse for them. Kyle went into the garden in tears, thinking it was all over.'

Grant assured them that they would do a proper session, but warned them against the drinking. The playing needed to get tighter. They needed to be better versed in the basics of playing live, even setting up their instruments and PA.

Creating a buzz was also important and The World Tour of Dundee seemed to tick all the boxes. 'It was every mental pub in Dundee,' says Kieren. 'The Ancrum Arms, The Rock, The Whip, but always coming back to The Doghouse in between.'

The crowds were getting larger and rehearsing for eight hours a day meant they were getting better. The numbers in some of the pubs were bigger than the landlords were used to and Pete says, 'I think everybody who owned the pubs was terrified.'

A gig at Drouthy Neighbours was cancelled following an over-enthusiastic spate of fly-posting by Kieren, Kyle, and a friend, Ryan McPhail. 'We littered the town with flyers. The trail went from Menzieshill to the town centre. It was in the paper the next day, so the boy from Drouthy Neighbours pulled the gig. We really didn't know that we had to ask.'

Friends of the band were more than happy to help out with the promotion. 'All our mates thought they were in the band as well,' says Pete. 'They all quit their jobs as well – apprenticeships were going down the drain. They just thought they would jump on the tour bus with us . . .'

One example of this DIY promotion can still be seen at the Dryburgh circle [roundabout]. Drive towards the band's home turf and you'll see a green spray-painted 'The View'. 'It's the only bit that the council hasn't painted over, so they must like it,' laughs Kieren. 'I remember before it was done, everybody was saying, "So before this goes up, it definitely IS the name eh?"'

The next sessions at Tpot, to record *The View* EP, were more successful. 'We did the EP to play to other people really,' says Grant. 'We were always going to go after a bigger deal. They always said that they wanted to sign to Rough Trade because they were such big Libertines fans at the time.'

James Endeacott, who had signed The Libertines to Rough Trade, had been sent a copy of the EP and then, in September 2005, Babyshambles were in Dundee playing at Fat Sams. Grant saw this as an opportunity to grab the perfect high-profile support slot. He wasn't alone.

Grant phoned Colin Rodger at Fat Sams and got the OK for his plan, which was to load the van, stick in front of the loading bay, get the band down and find a way to get fifteen minutes.

'Sergeant were outside as well,' says Kieren, 'they had been at the gig the night before and said they had already been told they could play. We said, "Nah yir no'." That was the first time we met and we're good pals now, but any spare slot – we were playing it.'

The bus driver videoed the band and it was passed on to Endeacott who matched it up with the EP he had received. He called Dundee and asked the band to come to London and play at The Windmill in Brixton.

Grant was also negotiating publishing deals and organised a support slot with The Kooks at Dundee University. 'Somebody from Universal Publishing was coming up from London, but his flight didn't land in time to see the band. I told him we could play again for him and would be set up in The Doghouse within the hour. I phoned ahead and told them to cancel whatever band was on that night. The crowd moved over from the university with us and it was a great night. At the end of the gig he said, "I'll give you whatever you want."'

James Endeacott established his own 1965 Records label as an offshoot of Sony BMG/Columbia in 2006 and The View got their wish to work with the man who signed The Libertines. Things couldn't get much better when they were put into the studio with Owen Morris, who had produced Oasis and The Verve.

'My dad was there when we signed,' says Pete. 'He was a bit happier then.'

The first single, 'Wasted Little DJs', charted in August 2006, followed closely by 'Superstar Tradesman' and 'Same Jeans'. 'We had really strong singles so wanted enough time to let songs bed in,' says Grant. 'We tried to have a top 10 hit before the album came out and we did. [Journalist] Billy Sloan told me that he looked up the stats and The View's album had more sales in the first week than any other Scottish band ever.'

Released on 22 January 2007, *Hats Off to the Buskers* was number one by January 28. 'Things went crazy,' says Grant. 'I hadn't been used to that level of requirement. Not just by the band but there were so many things to consider from the label and decisions to be made. I didn't know 24/7 really existed before that.'

That also included meetings in Japan and the US about the next steps for the band. 'I kept saying, "Don't get caught with drugs." Having a bigger involvement with the music business brought cocaine into the equation – I would give them money for a few pints but never for drugs.'

It had been a couple of years of hard work, however, and as eighteen-year-olds, they deserved some fun. 'We stayed in the Chelsea Football Club hotel and I took out £20,000 in cash from the publishing advance and dumped it on the bed, just so they could roll about in it and throw it up in the air.'

The level of attention was extraordinary, with the band gaining countless new friends. 'They're all pretty shy, really. With so many interviews to do, and people being nice to them because they had got to number one, it was weird for them,' adds Grant.

When Tom Doyle interviewed the band, he had a better handle on their backgrounds than most. 'They are a real talent. At first I thought, "Ach, it's just The Libertines from Dundee" – but they are much more than that. They were the first band I had interviewed since the Happy

Mondays that I thought, "You genuinely don't give a f*ck." I'm glad they've pulled it in a wee bit now.'

The indulgence wasn't always chemical or alcohol-based, however. With some money in his pocket, Kyle visited a toy shop and bought a Scalextric set and other toys that he never had as a kid.

For the band, the period following the first Windmill gig was non-stop playing. 'I think we did about 250 gigs in the first year,' says Pete. 'A few support tours and loads of toilet tours to build a fan base. It cemented us as a band, but it was chaos as well.'

One night saw them come off stage at Cardiff Barfly and travel straight to London for a gig at Brixton Academy. 'We had been too drunk to be on stage in Cardiff, so by the time we got to Brixton, well I can't really remember,' says Kieren. 'We got really good at playing drunk, well we thought we were really good. There was this reputation of the chaotic band – up for the good time and all that – but we probably took it a bit too far sometimes. What can you do?'

Pete remembers it as, 'A massive bender with your mates and getting paid for it. That's what we've always had in our favour – we've always been solid. There have been loads of fights, real roll-aboot fights with each other, and there will be loads more. When you spend so much time in each other's pockets it's bound to happen. Then the next day it's all, "I'm sorry. . ." ' he laughs, extending his arms to Kieren.

On the headline tours, a buffer was the fact that The Law and some-times Luva Anna were first-choice supports. 'It was like the Bash Street Kids on tour – just the best times. We were staying in Travelodges and The Law were in tents outside, but we didn't sleep in the rooms, we crashed in the tents with them. It's the gang mentality,' adds Pete. It was just as well, as Travelodge banned them in 2007 after they caused damage to one of the chain's Liverpool hotels.

Dave Webster remembers a tour when the three bands were on a bus driven by Grant. 'He had tried to blag us into a safari park by saying we were all no' right or something, but the guy wasn't having it. So we saw a way of sneaking in. We got over a fence and were straight into the monkey enclosure.'

There were early dates in the US and Japan. The sight of young Japanese fans sporting Dryburgh Soul T-shirts and singing lines from 'Superstar Tradesman' about having 'a house in the Ferrrrrry' was a surreal experience. 'That was the first thing that properly freaked me out,' says Pete. 'They're going mental and shouting your name and giving you presents.'

Kieren felt, 'The T-shirt thing was weird. It's all about getting your name out for the scheme, and we've got people in Japan wearing Dryburgh T-shirts.'

If the tours had been carnage up until that point, then a support tour with Babyshambles was 'an introduction in how to be really rock'n'roll', says Pete. 'We got a wee bit of a lesson on that tour. My favourite tour was supporting Primal Scream, though. The first time Bobby Gillespie walked past I couldn't speak, but then I played for them a couple of times.'

The video shoots were kept close to home, with 'Superstar Tradesman' done in Kyle's backies. The original idea had been to play on the roof of the Dryburgh shops, but health and safety nixed the idea. 'So many workies downed tools that day to come and watch,' says Pete.

The video for 'Same Jeans' was filmed in Kieren's granny's house. 'That party looked like a fake party. We couldn't wreck my granny's house, but she's had more mental parties than that. They should have filmed in the place we had a party the night before,' he laughs.

The live reputation was growing, from the T Break stage at T in the Park in 2006, they played twice at Glastonbury in 2007, on the Pyramid and Other stages. In between those shows that weekend, they also supported The Who.

'Right through all this, Grant did everything,' says Pete. 'He drove the van, sold the T-shirts, spoke to everybody. We were lucky to get someone so dedicated. I think it would have still happened, but not as fast without him. But you never know if it would have or not. He's the original fifth member.'

The fifth member was about to face a few challenges with the other four. 'We were six months in and nothing had gone wrong yet. Everything had gone to plan,' says Grant. 'And then "Same Jeans" was on the radio so often that they were sick of it and thought they had sold out. The record company had conversations with Radio 1 about the next single and the thought was "Street Lights". The guys wanted to put out "Skag Trendy" – not the most radio-friendly song in content. So many guys flew up from London to talk to them about it, and soon it seemed my position went from the guy who helped them to the guy who was on the record-company side and wanted to turn them into a boy band ... So much had happened so quickly. There was too much going on to think straight.'

Then Kyle was caught with cocaine and the American tour was off. The final straw for Grant was the Mercury Music Awards ceremony in 2007. What should have been a celebration of a nomination turned into what would be described in Dundee as 'a bit of a rammy' at the table. He walked away that night and when the band came to him with a problem two days later, he told them he was no longer their manager and shut the door.

'I had been looking after Luva Anna and The Law in my spare time. We nearly had The Law away on Relentless EMI but all the bands were dropped when EMI went up for sale.'

Although Grant wished them well, he knew that a London management company wouldn't make any allowances. 'I was managing lives rather than just a band, and no management company were going to do that.'

They kept in touch and Grant visited the band in their London rehearsal room to hear the songs they were planning for the next album. 'We went back to the flat and I knew it was going to sound bitter, but I told them I didn't think they had the radio hits they had on *Hats Off to the Buskers*.'

'The second album crept up on us,' says Kieren. 'We all got great girlfriends and had a good time and totally forgot to write new songs. The first album was the party and the second was the comedown. But imagine sitting in a mansion when you're fifty and saying, since I was eighteen I played every card exactly right. I never burned any bridges; never got too mental. How pissed off would you be?'

While *Which Bitch?* didn't disappear, entering at number four in February 2009, it dropped back down quickly and didn't have the hit singles. 'It's a different album and a lot more experimental, but there was too much nonsense,' says Pete. 'The first album was about our experiences and now Kieren and Kyle are writing about different things because they have different experiences. And, after the first album, come on, we were eighteen and nineteen and it was the first time any of us had had any money, ever . . . what are you going to do?'

It didn't diminish their reputation as a live act and that year they climbed the bills of festivals, headlining the King Tut's Tent at T in the Park.

Pete says, 'The noise of the crowd before we went on was ridiculous. I get goosebumps just thinking about it. When the roar went up when we went on, I sh*t myself a wee bit. We also played Oxegen in Dublin that weekend and got a helicopter over. That feels like real rock-star stuff.'

Grant had been concentrating on his other Two Thumbs artists when he bumped into Kieren. 'I was washing my car and, without actually saying the words, he let me know that things weren't really working out with the new management.' They got together to have a chat and Grant said he was interested in coming back, but things would have to be done differently.

If the first album was the party and the second the comedown, then the third was a time to get back on the level. *Bread and Circuses*, released in 2011, also didn't emulate previous sales, but it received favourable reviews, which applauded the band's ability to rein in the caning to work on the music. Producer Youth's alcohol ban meant that studio certainly didn't have the atmosphere of Owen Morris's. 'He can create an atmosphere, I tell you that,' laughs Pete. 'Comparing it to what we've done before, the experience was a bit dull for me.'

Kieren thinks they need to find a middle ground between the full-on mayhem of *Which Bitch?* and Youth's regimental approach.

Now that Kyle's visa restriction is lifted, they need to start again with America. 'Trying to turn a negative into a positive, maybe us not being there has created a wee bit of hunger and a buzz,' says Pete. 'If we had gone over after the first album, we would have been a bigger band. But I reckon someone was looking after us. If we had gone then, we could have been in a whole other kind of trouble over there,' he laughs.

A one-off project in 2011 gave them the opportunity to give something back to Dundee. Record Store Day is a way of promoting those independent stores that are battling against the torrent of downloading and Grant met with James Endeacott to discuss submitting something by The View to be a contender for the day's official anthem. Straight after the meeting, he was playing a compilation of power-pop B-sides that Grant had given him. 'He heard a song and thought, "That's The View. That would suit them perfectly." It was a 1980 song by The Tweeds called "I Need That Record" and when he sent me the link, I could feel myself grinning,' says Grant.

The record was recorded at Seagate Studios with Graeme Watt, and the video shot in Groucho's, with the lyrics also being changed to reflect the location. 'I thought, "Why pay a producer vast amounts of money, when this could be made in Dundee just as well for a lot less?" When I heard it, I knew it had to be the best contender. I knew how good Graeme was as an engineer and I hope we can do more stuff with him. The whole thing cost less than half a day's studio time in London. It was just a perfect fit.'

Epilogue

Music may be a lifelong passion, but in every city and town the scene is constantly shifting. Bands spring up, apparently from nowhere and many disappear into obscurity just as quickly. Even as this is being written, there will be songwriters in bedrooms toiling over lyrics, guitarists toughening up fingers for barre chords and singers trying to find their voices. They may be on stage before the book has reached your hands.

There are so many elements to the musical life of a city that there will be many characters that do not appear in these pages, but that in no way lessens their role in the story as a whole.

Michael Marra's 'Beneath the Underdog' theory holds true. Still the target of comedians' wisecracks, the city has inspired artists to work harder at their craft, even if that diligence isn't always matched by natural talent. The dedication has never been in question, whether it has resulted in success or not. It also speaks volumes for what Dundee *does* offer, which many of those who have achieved success choose not to leave and instead continue to be inspired by the city that shaped them and consequently their music.

The historical influence of Irish immigration to find work in the thriving jute industry cannot be underestimated. Working hard and playing hard is not a cliché in working-class towns and cities like Dundee, with many of the musicians holding down full-time jobs while playing several times a week. Sure the money comes in handy, but that's not what humping the gear around and playing in front of occasionally apathetic audiences is about – it's a sheer love of the music and, as Ali Napier puts it, 'being in a room with your pals, having a laugh and making a lot of noise'.

For many the fuse was lit while performing between shortbread and blackcurrant cordial fixes at family parties, with everyone expected to do a turn. Those sing-songs, whether it was traditional melodies or a rousing Guy Mitchell tune, were a bonding experience and like all community singing, always a happy time. Who wouldn't grow up thinking that this would be a rather enjoyable way to make a living?

Kit Clark recalls that there was no differentiation between those who were 'musicians' and those who weren't. Every performance in the room was given equal attention and respect.

Performing at parties has been significant through the generations, from Donny Coutts to Kit and Gary Clark. It has even had a lasting effect on younger performers such as Kyle Falconer of The View, who can pick up a guitar and entertain a room for hours on end; an eternal human jukebox. There's a good chance that it wouldn't be allowed, however, with the insistence that someone else get 'a shot'.

That sense of egalitarianism has resulted in strong, lasting friendships between musicians who have known one another, and played together, for almost fifty years. However, it has also resulted in opportunities that may have led to 'bigger things' being sacrificed for the sake of that Dundee fairness.

That sense of camaraderie runs across the generations with Peter McGlone and Howard McLeod as much a part of Paul Wright's Lefty and Friends band as Stevie Anderson. This is one of many bands as eclectic in their music choices as they are in the choice of personnel.

Music writers will always look to sum up the sound of a city, but that's a difficult job in Dundee. Unlike the beat boom of Liverpool, the psychedelic trance dance of 'Madchester', or Glasgow's Postcard Records and 'The Sound of Young Scotland', there has been true diversity. Whether that has come from its geographic location, divorced from other large centres of population, or from that 'Beneath the Underdog' banner, where they may as well do what they like.

That makes the prediction of what comes next impossible. Young teenage boys may be fantasising about being the next View, but they'll find their own sound through the influences of family, friends and peers.

If Dundee does have a strain running through its musical DNA it's one that shirks pretension and embraces those who are willing to put themselves out there for the crowd, for the crack and for the tunes. That's one thing that is sure to stay the same.

Appendix

WHO'S WHO

A list of people interviewed in this book, with a selection of their bands

Carol Air: musician (Adam 812)

Lloyd Anderson: musician (The Edge, No Fixed Abode, Spies, Sweden Through the Ages, solo, LAKE)

Stevie Anderson: musician (The Law, Anderson McGinty Webster Ward and Fisher)

Steve Aungle: musician (The Blush, Billy Mackenzie, solo)

Jackie Bird (née McPherson): musician (Street Level, St Andrew); broadcaster

Alan Breitenbach: musician (Bedlam, Havana Swing)

Liam Brennan: musician (The Hazey Janes)

Alastair 'Breeks' Brodie: Owner of Groucho's record store

Mike Brown: producer and musician (Better Backwards, Jih)

Jan Burnett: musician (Spare Snare)

Dave Burnett: musician (The Destinies, Talkin' Walls, The Phoenix, The Accelerators)

Alison Burns: musician (The Junkies, The Rainmates, Big Blue 72, Penny Dainties, solo jazz singer)

Gary Clark: writer, producer and musician (Clark's Commandos, Danny Wilson, solo, King L, Transister)

Kit Clark: musician (The Very Important Men, Danny Wilson, Swiss Family Orbison, solo)

Stuart Clumpas: promoter/manager

Alan Cormack: musician (The Sandflowers, Muppet Mule, Spare Snare)

Donny Coutts: musician (The Spotlights, The Wise Brothers, The Syndicate, The Vikings, The Right Time, Sleepy People, Mafia, Quicksilver, Big Blue 72, St

Andrew and the Woollen Mill, The Carlin Rose Band, Junkyard Dogs, Drew Larg and the Buzzards)

Simon Ciampi Deuchar: musician (Another Sunday)

Grant Dickson: Manager of The View and musician (Yellow Car)

Gordon Douglas: musician and theatre writer (Wells Fargo, The Cows, Seconds, Spies, The Careful Movers, The Prisoners of Fender)

Tom Doyle: writer, author and musician (Pavlov Orange, The Ashen Heart, Float, Electric Music AKA, Boo Hooray)

Jock Ferguson: performer and musician (Beaver Sisters)

Stuart Fleming: Jagged Roots management and music label

Helen Forbes: musician (Blon a Gael)

Gus Foy: musician (Hen's Teeth, Skeets Boliver, St Andrew and the Woollen Mill, MFI, Fabulous Specky Boys) and Woodlands folk club organiser

Steve Gaughan: musician (Go East, Lorna B, Penny Dainties)

Barry Gibson: musician (Better Backwards, Beaver Sisters, Readers' Wives, Muppet Mule, Spare Snare)

Alan Gorrie: musician (The Vikings, Scots of St James, Forever More, Average White Band)

Ged Grimes: musician (Grimes Folk Four, The Blue Macs, Danny Wilson, Eddi Reader, Deacon Blue, Simple Minds)

Stewart Ivins: musician (Mort Wriggle and the Panthers, Skeets Boliver, St Andrew and the Woollen Mill, The Headsquares)

Ronnie Jack: musician (The Castaways, The Bluebeats, Snowy Wood, The Flamingos, The Niteflys)

Steve Knight: musician (The Associates, Sweden Through the Ages)

Lou Lewis: musician (Wells Fargo, The Cows, Seconds, The Headboys, The Careful Movers)

Andy Lothian Jnr: musician (double bass with the East Coast Jazzmen) and music promoter/manager

Brian McDermott: musician (Badge, Skeets Boliver, Danny Wilson, Sweden Through the Ages, Del Amitri)

Steve McDonald: musician (Elegy, McDonald's Farm, Ringer, Tripper)

Pete McGlone: musician (Elegy, Skeets Boliver, Mafia, St Andrew)

Stuart McHardy: musician (solo), storyteller, lecturer and Scots language specialist

Ailsa McInroy: musician (Adam 812)

Keith McIntosh: music store owner and musician

Howard McLeod: musician (The Flamingos, Rokotto, solo)

Alice Marra: musician (The Hazey Janes)

Christopher Marra: musician (Hen's Teeth, the 45s, John Parr, Danny Wilson, Sweden Through the Ages, The Rainmates, Ringer)

Matthew Marra: musician (The Hazey Janes)

Michael Marra: musician and theatre writer (Hen's Teeth, Skeets Boliver, solo, St Andrew)

Dougie Martin: musician (The Hep Cats, The Mystery Men, The Johnny Hudson Hi-Four, The Poor Souls, The Cyclones, Cosa Nostra, Mafia, The Dougie Martin Soul Band)

Keith Matheson: musician (Big Blue 72, Marshal Curtis, Swiss Family Orbison, Bikini Machine, The Pearlfishers)

Andrew Mitchell: musician (The Hazey Janes)

Ali Napier: musician (Joe Public, Big Blue 72, Citizen Kane, Swiss Family Orbison, Dougie McLean, Freda Morrison, Paul Anderson, Miami Vince)

Rab Noakes: musician (solo)

Graeme Ogston: musician (The Hate Foundation, Spare Snare)

Dave Oudney: musician (Boogalusa)

Russ Paterson: musician (The Inn Folk) and promoter at Dundee Folk Club

Andy Pelc: musician (St Andrew)

Gregor Philp: musician (Another Sunday, Big Blue 72, Swiss Family Orbison, Heavy Little Elephants, Deacon Blue)

Pete Reilly: musician (The View)

Gus Robb: manager and promoter The Westport Bar and Fat Sams, and musician

Ricky Ross: musician (Deacon Blue, solo)

Tom Simpson: musician (Snow Patrol)

Gordon Small: First editor of *Jackie* magazine

Martin Taylor, MBE: jazz guitarist (solo, with Alison Burns, Spirit of Django, Gypsy Journey)

Chris van der Kuyl: musician (Citizen Kane, Big Blue 72)

Gordon Walker: musician (The Quick Spurts, Dirtbox, Slim Disney)

David Webster: musician (Luva Anna, Anderson McGinty Webster Ward and Fisher)

Kieren Webster: musician (The View)

Alan Wilson: music writer for the *Dundee Courier* and musician (Boogalusa)

Nick Wright: promoter and artist

Unfortunately, some of the people mentioned are no longer with us. In tribute to: Andy Lothian Snr, John McLevy, Jimmy Deuchar, Tony van der Kuyl, Jonathan Ogilvie, Steve Falconer, Gerry McGrath, Robbie McIntosh, Bob Quinn, Billy Mackenzie, Alan Matheson, John Mackenzie, Chris Taylor and Eric Pressly.

Bibliography

Doyle, Tom. *The Glamour Chase – The Maverick Life of Billy Mackenzie* (Bloomsbury 1998).

McCluskey, Mick. *The Rock 'n' Soul of Dundee* DVD (1994).

McNab, Ken. *The Beatles In Scotland* (Birlinn 2008).

Reynolds, Maureen. 'Dundee's Dancing Years' *The Scots Magazine* (February 1989, Volume 130).